"Benjamin Mark Cole **spotlights Wall Street's corrupt system of research analysis** in a fast-paced, name-the-names investigative style. No worries about finding the customers' yachts here."

HERBERT A. DENTON
President, Providence Capital, Inc.

**"What an eye-opener!** I'll look at the reports of sell-side analysts in an entirely different light now."

DENNIS E. LOGUE
Steven Roth Professor of Management
Tuck School, Dartmouth College

"Lynched by Peter or Merrill? Bagged in the great dot-con? This is the book for you. **The most honest book about Wall Street in years.**"

WILLIAM MASON
Finance Professor, Pepperdine University
Portfolio Manager, Cullen Fortier Asset Management

"…the work is **a provocative and lively read,** reminding all that the pricing system can emit false signals."

JOHN LONSKI
Credit Market Economist, Moody's Investors Service

**"A shoot-from-the-hip look** at America's hidden scoundrels and a few unsung heroes. Must-read material for today's financial set."

BEN SULLIVAN
Editor, *The Zone News*

"This book is a must-read for serious investors looking for **an unbiased, honest, objective, fresh view of Wall Street research.**"

MARSHALL B. FRONT
Chairman, Front, Barnett Associates, LLC

# THE
# PIED PIPERS
# OF
# WALL
# STREET

# THE
# PIED PIPERS
# OF
# WALL
# STREET

*How Analysts Sell You Down the River*

Benjamin Mark Cole

BLOOMBERG PRESS

PRINCETON

Books are available for bulk purchases at special discounts. Special editions or book excerpts can also be created to specifications. For information, please write: Special Markets Department, Bloomberg Press.

BLOOMBERG, BLOOMBERG NEWS, BLOOMBERG FINANCIAL MARKETS, OPEN BLOOMBERG, BLOOMBERG PERSONAL FINANCE, THE BLOOMBERG FORUM, COMPANY CONNECTION, COMPANY CONNEX, BLOOMBERG PRESS, BLOOMBERG PROFESSIONAL LIBRARY, BLOOMBERG PERSONAL BOOKSHELF, and BLOOMBERG SMALL BUSINESS are trademarks and service marks of Bloomberg L.P. All rights reserved.

First edition published 2001
1  3  5  7  9  10  8  6  4  2

Cole, Benjamin Mark
The pied pipers of Wall Street: how analysts sell you down the river /
Benjamin Mark Cole.–1st ed.
p. cm.

Includes index.
ISBN 1-57660-083-1 (alk. paper)
1. Investment advisors – United States.  2. Stockbrokers – United States.
3. Investment analysis – United States. I. Title.

HG4928.5. C65 2001
332.6'0973–dc21                                              2001016197

Acquired and edited by Kathleen A. Peterson
Book Design by Laurie Lohne / Design It Communications

*To my son, Max, and to Araceli, who bore him.*

*And to Evelyn, who bore me.*

*And to my father, who loved books so well.*

# Contents

# Acknowledgments

I HAVE DEBTS DECADES OLD and collecting interest daily, to city schools and libraries, to state universities and teachers, to family and friends. I also want to acknowledge Kathleen Peterson, Bloomberg editor, who read the manuscript of this book and pronounced it worthy despite its controversial nature, and Dan Taub, Bloomberg reporter, who recommended Bloomberg Press to me.

# Preface

THE NEW STARS OF WALL STREET are the brokerage, or "sell side," stock analysts, thrust from behind the scenes to near celebrity status in the 1990s and into the 2000s. Where once brokerage researchers toiled in obscurity and were granted a measure of independence in their firms, now they are often the face and public persona for major stock brokerages. Their job today is to entrance the market with their flute work, to provide the captivating music that helps stocks rise, and rise again.

In part, this is the result of an explosion of financial media that has occurred since the 1980s, with the emergence of all-business-news cable television shows and an avalanche of financial magazines and newspapers. The Internet, seemingly invented for Wall Street, is throbbing with stock market Web sites, all manner of financial information and news, and, of course, online trading. It helps immensely that analysts' songs are today sought by legions of financial journalists and broadcast to an audience that largely has never seen a sustained bear market—until recently, anyway.

Certainly, by 2001 many individual investors had lost a lot of money in the stock market and felt like they were getting killed—or perhaps it is more accurate to say they had been led to slaughter. With millennial finality, the market fever of the late 1990s had broken in 2000, and broken hard. The Nasdaq Composite, which so captured the rise of Internet stocks and tech skyrockets, in 2000 fell to about half of its peak, the worst year for any major index since the Depression era.

In addition to the Nasdaq Composite, stock indices such as the venerable Dow Jones Industrial Average and the Standard & Poor's

500, had each breached all-time records in 1999. The S&P 500, for example, had more than quadrupled in the 1990s, reflecting a bull market to hold its own against any other in history. It was a market unknown to veterans, even as it was taken for granted by growing millions of Americans, who in the 21st century own stocks by far greater percentages than ever before. Yet as investors are learning anew, it isn't always sunny on Wall Street, even if the widely quoted brokerage analysts are forever promising blue skies.

In the swoons on the major stock indices after 2000, a massive $3.5 trillion of paper wealth (some might call it "digital dollars") had been unceremoniously wiped out on Wall Street. Stocks that millions of Americans had been told would soar—Amazon.com, eToys Inc., Priceline.com, and even solid performers like Microsoft or Cisco Systems—instead tanked, losing half, 80 percent, or in the case of e-tailer eToys and shopping service Priceline, nearly all of their value on the exchanges.

And yet, in early 2000, weren't all the brokerage seers predicting another year of the bull? Wasn't Abby Joseph Cohen, the chief investment guru for Goldman Sachs, invincible? Wasn't everybody on CNN in agreement?

Brokerage analysts today—many of whom work for global behemoths, with thousands, and even tens of thousands of stockbrokers—have linked arms with their investment banking departments, to help smooth the road for the successful issue of IPOs (initial public offerings), of secondary equity offerings, and of bond offerings. Analysts are there to help the huge trading institutions, the money managers, and the mutual funds ease in and out of positions, profits in hand, even if the retail investor is left holding the bag. Much like lawyers, the brokerage analysts' job today is to make a "best case" for a stock, not to be objective skeptics of a company's future performance.

Ironically, the body of federal securities law that pertains to brokerage analysts, largely developed fifty and more years ago and affirmed in the famous *SEC v. Ray Dirks* decision in 1983, grants safe harbor to these professionals. The law assumes analysts are still in their traditional garb of pure researchers, separated from investment banking and trading departments by the noble (if now nonexistent) so-called Chinese wall. Thus, under the law, analysts are granted the latitude to be almost completely unhindered when expressing their views, as if they were journalists or pundits. But financially, they are beholden to their employers and largest clients. Even the recently passed SEC Regulation FD implicitly embraces the hope that analysts wish to do a good job, and just need less baggage or some minor rule-tinkering to do so.

The law and current regulation don't recognize what almost every Wall Street pro no longer even considers controversial: that Wall Street today is a half-century and a world away from that business climate embodied in SEC regulations. Where the law sees a stock market researcher hunched over his slide rule, pros take for granted the present-day constellation of analyst hype, market fever, ubiquitous financial news, cyberized trading, and gigantic brokerages and mutual funds armed with mega-dollar advertising budgets. Where once independence was their hallmark, analysts today are effectively part of the investment banking and marketing departments of brokerages.

This book takes a hard look at stock market analysts and their role in the changed brokerage industry and the financial media. It is not a reassuring examination. For one, numerous academic and industry studies have concluded that analysts' "buy" recommendations, as a group, actually underperform the general market. The reason for this has much to do with the nature of the compromised relationships described here.

In tracing how the role of the securities industry analyst has been transformed, *The Pied Pipers of Wall Street* presents first a microcosmic view of one analyst's conflicted actions. It then looks more broadly at the evolution of Wall Street and how it got to where it is. Highlighted are a number of interesting, sometimes outrageous, IPOs and secondary offerings that have been flogged by analysts at major firms. Also examined are the antics of Wall Street Minor—the financial shenanigans of regional or single-shop brokerages and self-styled analysts, whose dealings mimic many actions of the big houses. In addition, the book reviews short traders and how they can serve as a valuable tonic on the market—yet how the Street has nearly wiped that breed of investor out of existence. Also provided is a compilation of some independent and highly regarded research outfits that can be of real value to the individual investor seeking unbiased guidance, and a final chapter on the Securities and Exchange Commission and possible regulatory reform.

If more investors knew of the changed market realities of the 1990s and beyond, they might tread with more caution, but unfortunately, in the words of the old saw, experience is what you get after you need it. In 2001, with the Nasdaq still off about half from its peak, many investors had already figured out it was too late to learn the new score on Wall Street. Their portfolios have been crippled, and it is hard to envision full recovery. One can only hope that other investors may learn from their experience, and not repeat it.

# 1

# THE MAN ON
# THE TELEPHONE

The man on the telephone oozed confidence.

*"And how did I know?" he asked rhetorically. "Well, Soros is
my client... and I know he is short on the stock."*

S oros is my client. No wonder the man seemed smug. On Wall
Street and in the world of money managers, George Soros
was—and still remains, despite recent setbacks—a leviathan.
An investor of legendary skill, daring, and reach, Soros was "the man
who broke the Bank of England" by shorting the British pound sterling in 1992, and he took home $1 billion in lucre doing it.

Through most of the 1990s, Soros was more a financial force of
nature than an investor, a money titan who could manhandle the
economies of entire nations. Invoking his name in the world of high
finance was akin to a medieval cardinal claiming "The Pope said so."
Soros managed billions of dollars, and he wasn't shy about borrowing
billions more to wager on Wall Street, or anywhere else. And now the
man on the telephone was saying that the great Soros was his client,
that Soros actually listened to him and took advice from him. The
man on the phone had Soros's ear!

The man on the phone was drug industry securities analyst Hemant
K. Shah, the principal of HKS & Co., Inc., a one-man research firm he
ran from his home in suburban Warren, New Jersey. On this May
afternoon in 1996, he was telling the manager of a large investment
fund that his "client" Soros was shorting the fledgling drug company

Biovail Corp. International, based in Toronto, then listed on the American Stock Exchange (since switched to the Big Board).

Just as Soros had wagered against the pound, now Soros was straddling Biovail like the Colossus of Rhodes, Shah explained in knowing tones. It didn't take a wild imagination to figure out what was going to happen next to a small-cap stock like Biovail—a company then posting less than $70 million a year in sales. Biovail was going to get crushed.

In retrospect, it might seem ludicrous that a figure of Soros's stature would even know Hemant Shah's name, let alone take advice from him. But in the mid-1990s, when it came to companies like Biovail, Shah had credibility, and more than a little. When the topic was drug stocks, he was a darling of *The Wall Street Journal* and its cousin, the Dow Jones Newswire, and other business wire services, such as Reuters. Newspapers the likes of *The New York Times*, the *Los Angeles Times, Investor's Business Daily*, and Britain's *Financial Times* all turned to Shah on a regular basis for commentary on what was hot and what was not in the pharmaceuticals industry. So did the two financial cable-TV channels, CNBC and FNN. Shah was good at talking, and he knew the best-kept secret in PR: those who quickly return reporters' calls, banter a little—and give a pithy sound bite—get quoted.

Too, there were plenty of good reasons to air Shah and his views. He did win *The Wall Street Journal*'s "All-Star Analysts" stock-picking contest in 1996 and 1997 in the drug stock category, and he wrote a monthly newsletter on the pharmaceutical industry. He had been a pharmaceutical analyst (in New York) with Japan's Nomura Securities, and his record with regulatory agencies was clean.

Before that, he had worked as a financial analyst for some drug giants, including Pfizer, Smithkline Beecham, and Merck. Moreover, early in his career, before earning two business degrees, he had actually been a pharmacist. Give credit where credit is due—Shah knew the drug industry, and there were no official black marks against him. Appropriately, the financial magazine *Forbes* said of the star analyst, "Shah's opinions are widely sought and followed."

But most of all, he was there for reporters with the collegial banter, the quick quote. He knew how to make the media into unwitting allies in his stock gambits—by one online literature search, Shah was quoted by name in major business newspapers and magazines more than 2,500 times in the 1990s, and 28 times alone on Biovail, in major publications.[1] And so when it came to drug stocks, Shah was a Wall Street fixture, a regular at the panel discussions organized by the New York Society of Securities Analysts, a bon vivant in the financial pages, a talking head for TV—in short, he was a player.

In the investment world, this visibility translates into influence. Shah's popularity with the media gave him the ability to mount campaigns—the power, with a well-placed whisper, a published opinion, or a memorable video sound bite, to help push a stock up or down, particularly the less-followed stocks of medium-sized or smaller companies.

Shah's visibility also brought him clients, dozens of them, mainly fund managers but also stockbrokers and tycoons, clients with millions, hundreds of millions, cumulatively even billions of dollars at their disposal. They paid for his advice, his insights, his views on the pharmaceutical sector and where it might be headed, for his say-so on which stocks to buy—and which to bet against.

In this regard, Shah was something of a dwarf version of the combination seen today on Wall Street of big brokerages, their trading departments, and huge mutual funds—if the funds follow an analyst's "buy" or the rare "sell" signal (which they often get before the rest of the market), the analyst's call becomes something of a self-fulfilling prophecy, at least in the short term. Sometimes this combination of brokerage support and institutional ownership of a favored stock is known as "sponsorship." The industry never calls it "manipulation."

Shah, with his coterie of client investors, had replicated in small scale the brokerage analyst/mutual fund combines of Wall Street Major. Sensibly enough, Shah recognized his smaller amount of firepower and usually took positions in small-cap stocks, where his artillery could win a stock skirmish. And in May 1996, Hemant Shah was definitely in the middle of a skirmish. Actually, it is more accurate to say he was in a war—a one-man war to destroy Biovail.

Shah was short on Biovail stock, and he had convinced clients to short the stock. (A short position is a financial bet that the price of a stock will go down, not up. A short is accomplished by borrowing target stock from an owner and then selling it immediately. The short trader hopes to buy the stock back later at a lower price and return it to the original owner—having profited on the spread between the price when the stock was first sold and the lower price when it was repurchased.)

Unfortunately for the financial media and investors, the public didn't know about Shah's covert operations. Even as he was bandying the name of Soros around, Shah had an agenda, a governing but buried passion hidden from his clients, from the media, from other investors. There were intense conflicts in Shah's professional life. There were reasons for Shah's whispering about Soros, which later were revealed—although too late to help the many Biovail investors who were hurt.

They didn't know then what has been learned since and exposed in the proceedings of a civil suit: that Shah was being tape-recorded, even as he dissembled about Soros being a client, about Soros being short on the stock, and while spreading other falsehoods about Biovail.

On Wall Street today, brokerages and institutional money managers routinely tape-record their telephone calls, so that trading disputes can more readily be resolved—a fact Shah must have known but evidently disregarded in his zeal to sink Biovail, or perhaps he thought no one would ever know about or subpoena the tapes. The phone calls, and other depositions, became record in the 1998 civil case *Biovail Corp. International v. Parker Quillen et al.* and in other legal proceedings.[2] Indeed, Shah was getting caught in a web of contradictory statements, from which ultimately he could not extract himself with honor. The Soros tall tale was hardly the worst of it.

IT WAS MAY 20, 1996, AND SHAH was in temporary retreat in his jihad on Biovail. In a remarkably bad turn of luck (for Shah), the market was rife with rumors that Soros, the money potentate, was going to take a big stake in Biovail—obviously, a bullish signal. The stock was rising, and rising again. It had nearly doubled in less than two months. With several hundred thousand dollars of his own dough on the line in short positions, and millions of his clients' money also at risk, Shah was hurting. So Shah got a fund manager on the phone, and he was doing the Shah thing—talking, hinting, schmoozing, trying to turn market participants, trying to turn the media, trying to turn the market itself against Biovail.

> *Shah:* Somebody is creating these rumors to push the stock up. On bad numbers...
>
> *Fund manager:* On the floor [of the New York Stock Exchange]?
>
> *Shah:* On the floor—I mean, you tell me.
>
> *Fund manager:* What was the rumor?
>
> *Shah:* That Soros was going to take 10 percent of the company. He was going to announce on Monday that he owns 10 percent. Well, let me tell you. Soros is my client.
>
> *Fund manager:* Soros is your client?
>
> *Shah:* Yes!
>
> *Fund manager:* Okay.
>
> *Shah:* Ha, hah!
>
> *Fund manager:* So you are saying the rumor is not true?
>
> *Shah:* Of course [it is] not.[3]

## IN THE BEGINNING

But why? Why, of the thousands of publicly traded stocks, had Shah targeted Biovail? And why did Shah—who was presented to investors and readers of financial pages as an analyst, a cool, objective observer—campaign against Biovail in such a sustained and unrelenting manner? Nor were Shah's actions those of a simple short strategy: usually, when events contrive against short traders, they retreat, and for good, in search of easier prey. But Shah was resourceful, tenacious, cunning, and seemingly never daunted by setbacks.

There was another curiosity. Shah wasn't born into the business of destroying Biovail stock. Quite the contrary. He was an ally first, then a turncoat. There was a lot behind the Shah story, and it starts with Eugene Melnyk, an ebullient young Canadian entrepreneur, who has built Biovail into a company that by 2001 was worth $5.58 billion on Wall Street.

The son of a Toronto physician, Melnyk was a medical book and journal publisher in 1989, the year he took over Biovail. He was still under thirty. As he earned his ink stains, Melnyk saw more-effective medicines being introduced every year, but he also saw that doctors faced a frustrating problem: patients didn't always follow increasingly complicated pill-popping regimens. As a result, there was a fat niche shaping up for makers of controlled-release drugs—cleverly designed pills that deliver their active ingredients over relatively long periods. That makes for "hassle-free" pill-popping—and better medicine.

With his doctorly bloodlines and medical publishing background, Melnyk was quick to recognize the potential of sustained-release prescriptions, and also cheaper generic pills. To that end, in 1989 he acquired a small Swiss medical research firm called Biovail SA, which was run by a pioneer of drug-delivery technology, Dr. Arnold Beckett. Melnyk's business plan for the renamed Biovail Corp. International, with its small research lab in Toronto and manufacturing facility in Manitoba, was simple conceptually, if difficult in practice: invent controlled-release versions of name-brand drugs and then license them to major pharmaceutical manufacturers and distributors.

Although Biovail had a number of different arrows in its quiver, a major focus in the first half of the 1990s was its blood-pressure drug, brand-named Tiazac. A generic version of diltiazem, a once-a-day calcium channel blocker used to treat angina and hypertension, Tiazac offered physicians a less expensive alternative to Hoechst Marion Roussel's Cardizem and Rhône-Poulenc's Dilacor, two hugely successful drugs that were together racking up annual sales of nearly $1 billion.

Bringing a new drug to market is a complicated, expensive, and time-consuming procedure, involving painstaking patent searches, carefully scrutinized clinical trials, and red-tape wrestling with the

U.S. Food and Drug Administration (FDA). As it happened, Biovail was able to move Tiazac along relatively quickly. Even so, the company's profit-and-loss statement showed red ink. In 1992, with revenues of just under $6 million, Biovail posted an operating loss of nearly $7 million.

If Biovail was to succeed, it had to grow, and to grow it needed to raise new capital. But how? Melnyk didn't want to borrow money; the drain of interest payments could strangle his fragile young company. Anyway, start-ups have trouble borrowing at all. But if debt wasn't the answer, equity financing seemed equally impractical.

A larger, more-established publicly held drug company could simply turn to a Merrill Lynch or a Salomon Smith Barney and say, "We want to do a follow-on offering." The investment bankers would appear with their spreadsheets, the brokerage analysts would be summoned to ready a "buy" recommendation, and voilà!—a secondary issue of stock would raise the needed funds.

But in 1992 Biovail was too small and too speculative to interest the big investment banks, or even the regional ones. To be sure, there were venture-capital firms, but where the banks might fear to tread, the venture capitalists usually demanded a company's heart and soul—probably even a controlling equity stake—in repayment. Melnyk wanted to keep what he built, and he wasn't about to give away a great idea to a bunch of V.C. "suits."

So Melnyk, then just thirty-three, began asking around. "How does a small, publicly held drug company get new equity financing?"

Enter Hemant Shah.

The chief executive of a major drug company first mentioned Shah to Melnyk. "He was positioned as an analyst who had a lot of connections," Melnyk recalls. In other words, he was an analyst who dabbled in the investment-banking side of the securities world, in small-cap stocks. He could help raise money for a small-cap company and maybe even boost the stock while doing it.

Indeed, a few years later Shah would tell a reporter that his real American Dream was to become an investment banker and venture capitalist, to set up a $50 million fund to invest in start-up drug companies. That was why he had immigrated to the United States from his native India, why he had become a securities analyst, why he had started HKS & Co. "There [in India], it is not so much what you know but who you know that matters," he said. "The kind of corruption you see in financial markets would not be tolerated here even for a second. That was why I started my own firm and focused on a few selected clients."[4]

Given that securities analysts are expected to render impartial opinions on publicly traded companies, Shah's ambitions of investment banking and deal making should have raised red flags. Raising money for a company and touting it as a "buy" are two different functions. On the one hand, an investment banker could very legitimately raise money for a company thought to be fully valued on Wall Street (thus, not a "buy") or could very justifiably underwrite bonds even if the company was somewhat overvalued on Wall Street. By contrast, an analyst—at least as far as investors are concerned—shouldn't tout or bad-mouth a stock unless it is independently seen as going to outperform or underperform the market.

Wearing both hats doesn't work; analysts can't very well put a "sell" signal out on a company and then try to raise money for the company, too. Awkward, to say the least. A "buy" signal is incumbent in the situation. Because of this conflict, for generations the idea of analysts as investment bankers, or of analysts even having relations with traders and investment bankers (the guys who issue securities), was something seen only on the rinky-dink side of Wall Street, in smaller regional firms and fraudulent "bucket shops" (brokerages that often rely on telephone "boiler rooms" and aggressive salespeople to push stocks, regardless of merit).

But in the Wall Street of the 1990s and the millennium, analysts—even those at major stock and bond brokerages such as Morgan Stanley Dean Witter or Salomon Smith Barney—were more and more taking a role in investment banking activities.

Melnyk knew that taking on an analyst investment banker to help raise funds was a bit on the shabby side of Wall Street. However, Shah had been recommended, and Melnyk needed the money. Pushing aside his concerns, Melnyk called him up.

## MELNYK AND SHAH

While it wasn't exactly a marriage made in heaven, the honeymoon certainly went well enough. In the early days at least, Shah and Melnyk hit it off, if awkwardly at times, entertaining each other's families on their respective yachts and jabbering on the phone, Melnyk's Canadian-Midwest twang mixing with Shah's Indian inflections. Melnyk became aware that the wavy-haired, olive-skinned Shah, then turning forty, had a large share of eccentricities—for example, he took two-month vacations, leaving clients in the lurch—but they seemed to be balanced by results. Over the next two years, Shah raised roughly $15 million for Biovail through two rounds of "private equity financing," or shares issued privately to investors, not sold in public offerings.

At the same time, Shah also began touting the company's stock to his roster of client money managers. Shah's touting of an investment banking client was not a good idea, but a flamboyant entrepreneur like Melnyk wasn't going to scrutinize someone's personal habits or private business. The results were what counted, and the results were good.

By 1995, Shah was working on an even bigger deal for Biovail: a licensing agreement for Tiazac, Biovail's star blood-pressure drug. Under Biovail contract, Shah was talking to Hoechst-Roussel (now Hoechst Marion Roussel), the American arm of German pharmaceutical giant Hoechst AG, which seemed willing to pay Biovail a hefty royalty in exchange for the exclusive rights to distribute Tiazac in the United States. It looked to be a good deal for both companies: Hoechst would get a piece of a promising new drug, while Biovail would get the credibility and marketing muscle it needed to be able to penetrate the U.S. drug market. Biovail would also get money for expansion.

A good deal, yes. But the best deal? No. The youthful Melnyk was no sit-behind-a-desk executive, nor a slouch at deal making. He knew how to talk on the phone too, and just as he wasn't going to get outmaneuvered by some venture capitalists, so too he wasn't going to hook up with the first big distributor who talked sweet.

Melnyk eventually wrangled an introduction to some players at

New York–based Forest Labs Inc., another drug house. The affable but sharp-eyed Melnyk—an owner of stakes-winning racehorses—is probably at his best in cutting a deal. And cut he did, with such speed that the Forest Labs negotiators felt rushed to keep up. In return for U.S. distribution rights to Tiazac, Forest agreed to pay Biovail a $20 million cash advance against royalties *and* buy a 20 percent stake in the company.

Melnyk's deal was a stroke of business genius. By requiring Forest to purchase an interest in Biovail, the deal gave the larger company— a distributing company, no less—a major incentive to make sure Tiazac was a success. If for no other reason than to protect the value of its Biovail stock, Forest would tell its salespeople and manufacturers' representatives to push Tiazac.

Melnyk's Forest Labs strategy worked. Tiazac won FDA approval in September 1995 and quickly made inroads in the U.S. market. As Tiazac sales soared, so did the price of Biovail stock. From the $2.34-a-share level at which Shah had sold it to his private clients in 1993 and 1994, Biovail exploded to $40 by the spring of 1996. Investors were hitting "ten-baggers" (1,000 percent returns) and more on Biovail stock, and there were high-fives all around.

Well, all around except for the mustachioed Shah. To the contrary, he felt burned. To hear him tell it—and a number of his clients did, according to depositions and recorded phone calls—he had been unfairly cut out of the Forest deal. And he had been shunted aside in the deal-making process. From his point of view, he had been wounded, and then salt was rubbed in deep.

One Shah associate, Robert Parrente, was deposed in the aforementioned *Biovail v. Parker Quillen* civil case. In depositions, Parrente said Shah told him that he "had been hired by Biovail as a consultant to do a deal, and he wasn't paid, so I guess there was bad blood."

Another hedge fund manager (who spoke on condition of anonymity) who had worked closely with Shah for several years on several stocks, including on Biovail, also observed Shah's change in temperament. "I thought he [Hemant Shah] was probably better than most analysts. But Hemant did say to me that Biovail had not honored its fee obligations. I was aware they had had an investment banking agreement, and Hemant felt they owed him. After that, Hemant was too pessimistic on the company, he probably overreached and let his anger influence him. Was Hemant wrong on Biovail stock? Yes, we are all wrong at some point."[5]

Shah felt he should at least have been paid for the work he did on the nixed Hoechst deal. He even griped, perhaps injudiciously, to the media, complaining to the magazine *Financial World* in November 1996 that he had done consulting work for Biovail "but had never been paid."

Of course, to Shah, who was self-described as a would-be investment banker/financier, being left on the sidelines during the Biovail-Forest talks was not just about the lost fees. The Biovail-Forest arrangement was both literally and figuratively a Big Deal. To have been able to claim credit would have propelled him mightily into the role of investment banker—along with the more-lucrative fees and pre-IPO equity stakes such deals would bring. But instead he was set aside. From the outside, it looked like he was a wallflower—maybe even uninvited—at what should have been his coming-out party.

There were other reasons for Shah's animus toward Biovail. Before leaving on an extended European vacation and cruise in October 1995, he had recommended to his clients that they toss overboard their Biovail holdings. At the time, Biovail stock was trading in the low teens—a nice multiple over the $2 or so most of them had originally paid for it, but nowhere near the levels it would attain over the next few months. The clients who took Shah's advice thus missed a great run-up, even by 1990s standards. That's not exactly what an analyst wants to be known for, and Shah wanted to correct the impression that he had made a bad call. If the run-up were seen as flaky, all the better.

Surely, even more than most analysts, Shah needed to preserve and enhance his reputation. After he left Nomura Securities in 1988, Shah had never again latched on with a name-brand brokerage firm. Perhaps unfairly, he had to work harder to be taken seriously than someone who could hand over a business card embossed with a big brokerage name like Merrill Lynch or Morgan Stanley Dean Witter. That was one reason to work with the press so closely—to keep his name out there, to keep the image of being recognized. Shah lived every day on his record, his calls, without the presumed authority of a major Wall Street house to fall back on. Admirable, but tough, too.

As Biovail founder Melnyk put it some years later, "Shah had always loved to position himself as an outsider, often on the other side of a mainstream analyst's recommendation. Of course, that's a vulnerable place to be. When his recommendation to sell Biovail blew up in his face, it doubled the humiliation. I think he desperately tried to show in 1996 that his recommendation to sell in 1995 hadn't been wrong. Being wrong hurt as much as the fee, I believe. Probably more."[6]

However much Shah felt Biovail had betrayed or humiliated him, he evidently didn't feel it was an issue for the courts. He never filed suit. Instead, he decided that he would extract his revenge in his neighborhood—on Wall Street. On this turf, in this particular battle, for right or wrong, Shah would prove a formidable opponent.

## THE FIRST ASSAULTS

Burning from his sidelines role in the Forest-Biovail deal, Shah began to lay the groundwork to sink the company's stock. As Halloween 1995 approached, Shah conceived of a plan to spook Wall Street about the company's new pay-dirt medicine for hearts, Tiazac. If Biovail's fortunes were hitched to the star drug Tiazac, what would happen if Tiazac turned out to have ghoulish side effects?

Of course, for Shah to achieve his ends, Tiazac didn't really have to be a horror story. All that was necessary was for Wall Street to believe—or even just worry—that Tiazac *might* be the grave digger's friend.

Shah's first salvo assumed the nebulous form of a whispering campaign pitched at financial reporters. The message: Tiazac wasn't moving, it wasn't meeting expectations, something was ghostly about the sales figures.

In fact, Biovail and Forest had yet to formally launch the drug in the U.S. market. That notwithstanding, the respected Dow Jones News Service fell for Shah's pitch, and in a piece that went out over the wire on October 29, 1995, repeated his spiel virtually verbatim.

As the story put it:

> Some short-sellers and bearish analysts have speculated that the
> initial strong sales of Tiazac reflect a built-up inventory, and not
> actual patient demand. They said Forest has bought product from
> Biovail but isn't selling much to patients. Hemant Shah, an out-
> spoken independent industry analyst, estimates that year-to-date
> there has been only $10 million to $12 million in end-user Tiazac
> sales (about one-third of expected levels).

The substance of this report was as baseless as its description of
Shah as an "independent" analyst. With his investment banking relations to Biovail and the subsequent falling-out, Shah was almost certainly the least-independent analyst covering Biovail, and certainly
one who appeared to have an axe to grind. Furthermore, Biovail was
selling a lot of Tiazac to patients.

With his Halloween offensive underway, Shah also began circulating an even more troubling rumor: that the U.S. Food and Drug Administration was concerned about calcium channel blockers (CCBs)
in general and Tiazac in particular. Depending on whom he was talking to, Shah insisted the FDA was thinking of banning the drug, or
limiting its use, or requiring it to carry scary warning labels. Shah created a frightening apparition for Biovail shareholders: although
Tiazac was well past the testing stage and gaining increased penetra-
tion in Biovail-Forest test-marketing, Shah claimed it might suddenly
be yanked out of hospitals and pharmacies—the result of a pending
(but imaginary) FDA ruling that it had harmful side effects. D day, he
said, would be January 25, 1996, when an FDA advisory panel was
scheduled to hold a public hearing—at which, Shah claimed, it would
announce that the use of Tiazac and other CCBs should be restricted. One Shah client, Associated Capital LP of New York, a money
fund run by the storied Jay and Selig Zises, was worried enough by
Shah's incantations to send not one but two lawyers to attend the
FDA hearing, to get the skinny direct.

Playing on his many years of experience in the industry and his
reputation for being well-connected, Shah told anyone who asked

that his information came directly from secret sources deep inside the FDA. According to his account, the FDA had determined that CCBs increased the risk of heart failure, and on that basis the agency was taking aim at Tiazac and its rivals. His friends at the drug companies, he added, were "scared to death."

What made this dirge so bewitching—or unnerving—was that it was played with some relevant background music. As would happen many times in Shah's war on Biovail, his flute played some true notes—in scores with which he recomposed reality to suit his purposes.

As it happened, medical evidence did exist that raised questions about CCBs. In 1995, published research indicated that some CCBs might actually trigger heart attacks. The culprits, however, weren't the controlled-release (or long-acting) CCBs such as Tiazac. Rather, they were the short-acting CCBs, those that quickly release a relatively large amount of calcium-blocking drugs into the body, that posed danger. There has never been any evidence, not in 1996 nor to this day, indicating that long-acting CCBs such as Tiazac are in any way harmful.

But that's not how Shah played the tune. On January 18, 1996, Shah was caught in a tape recording telling a client that the FDA had found danger signals in a retrospective study of long-acting CCBs, which he referred to as "slow release" or "sustained release."

Shah's pitch went like this:

*Shah:* I know for a fact that the FDA has found similar evidence with k—one other fast-relea—slow-release calcium channel blocker. I don't know which one it is.

*Client:* Really?

*Shah:* My, my gut feeling is…

*Client:* Now, where is this evidence coming? This is the first I've heard of that.

*Shah:* From the FDA.

*Client:* FDA internally?

*Shah:* People I know, yes.

*Client:* They did their own study?

*Shah:* No, what they did is they looked at all the adverse-reaction reports filed, and they did a statistical analysis on that.

*Client:* So, it's—it's retrospective, but—

*Shah:* But it is based on fact.

*Client:* Okay.

*Shah:* It's based on, you know—

*Client:* And it's based off the—the time release or …

*Shah:* This is sustained release.

According to another client (a large hedge fund manager) of Shah's who testified under deposition, Shah predicted that the FDA action resulting from this (nonexistent) "statistical analysis" was likely to devastate the market for Tiazac, causing sales to plummet by 80 percent or more.

Shah wasn't only talking, he was putting his money down. Between January 18 and January 24, 1996, he shorted 7,000 shares of Biovail stock, at $26 to $28 a share. At that point, Shah had shorted at least $182,000 worth of Biovail stock, but he would take much larger short positions in the future.[7] Perhaps he thought he would win back in the market what he had lost when Melnyk's deal with Forest deep-sixed his negotiations with Hoechst—while simultaneously driving down Melnyk's net worth (Melnyk is the major shareholder in Biovail). Perhaps by Shah's reckoning, that was fair play.

In any case, although it is hard to credit moves in a stock's price to the murmurings of any particular short trader or analyst, it is worth noting that Biovail stock weakened suddenly after January 18, falling from around $26 a share to about $21 a share the following week. Given Shah's prominent role in all things Biovail at the time, however, it wouldn't be a stretch to credit him with a significant portion of the tailspin.

Of course, the day had to come when the FDA actually held its meeting, and indeed on January 25, 1996, the FDA advisory panel held the anticipated public session. Shah had the date right, anyway. But he had everything else wrong. The panel did not recommend any restrictions or any other FDA action regarding Tiazac or the other long-acting CCBs. The FDA panel did vote to "discourage" the use of *short-acting* CCBs—in commercial terms, actually a positive outcome for the alternative form, which is long-acting Tiazac.

Why did Shah concoct and spread such a brazen fabrication, one that he had to know would surely be exposed as a falsehood when the FDA panel finally met? Most likely, it was because he knew he could get away with it. Maybe he had made money on his short positions in the meantime. Maybe his clients did, too. In any case, when was the last time the SEC prosecuted an analyst? And the media don't compile batting averages on analyst predictions.

And even if the FDA hadn't slammed the door on Tiazac for now, maybe Shah had raised the shadow of doubt that Tiazac was a shaky drug, possibly subject to future FDA restrictions. How many investors actually read minutes of FDA meetings anyway? How many know the difference between long-acting and short-acting CCBs? To create worries about a stock is enough on Wall Street.

IF SHAH HAD BEEN A SIMPLE short trader, he might have disappeared back into the woodwork after his FDA visions were so clearly contradicted by events. But Hemant Shah was just getting started. Indeed, between February 13 and February 23, 1996, Shah shorted an additional $835,100 worth of Biovail stock, at about $30 a share (obviously, the stock rebounded after the January 25, 1996, FDA meeting).

About the same time, he started a new round of rumors about potential obstacles facing Biovail. Although he could no longer claim that the FDA was about to ban Tiazac, he nonetheless insisted to reporters and money managers that the "controversy" about CCBs was bound to hurt Tiazac sales. He began this effort with a broadside in the February 2, 1996, issue of his newsletter. In part, it read:

We believe that ... expectations [about Biovail's profits] may be just too optimistic, and may be difficult to meet under the current controversy surrounding calcium channel blockers.... Before the eruption of the controversy related to calcium channel blockers (CCBs), we had expressed an opinion that ... Tiazac could easily achieve $100 million in annual sales.... We currently believe that due to a dramatic deterioration of the CCB market place ... performance of ... Tiazac may be well below our previous expectations, and below the expectations of Wall Street.

Later that month, Shah's argument appeared to be independently buttressed when a Canadian brokerage issued a long research report that came to some remarkably similar conclusions. Written by director Jim Wilhelm of the now-defunct firm of Richardson, Greenshields, it included this downbeat assessment:

It is believed the stock of Biovail is one of the most overvalued and least understood stocks currently in the health care field.... The current controversy surrounding Calcium Beta Blockers (CBBs) [sic] has impacted their use....[8]

Wilhelm went on to predict, "Due to the adverse publicity surrounding CBBs, it is believed Tiazac's sales will be closer to $25 million rather than the predicted $300 million."

Wilhelm's grasp of the subject was as dubious as a $3 bill. For one thing, he confused Tiazac, a long-acting calcium channel blocker, with an entirely different class of blood-pressure drugs known as beta-blockers, conflating the two into a nonexistent amalgam he called a "Calcium Beta Blocker." It made for interesting literary alchemy, but it was hardly analysis. For another, despite his assertion that Tiazac sales had been "predicted" to reach "$300 million," the fact was that nobody—either at Biovail or in the analyst community—had ever predicted sales on such a grand level. Biovail's 1996 total sales were $66.4 million (with a healthy $22.7 million of net profit). Wilhelm's lack of expertise should not have been surprising, given that he had never before published anything about the drug industry, nor has he since.

These lapses, however, did not prevent the Dow Jones News Service from taking note of Wilhelm's conclusions and wiring an account of them to investors around the world. For the second time in just over three months, Dow Jones had been unwittingly enlisted as an ally in Shah's war on Biovail. While it may have looked to outsiders as if Shah's gloomy forecasts had been seconded by a second, independent expert—one credible enough to be quoted by Dow Jones—the similarity of Shah's and Wilhelm's views on Biovail was no coincidence. Shah effectively conceded as much in a March 5, 1996, tape-recorded telephone conversation with an unidentified speaker, in which he worried about being exposed in the pending discovery proceedings connected with the *Biovail v. Parker Quillen* lawsuit.

*Shah:* Ah … there's an awful lot of things in that [Biovail] file.

*Speaker:* Right.

*Shah:* And, you know, the worst part for me is this—the worst thing that happen, that can happen to me is that I, I, you know—there's a discovery …

*Speaker:* Uh huh—are you connected to Richardson, Greenshields?

*Shah:* Right.

*Speaker:* You are.

*Shah:* I was connected.

*Speaker:* Uh huh.

*Shah:* You know … everybody knows that …

*Speaker:* Okay.

*Shah:* … this man apparently visited Biovail …

*Speaker:* Uh huh.

*Shah:* … with [name withheld].

*Speaker:* Right.

*Shah:* So, if I am discovered …

*Speaker:* Uh huh.

*Shah:* … I have to hand over all my files …

*Speaker:* Right.

*Shah:* … to their attorney.

## THE CARDIOLOGISTS' MEETING

While Shah was scare-mongering the problems supposedly associated with long-acting CCBs, the medical community was doing exactly the opposite. At the annual meeting of the American College of Cardiology held in Orlando, Florida, at the end of March 1996, researchers reported glowingly on the safety and effectiveness of long-acting CCBs. In particular, they pointed to a just-completed study of 30,000 hypertension patients that demonstrated clearly that long-acting CCBs did not increase the risk of heart attack. As a result of this finding, the assembled cardiologists were told that the FDA was suggesting that doctors might want to consider taking patients off the short-acting version of the drug and switching them to the long-acting version.

In other words, to the extent there was any sort of medical concern involving CCBs, it was bound to help—not hurt—the sales of Tiazac. Of course, Shah never shared this information with any of his clients or the journalists who liked to quote him. Nor did he make any distinction between long-acting and short-acting CCBs. Rather, he told a reporter covering the Orlando convention simply that "overall prescription usage [for CCBs] has been declining in the last eight months, and it's because of the controversy."

In fact, data collected by IMS Health, an organization that tracks prescription sales, indicated that demand for Tiazac was growing steadily, even spectacularly, in the early months of 1996. In January of that year, Tiazac claimed less than 1 percent of the market for long-acting CCB prescriptions. Over the next month, its market share more than doubled; it climbed to 2.6 percent in April, and by June had reached 4 percent. (Tiazac's market share, in fact, steadily increased through 1996 and 1997, according to IMS Health data.)

As Tiazac went, so went Biovail. As a result of the success of its new drug, the company was transformed from an iffy start-up venture into an extremely profitable and fast-growing concern. Both earnings and revenues exploded in the first half of 1996, jumping roughly fivefold from the year before, to a net of $10.4 million on sales of $34.6 million.

The facts, however, were not going to get in the way of Shah's new mantra. Throughout the first half of 1996, he continued to tell all who would listen that the CCB "controversy" was wreaking havoc with sales of Tiazac, and that as a result Biovail was in trouble. The following April 22, 1996, telephone conversation between Shah and a client was typical:

*Shah:* Uh … you know I, how um, I get data early from couple big drug companies I work with?

*Client:* Right.

*Shah:* I kind of asked them you see if … the, they, they sell … they, they probably buy $2-$3 million of data from the scrip—from Prescription Audit Services.

*Client:* Right.

*Shah:* So, I asked them if they could use their influence and try to get some early peek because, you know, they get a lot data a— ahead of time, so they have data for at least several days for the week ending April 19th.

*Client:* Okay.

*Shah:* And, based on this spot check, it looks like Tiazac will be down another 15 percent or 16 percent.

*Client:* This is based upon preliminary data that these drug companies have had … have seen … have gathered?

*Shah:* Based on the data gathered by the audit service.

Two days later, Shah was back on the phones with another client, this time armed with information, he said, from inside drug giant Forest (which had taken the stake in Biovail and which distributed

Tiazac). Shah is at his conspiratorial best, and it's hard not to admire his stock-sinking skills just a bit:

*Shah:* You cannot mention this to anyone.

*Client:* Okay.

*Shah:* We got … You know I am getting sales projections within Forest, and they had a sales projection of $50 to $55 million for calendar '96.

*Client:* I'm sorry, $50 to $55 million?

*Shah:* Right, in the beginning with the product was—

*Client:* For Tiazac?

*Shah:* Right, for Tiazac. Then it was reduced to [the] $40 to $50 million range.

*Client:* Right.

*Shah:* Then it was reduced sometime toward the beginning of March. You know, when it was launched they immediately lowered the number because they were beginning to see the resistance. Then some time beginning of March, the numbers were lowered to $25 to $40 million, and right now the number is between $15 to $25 million.

*Client:* And they … [unintelligible]

*Shah:* These are from internal memorandums!

*Client:* Internal memorandums from …

*Shah:* Within marketing department of Forest.

Later in the same conversation:

*Shah:* You still have probably another month, at the most, because next week is going to be a disaster week, in my opinion, for Biovail.

*Client:* Because of script numbers [i.e., the volume of Tiazac prescriptions].

*Shah:* Because the script numbers are going to be terrible …

Of course, the figures Shah cited, both in this conversation and in the April 22 tele-chat, were wrong, as was revealed when the figures became public. But his clients took them seriously. After all, Shah was one of the most widely quoted securities analysts covering the pharmaceuticals industry.

As Shah told it, Tiazac was stumbling so badly that Forest was pressing to renegotiate its contract with Biovail. On May 8, Shah was caught on tape telling a client that Forest wanted to "substantially reduce" the royalties it paid Biovail under their licensing agreement. "[T]hey are going to be making some major, major decisions as far as ... Tiazac is concerned," Shah warned. "One of the things, I'm almost certain, would be to renegotiate the deal."

But in fact there was no such renegotiation. It was just Shah playing a new song for his clients.

### DIEHARD BIOVAIL

Despite all Shah's efforts, the price of Biovail stock continued to lurch upward after mysterious downdrafts, from $20 a share in January 1996 to $30 in February. By May, it was heading toward $40. In part, the problem was George Soros.

For months rumors had been circulating that the Brobdingnagian speculator was stomping around Biovail. By the middle of May, the buzz was that Soros would grab a 10 percent stake in the company. The ground was shaking, and traders skittered about to buy Biovail and liquidate short positions. To make matters worse for Shah, Soros wasn't the only heavy hitter supposedly interested in Biovail. There was also talk that the pharmaceutical giant Pfizer was thinking about acquiring the company outright. Biovail was getting to be positively sexy on Wall Street.

At the time, Shah's personal short position totaled some 29,000 shares of Biovail stock. Facing huge losses, and with his reputation on the line, he once again began working the phones. As noted earlier, first Shah told clients and others that Soros was also a Shah disciple and that Soros wasn't going to buy Biovail stock. Shah was equally dismissive of the reports of Pfizer's interest in Biovail, telling one fund manager that "the Pfizer rumor under any circumstance cannot be true." How did he know? Once again, Shah portrayed himself as the indispensable guru, in this conversation taped on May 20, 1996:

*Shah:* I told you, two of the most senior [Pfizer] officers listen to me. I give them stock ideas.

*Fund manager:* Right.

*Shah:* One of those ideas was to short Biovail.

*Fund manager:* Oh, you told Pfizer [to short]?

*Shah:* That's right!

*Fund manager:* Uh-huh.

*Shah:* One of the executives, not the company…. If they short the stock, do you think they would buy the company?

*Fund manager:* Certainly wouldn't make much sense.

With what can only be called poetic justice, Shah found himself losing money on his Biovail short positions in May 1996, along with his clients, as the Soros rumor boosted Biovail stock. His short positions were killing him—as Shah himself complained to a client, also on May 20, 1996:

*Shah:* What happened is, because of my report, a lot of people have shorted the stock apparently.

*Client:* Right.

*Shah:* Some may be short, some may have covered. Some may have gotten burned.

*Client:* Right.

*Shah:* What has happened is I have a lot of upset clients.

*Client:* Right.

*Shah:* And you know, I write, I have to write more [short more stock and hope for a price drop] as a result. It's like a vicious circle.

*Client:* Are you going to continue to write?

*Shah:* I have no choice.

Unfortunately for Shah, locked in a battle of his own making from which he evidently felt he could not escape, poetic justice ruled the day. Like cymbals crashing in the middle of his flute song, on May 22, 1996—just two days after Shah had scornfully snubbed speculation that Soros would buy into Biovail—a group led by Soros announced it had acquired not a 10 percent stake but a *20 percent stake* in Biovail. Soros had decided to take Forest's one-fifth position in the company. Soros liked the stock, evidently. A lot.

### REGROUP, ATTACK AGAIN

With a drumroll and a full orchestra in forte, Soros had drowned out Shah's song. The Wall Street warrior must have asked himself, "Now what?" How could he make it seem to clients as if he still could play to a beat, recognize a tune? How could he rescue his short positions?

Some defense lawyers have a saying, "If the facts are with you, argue the facts. If the facts are against you, challenge the facts." And so the relentless Shah began to challenge the facts, launching a fresh campaign of misinformation, half-truths, and outright whoppers—all aimed at raising doubts about information that was actually rock solid.

His first target was a fact that seemed patently undeniable: the Soros group's purchase of Forest's interest in Biovail. Shah's spin was as cock-eyed as it was untrue: Soros wasn't really investing in Biovail—that was just for public consumption. What Soros was really doing was manipulating and speculating. While publicly announcing his purchase of a 20 percent interest in Biovail, he was actually shorting the company's stock in secret, and possibly buying "put" options (another way to bet that a stock would go down in value). By judiciously selling portions of his stake from time to time, Soros could drive down Biovail prices and make huge profits on his short positions, Shah hinted.

Shah began circulating this novel notion the same day the Soros group announced its purchase of the Biovail equity, as this May 22 telephone conversation shows:

*Shah:* Uh, remember I told you the Soros story is not true?

*Client:* Right.

*Shah:* And how did I know? Well, Soros is my client.

*Client:* Right.

*Shah:* And I know he was short the stock. Now I know why he is short the stock.

*Client:* Okay.

*Shah:* The rumor is that he has already presold at least one-third of his position. I mean this is typical George Soros, and that's why he is a billionaire, and we are not. Ha, ha, ha. What a masterstroke. What a masterstroke! This is unbelievable.... I bet he [Soros] is going to have a 50 percent return in one month.

*Client:* You think [Biovail is] dropping 50 percent in one month?

*Shah:* No, no. no. He is going to have a 50 percent—at least 50 percent—return in one month.

*Client:* Hmm.

*Shah:* That's without a doubt, ha, ha. But think about this. What a masterstroke. I mean, you know, Eugene [Melnyk] should have shown the stock to us. You and me.

*Client:* Hmm. So his strategy in your eyes is to—

*Shah:* Not eyes, ha, ha, ha. This is not a George Soros stock!

*Client:* Who knows? I mean, uh ...

*Shah:* I know!

*Client:* Okay.

*Shah:* He told me. He is my client!

*Client:* Hmm. So you think he'll be out of it—

*Shah:* Within a month.

*Client:* He'll be out of a complete position?

*Shah:* Oh yeah. He'll do options and everything else. He is a big options trader, you know that.

*Client:* Right.

Shah further muddied the waters in the next issue of his monthly newsletter, writing that Forest wouldn't have sold its Biovail stake to Soros unless it knew something troubling about Biovail's prospects—something that Soros himself was presumably too ignorant or dewy-eyed to see. "Maybe Forest knows something more about underlying fundamentals at Biovail than most investors, and assumes that Biovail stock is grossly overvalued in the marketplace," he suggested.[9]

Then again, Shah publicly wondered (with admirable gall), could it be that Soros "is trying to manipulate the stock? Maybe this is a great way to become a billionaire without regard to [sic] integrity of the U.S. financial markets, which I teach all my students and children to be the backbone of the financial markets."

Shah went on to say he had a "few questions" for "market participants, the billionaire, and regulators guarding the markets"—among them, "Why would Forest be willing to sell its stake in Biovail at well over 50 percent below the market price...?"

Shah was referring here to the fact that the Soros group had bought Forest's piece of Biovail for about $100 million, or roughly $20 a share—about half of what the stock was trading at on May 22, when the deal was announced. What Shah neglected to mention was that Soros's deal with Forest had actually been negotiated back in April, when Biovail was trading around $24 a share. The fact was, while Forest did indeed sell Soros its stock at below the market price (as often happens when such "jumbo blocks" change hands, but which does not confer a controlling stake in a company), the discount was a normal-sized 15 percent—not the "well over 50 percent" Shah had claimed. Further, Forest was known to be a company that was cash-strapped. It needed the money, even if it cut a deal for which it later was sorry.

David Farber, an on-air reporter with CNBC, on May 23 told the world that he had heard that Soros had actually been short on Biovail, but the stock had risen in price.[10] So Soros covered his short position by executing the purchase of the Forest holding in Biovail—in brief, the Farber report was almost certainly another bit of Shah-inspired airwave nonsense, and another subtle reminder how analysts can influence the investment climate for a stock.

Shah continued his disinformation campaign in a May 23, 1996, interview carried by Bloomberg News, in which he predicted that "based on prescription trends," 1996 sales of Tiazac would "be under $25 million." (In fact, they would wind up totaling more than twice that.)

As with the October 29 Dow Jones report and the CNBC report, Bloomberg seemed unaware that Shah was a onetime consultant to Biovail, that he and the company had parted ways with bad blood, and that he had disclosed in his newsletter that he might be trading in the company's stock. And, obviously, Shah didn't volunteer to Bloomberg that he was heavily short on the stock and taking a financial beating. All to show that even good reporters, on deadline, have to fly with sources that they don't really know much about—the inevitable curse of daily and wire reporting.

In any event, after the Soros debacle, some of Shah's efforts began to take on the air of "throwing mud on the wall to see what sticks." On June 24, he was tape-recorded almost whimsically telling a client that Tiazac was not approved for sale in the United Kingdom, hinting at the dangers of the drug. In fact, the Medicines Control Agency, Britain's version of the FDA, had approved Tiazac three months earlier.

Around the same time, he began spreading tales that Tiazac had been barred from Canada because Biovail had submitted false data to Canadian medical authorities. As it turned out, the only thing holding up approval in Canada was the foot-dragging bureaucracy of the Canadian Health Protection Board, which ultimately okayed Tiazac in 1997.

## WAR OF ATTRITION

After May 1996, despite frequent setbacks, Shah's relentless jihad against Biovail appeared to be taking a toll on the company, in something of a delayed reaction. After peaking at $40 in May, Biovail stock began drifting downward. By the end of the summer it was back in the mid-20s—despite improving fundamentals and an overall bull market. By November 1996, Biovail was one of the most heavily shorted stocks on the American Stock Exchange, with 2.8 million shares, or a sizable 11 percent, of the company's outstanding float in short positions.

The stock got a boost in the fall, when Biovail posted strong numbers for the third quarter, actually beating the consensus estimates. As is made clear in later chapters, that was a real feat, since analysts tend to be overly optimistic about companies they cover. The fundamentals looked good.

IMS Health, the independent prescription-tracking agency, reported that Tiazac was selling well, having captured more than 6 percent of the once-a-day diltiazem (sustained-release) market. Tiazac sales looked good. Nonetheless, the tide of war was starting to go Shah's way in mid- and late 1996. True, with Biovail revenues up sharply, he could no longer raise the specter of weak sales. But the cumulative effect of one story after another—remember, market participants back then didn't know what we know now—was shaking investor confidence. It should also be considered that the full record of Shah's actions is not known, only what he said when tape recorders were whirring and what showed up in court records. Shah may have dropped other and many bombshells on Biovail, never revealed.

Perhaps emboldened, Shah tried out a new song in the September 1996 issue of his newsletter, which warned investors, "We believe that company earnings performance is primarily driven by shipping of Tiazac from one warehouse to another, rather than sales of Tiazac to consumers."[11] Shah, with staggering mendacity, was asserting that while Biovail may have been shipping Tiazac to Forest warehouses, Forest wasn't actually selling the drug to consumers. Although this notion was clearly contradicted by prescription-tracking data, Shah still managed to get both investors and journalists to take seriously his inference that Biovail was somehow cooking the books.

One reporter who fell for Shah's tune was Dow Jones reporter Jesse Eisinger. On November 15, 1996, the Dow Jones News Service carried a story by Eisinger that described Biovail's accounting techniques as "aggressive" and noted that while the company "expects Tiazac sales in its first year to reach $50 million ... Hemant Shah, an independent analyst, said the drug will sell under $20 million." (As usual, Shah's relationship with Biovail, not to mention his large short position in its stock, escaped the reporter's notice, or at least wasn't reported.)

In November, Shah was quoted in the *Toronto Globe and Mail* financial paper, stating that "I work for the industry. A [sales] performance like this is considered a big disappointment. A drug that doesn't take off in the first nine months doesn't take off forever." [12]

To the eternal credit of the *Globe and Mail,* its reporter Stephen Northfield also reported that "Mr. Shah has claimed that Biovail stiffed him for work he did on the Forest deal." Northfield, unique among financial reporters, identified Shah as an analyst who "has figured prominently on the bear side of the Biovail debate." Northfield's qualifying statements are as exemplary as they are rare. Financial reporters cannot be expected to know the full facts and history of any particular stock or company as they pound away on deadline. But they can be expected to elicit from sources what biases they may have, and then present those biases to readers or viewers as well.

In any event, once again Biovail stock began to drift in a southerly fashion. Despite the company's strong operating results, it sank back to the $25- to- $30-a-share range in late 1996. The disconnect between Biovail's strong performance and its mediocre stock price was so striking that on November 22, analyst Jerry Treppel of New York–based Dillon, Read & Co. (now Warburg Dillon Read) issued a strongly positive research report on the company, in which he reiterated an earlier "buy" recommendation for its stock. Blasting what he called the "short seller assault on Biovail with its related plethora of misinformation"—and pointing out that there was nothing at all unusual about Biovail's accounting methods—Treppel noted that "those of us who have been in this business for any length of time recognize that knowledge of accounting, or pursuit of veracity, is not a hallmark of much of what passes for reporting in the financial press."

It should be noted that Treppel's brokerage had no underwriting business with Biovail, and little prospect of getting any—a conflict that, if it had existed, would have considerably lessened the weight of his comments, as is explored at length in later chapters.

Unfortunately, unlike Shah's apocalyptic (and consistently baseless) warnings, which Dow Jones and the other wire services had been dutifully relaying to the world, Treppel's reassuring conclusions received scant coverage in the business press. Evidently, Treppel didn't know how to play the press game, or felt it beneath his dignity.

Nor did the confirming opinion issued on December 5 by Biovail's auditors, the respected Big 5 firm of Deloitte & Touche, that the "Company's recording of sales revenues ... are all in accordance with generally accepted accounting principles," receive much publicity. It should be remembered that by issuing such an opinion, the deep-pocketed Deloitte & Touche was opening itself up to shareholder lawsuits galore—but only if it were wrong. It issued not a qualified opinion, but a full-throated one. Obviously, Deloitte & Touche felt comfortable with its opinion, which has never been challenged, legally or otherwise.

But Biovail stock languished nonetheless. As Shah understood, what matters most in the battle for Wall Street perceptions—at least in the short run—is not always the facts but rather who shouts the loudest (or has the best connections to financial journalists) and who can bring investor firepower to bear.

Through 1997 and 1998, Biovail was consistently dogged by short rumors, and the short position in the stock was enormous—despite improving fundamentals in nearly every quarter, and certainly on a year-over-year basis (see chart at right). As late as June 1997, Shah was telling the Dow Jones News Service that Biovail drugs in development were dubious. On June 11, 1997, he was quoted by the Dow Jones News Service to the effect that Biovail stock was rising only due to rumors of an impending buyout at $50 a share by a British drug giant. "Tomorrow, if there is a rumor that God will buy the company for $50 [a share], it wouldn't surprise me," Shah told the news service. (You have to give Shah credit—what wire reporter could pass by a quote like that? Again, no mention was made that Shah was a known bear on the stock and had had a falling-out with Biovail.)

Even as Biovail posted solid numbers, short positions (the number of shares sold short) in the company increased. In May 1998, a very heavy 6 million shares had been bought and sold by short traders, out of a total float of 25.6 million shares—remarkably, more than one-quarter of the stock's float was in the hands of short traders. But the tables were about to be turned.

## BIOVAIL CORP. INTERNATIONAL
## THE TRACK RECORD

| YEAR | REVENUES (MILLIONS) | NET INCOME (MILLIONS) |
|------|---------------------|-----------------------|
| 1999 | $176.5 | $62.5 |
| 1998 | 112.8 | 45.4 |
| 1997 | 82.4 | 35.2 |
| 1996 | 66.4 | 22.7 |
| 1995 | 20.6 | 5.9 |

Source: Securities and Exchange Commission

## AFTERMATH: THE DEPOSITION

Shah—the spinmeister on the phone, the confident confidante, the independent and outspoken Biovail expert, the media-savvy short— became a different man in depositions conducted in February and March 1998. Then, Shah was under oath, being questioned by Andy Levander, a lawyer hired by Biovail to try to break apart the short-trading ring they suspected was playing havoc with the stock.

Not one to fool with, Levander early in his career worked in the U.S. Attorney's office in Manhattan. If there is a training ground for sharp young lawyers, it is the Southern District of New York, as that office is called. Moreover, Levander trained under Rudolph Giuliani, the U.S. attorney who put junk bond king Michael Milken behind bars and then became widely hailed as the mayor tough enough to clean up New York City.

Transcripts of the deposition show a consistently evasive Shah, who suffers critical memory lapses frequently, to put it politely. Under Levander's relentless questioning, Shah suddenly wasn't sure if Soros was his client, or if he ever had had figures on Tiazac's true sales, or if he ever recommended to investors they short Biovail stock, or if he had suggested that Tiazac wasn't allowed for sale in the United Kingdom. At one point during the questioning, Shah actually bolted from the deposition room, shouting "I am just going to answer 'No' to everything!"

Beyond suspicious lapses in memory, Shah several times was caught in what it is difficult to interpret as anything but outright inconsistencies.

### SHORT ADVICE?

As seen in Shah's tape-recorded calls, he advised people to short Biovail, and even bragged about advising Pfizer executives to short the stock. Yet in deposition, Shah had a much different recollection of his history on Biovail.

*Levander:* Did there come a time that you began to recommend Biovail as a short?

*Shah:* No.

*Levander:* Did you ever recommend that anybody sell Biovail short?

*Shah:* Yes—no, I recommended as overvalued.

Later in the deposition ...

*Levander:* Did you recommend that people that didn't have a position in Biovail short the stock because it was overvalued?

*Shah:* No, I do not recommend that. It is up to them.

*Levander:* Did you ever recommend shorts?

*Shah:* No. [13]

It is difficult to reconcile Shah's testimony in deposition with his May 28, 1996, phone conversation with a client in which he states he advised Pfizer executives to short Biovail stock. Either Shah misspoke in deposition or he misled his client.

### THE IMS DATA?

As has been shown, Shah told money managers and others that he had advance knowledge of Tiazac prescription volume from IMS, the company that tracks prescriptions in the United States. In fact, IMS tracks prescriptions by computer, then releases results simultaneously to clients, and takes great pains to see that no data are leaked. Did Shah have access to IMS data, as he told clients? Here is how he answered under oath:

*Levander:* Do you ever have access to IMS data prior to its publication?

*Shah:* No.

*Levander:* Do you understand that IMS collects its data by computer and then releases it simultaneously to all its users?

*Shah:* I don't know how it works, no.

*Levander:* Have you ever been in possession of nonpublic, confidential information from anybody at IMS regarding the data that they are about to publish to its customers?

*Shah:* No.

*Levander:* Have you ever told anybody that you were in possession of IMS data that has not yet been published but is about to be published?

*Shah:* No.

As noted previously, Shah in a telephone conversation on April 22, 1996, told clients that sales of Tiazac were slow, and that he had access to IMS data—before the market—that revealed Tiazac sales to be slow. Again, he either lied in deposition, or he misled his clients.

## INTERNAL FOREST DOCUMENTS?
Recorded on tape on April 24, 1996, Shah told a client he had internal Forest documents, from within its marketing department, that showed a distinct slowdown in Tiazac sales. In deposition on February 23, 1998, Shah had a different story to tell.

*Levander:* Did you ever say in words or in substance to any of your clients that you were getting internal sales projections from within Forest and that the [Tiazac] sales projections had initially been

$50 to $55 million for calendar '96, that sometime in March the numbers were lowered in these internal sales projections to $25 to $40 million, and right now the number is between $15 and $25 million in the internal memorandums of Forest?

*Shah:* No.

Later in the deposition ...

*Levander:* Did you ever tell anybody that you had internal memoranda from Forest?

*Shah:* No.

Again, under Levander's questioning, Shah was caught on the horns of a dilemma: either he had to dissemble in deposition, or he had to go on the record as having misled his clients.

## TIAZAC NOT APPROVED IN THE U.K.?

On June 24, 1996, Shah told an investment client, in a taped interview, that regulatory agencies in Great Britain were not allowing Tiazac to be sold in that country. In fact, Biovail had been approved March 28, 1996, for sale in Great Britain, according to the Medicines Control Agency of the Department of Health. When questioned under oath, however, Shah denied he had ever raised the possibility that Tiazac would be blocked in the United Kingdom.

*Levander:* You are aware, are you not, that Biovail publicly announced [on March 28, 1996] that its Tiazac product had been approved for distribution in the United Kingdom?

*Shah:* Yes.

*Levander:* Did you ever suggest to anybody that there was a question as to whether Biovail's announcement was accurate?

*Shah:* No.

Again, Shah had a great deal of difficulty testifying under oath in a straightforward manner.

## THE SOROS STORY

It's hard to pin down exactly what was Shah's most outrageous false-hood, but near the top at least was his claim that Soros was his client and that Soros was short on Biovail stock, made in telephone conver-sations in May 1996 to clients, shortly before and after Soros assumed his big position in Biovail.

In fact, Soros purchased a sizable block of Biovail and held onto it for more than a year.

Shah later told a reporter for *Forbes* magazine that a certain indi-vidual within the Soros camp was his contact to Soros. But it turned out that that individual, Bob Raiff, had not worked for Soros since 1994—a full two years before Soros bought into Biovail—and doesn't remember talking to Shah since at least 1992, according to research conducted by *Forbes*.

One thing is for sure: In 1998, under deposition, Shah was no longer willing to state that Soros had ever been his client. Here is how Shah responded to the Soros question in deposition:

*Levander:* The sale by Forest of its stock to a group of investors, one of whom is Soros. Do you recall that last time?

*Shah:* Yes.

*Levander:* Did you ever tell anyone prior to the announcement of that deal that you knew for a fact that Soros was not buying Biovail stock from Forest?

*Shah:* I don't recall.

*Levander:* Is Soros a client of yours?

*Shah:* It was at one point.

*Levander:* Was it a client of yours in the spring of 1996?

*Shah:* I don't recall.

To say the least, it is unlikely that Shah, or any other investment adviser or analyst for that matter, would be unable to recall whether a major figure such as Soros had been a client less than two years earlier.

## DEEP IMPACT?

It is rarely possible to attribute a stock's move to a single event or a particular analyst's recommendation. Simply too many factors come into play. In addition to the fundamentals there are macroeconomic variables, such as the state of the overall economy and interest rates. Bull markets and bear markets wax and wane, and whole industries fade in and out of favor. Institutional investors, working in concert with brokerage trading departments and their analysts, can trade huge volumes and "defend" a stock, sink it (almost never a strategy), or send it into the stratosphere, if conditions are right. And lately, fads in investing have been inflamed by day traders and Web surfers, and a security may orbit into cyberspace, unfettered by earthly concerns, soaring even above levels that institutions and brokerages would defend ("sponsor") in a stock.

Nonetheless, it could be argued that over the course of 1996 and 1997 Shah's tireless campaign had a marked effect on the price of Biovail's stock. For example, although Biovail's fundamentals and outlook were strong—sales and earnings were up sharply in each quarter of 1996—its stock tumbled nearly 40 percent over the second half of 1996. Even by present Wall Street standards, that's odd market behavior. "My guess," says Biovail chairman Eugene Melnyk, "is that we traded about one-third below our proper level in the second half of 1996, based upon price-earnings ratios of other, similar drug stocks."

Yet as noted, Biovail was growing, in revenues and earnings, and had other promising drugs in the pipeline during and after this period. Like many other analysts, Shah probably knew when it was time to bring down the curtain and get his clients out of short positions, as the fundamentals can't be beaten forever. Shah apparently abandoned at least his public efforts against the company sometime in late 1997 or 1998, and by late 1998 the stock seemed to recover, once again piercing $40 a share. By 1999, Biovail stock had crossed over $60, and by 2001 was trading at around $170 a share (adjusted for splits). By early 2001, Biovail had eclipsed a $5 billion market capitalization on Wall Street.

The future looked even better. A consensus of analysts' projections, put together by Chicago-based Zacks Investment Research, was that Biovail earnings would rise to $3.92 a share in 2001, from $2.98 in 1999 (adjusted for the split). Additionally, Biovail, in September 2000, received FDA approval to begin marketing its Procardia XL drug, for the treatment of hypertension and angina. Clearly, Melnyk and Biovail had routed the short traders the old-fashioned way: with sustained, solid fundamentals. Quickly forgotten (by investors and financial journalists) were Shah's outrageously off-target predictions about a pending Biovail demise.

With Shah's whisper campaign fading, if not buried, under an avalanche of Biovail profits, the company was able to tap capital markets, raising $255 million in a common stock offering lead-managed by Donaldson, Lufkin & Jenrette Securities Corp. in March 1999, and then another $450 million in debt and equity offerings in March 2000. Biovail was poised to become a blue-chip standard on Wall Street—yet recall that this creation of Melnyk's only five years earlier had had to turn to Shah to raise a meager $15 million in private placements.

All's well that ends well? Perhaps. But remember, Shah's efforts in 1996 almost certainly depressed the stock, perhaps costing shareholders a cumulative $500 million in market value back then. Some individual investors may have been discouraged and may have sold out in 1996 and 1997, enduring losses or smaller profits than they otherwise would have, thanks to Shah. We don't see their faces, don't know if they suffered, with their dreams delayed or abandoned. They didn't know a gag was being run. Furthermore, Biovail's access to capital in 1996 and 1997 was pinched at times, certainly compared to what it would have been if the stock price had been higher. We don't know if Biovail could have made stock-swap acquisitions in 1996 or 1997—opportunities now lost forever—if its stock had been more richly priced.

And what has been listed in this chapter is just the bare-bones record of Shah's whisper campaign. Much more is on the tapes, and, of course, as noted before, it is not known what Shah may have said in unrecorded conversations. Suffice it to say that personally negative rumors about Melnyk, of mysterious origin, were spread, and likely hurt Melnyk's attempts to raise capital through 1998. In short, Shah's campaign left bruises, some of which may be hidden and may never heal.

## SHAH: WALL STREET WRIT SMALL

Hemant Shah may not be the typical securities analyst, but he is hardly unique. Moreover, the questions raised by his conduct toward Biovail—the conflicts of interest, the lack of accountability—are rife in his profession. In particular, his role as investment banker for Biovail—while touting the stock—is a murky reflection of Wall Street Major, but writ small.

In this sense, the shortcomings of Hemant Shah are the weaknesses of an entire industry. Too often, brokerage analysts are playing footsie with investment banking departments—if, as in the case of telecom analyst Jack Grubman of Salomon Smith Barney, they are not actively part of corporate finance operations and bragging about it.

Indeed, the only really unusual aspect of Shah's behavior, beyond its brazenness, was that he was not touting but trying to tear down a company, and that he was caught on tape—and ultimately trapped in a deposition—in so many compromising positions. It can be assumed that big-league brokerage analysts, smart and backed by powerful legal departments, are not going to get exposed like Shah.

Also, as a rule, Wall Street analysts tend to issue overly optimistic reports, not unduly negative ones. Brokerage analysts are tight with large institutional investors, who don't want a "sell" recommendation put out while they have a major stake in an issue, and also with brokerage investment banking departments, who need the analysts to flog initial public offerings and help generate lucrative investment-banking fees. Too, a brokerage trading department may assume a position in a stock before an analyst releases a pending "buy" recommendation, an arrangement entirely legal under current law and regulation.[14] As explained in later chapters, analysts have remarkable latitude, under the law.

There is another noteworthy aspect of the Shah saga: despite having been so completely wrong on Biovail, he is still a much-quoted Wall Street source on the health care industry. He was cited in 596 North America media stories in 1999 and 2000, according to *The Wall Street Journal*'s online publications library. Shah is still seen as a worthwhile observer of the drug industry.

For investors, the lesson of Shah is that analysts often, indeed usually, have agendas unseen by the media or the public. Another lesson is that the media have a short and faulty memory, and they don't keep batting averages on analyst predictions or commentary. The most important lesson is that, as with Shah on Biovail, the siren songs played by analysts more often than not take individual investors down the wrong path.

## 2

# AN INDUSTRY TRANSFORMED: FROM SLEUTHS TO SALESMEN

*"We used to call them customers' men."*

—BENJAMIN F. EDWARDS III
Chairman of A.G. Edwards & Sons Inc.

Benjamin F. Edwards III, the fifty-eight-year-old chairman of A.G. Edwards & Sons Inc., the conservative St. Louis–based securities brokerage his grandfather founded back in 1887, is talking about the good old days, when the securities business was a largely retail enterprise and stockbrokers were regarded as financial insiders, sharp, pinstriped guys who understood the market, had well-connected friends, and knew how people should invest. "They had desks at A.G. Edwards," Edwards remembers, "but it was very clear they worked for the customers. They weren't called stockbrokers or registered reps. They were 'customers' men.'"[1]

There is a whole world in that phrase "customers' men"—dear old days, dead but not yet beyond recall. It was the world of investing before the twentieth century's three-quarter mark, before the giant brokerages, mutual funds, and institutional investors grew to dominate Wall Street. Before analysts had to worry that the real profit centers—investment banking and institutional traders with their huge mutual fund clients—would go on the warpath after a negative report.

It was also before financial news came to dominate national discourse, spawning a flood of financial print publications and TV shows, not to mention cable offerings and ubiquitous financial Web sites. It was a world in which the bulk of Americans didn't own stock—and those who did huddled close to their stockbrokers.

In this world, a stockbroker with a solid "book"—that is, a strong list of loyal clients—could all but write his own ticket. That's because brokerages made their main money from fat commissions their stockbrokers charged for even simple trades they executed for ordinary "retail" investors. The practice amounted to price gouging—but commissions were fixed by federal law and regulation prior to May 1, 1975. This happy state of affairs not only made the business highly profitable for stockbrokers and brokerages, it also promoted employment for gimlet-eyed securities analysts.

After all, with trading commissions off the table as an issue, competition between firms was basically restricted to mannerly claims over who could offer customers the best service and the best advice. Among other things, this put a premium on the development and maintenance of first-rate, and usually independent, research departments, that could deliver buy and sell recommendations that helped their firms' retail customers make money.

For Wall Street professionals, it was a pleasant if highly artificial world. Then, on one fine May Day in 1975, it all came to an end.

STEPHEN BRYANT WAS ONE OF THE many thousands of young men who almost stumbled onto Wall Street and became stockbrokers in the 1960s. In many regards, his story shows the way things were. Born on the East Coast, Bryant left his Long Island, New York, home in 1960 to bang around Southern California. After earning a bachelor's degree from Occidental College, a small, well-regarded liberal arts college in Los Angeles, he took a job as a loan officer with the old United California Bank in downtown Los Angeles. Soon he found himself suffocating in the straitjacket norms of commercial banking. "I didn't like them, and they didn't like me," he recalls. "I think they had a rule for everything." Still, it was gainful employment. He even managed to save a little money.[2]

One morning, rushing on his way to work, Bryant stopped in at the downtown Los Angeles offices of Hayden-Stone Inc., a midsized brokerage of note in the 1960s, of which there were many in those days. He was twenty-five and was thinking about investing in the high-tech stocks of the period, and he hoped to get in a quick order. Ushered into a well-appointed office, the youthful Bryant was introduced to branch manager Parker Dale, a well-dressed, well-spoken stalwart of the securities business who had worked his way up the Hayden-Stone ladder. Back in those genteel days, a lot of Los Angeles securities men seemed to have names like Parker Dale's—names in which the first and surname could be switched around. One firm even boasted a Robert Edward Howard.

In any event, after lightning-fast pleasantries, Dale sized up his visitor and went to work—not *for* Bryant, but *on* him. Rather than stock tips, Bryant instead found himself spellbound by a Dale monologue on the manifold joys and virtues of the brokerage business. "He talked nonstop for three-quarters of an hour, rattling off one idea after another why I should become a stockbroker," Bryant recalls. "I never said a word, but when I left, I said to myself, 'Maybe he is right.'"

Bryant joined Hayden-Stone the following week. He started with nothing but a "desk and a telephone"—there weren't any computer terminals—and a goggle-eyed view of the handsomely remunerated senior brokers, some of whom earned upward of $1 million a year in gross commissions and took home maybe half of that. The merely good ones made $200,000 gross a year—this at a time when large homes in the best neighborhoods of Los Angeles might sell for $100,000, but usually less.

To build his "book," Bryant plunged into a whirlwind of business-oriented socializing that a later generation would dub "networking." He coached school sports, joined a country club, got involved with local charities, and signed up with the Los Angeles Athletic Club and the by-invitation-only Los Angeles Bond Club. "Any time you could meet people, you did," he says. "In large part, your social life was a way to meet people for your business."

He also took to giving lectures about Wall Street in school auditoriums, hotel meeting rooms, wherever he could find a big room for small rent. "You would send out a couple hundred pieces of mail, and maybe ten people would show up, and out of that group maybe one or two would become customers." Back then regional or midsized brokerages such as Hayden-Stone—the mainstay of the industry, before industry consolidation created nationwide behemoths—didn't have budgets for major media buys. It was stockbrokers who brought customers in. The regional firms could hardly buy national time on mass media—and anyway, the industry was so genteel that advertising was seen as somewhat crass. Professionals—doctors and lawyers, and also brokerages—didn't hawk their wares in those days, often prohibited by law. Again, that meant the stockbrokers, with their ability to bring in customers, were vital.

Before long, Bryant had developed both a solid book and a position of respect in the community. No mere order-taker, he was a family friend, a trusted adviser. In general, this image of rectitude and prudence was carefully cultivated and diligently maintained by the securities industry. Not only was a stockbroker expected to join the right clubs, but his firm likely occupied exclusive space in the local financial district, its office decor often mimicking the formal style then favored by banks and courthouses, with their reassuring marble pillars, equestrian portraits, and haughty secretaries.

The individual stockbroker's aura of expertise was both real and exaggerated, of course. In the case of Bryant, for example, though his concern for his clients' welfare was genuine and he was a shrewd investor, much of his actual stock-picking advice was a rehash of reports issued by Hayden-Stone's research department. Toiling away in relative obscurity, the firm's analysts would forecast overall economic trends and the likely potential of individual industries and stocks. Their findings (on paper only, back then) were dispatched on a regular basis to brokers in the field like Bryant. Make no mistake, however—if Bryant didn't like a report, he didn't show it to his clients.

Nevertheless, the information and insights contained in the Hayden-Stone reports in those days were hot stuff. It's easy to forget today, but back then the investing public had access to only a trickle of stock-market data. Reading the stock tables in the afternoon paper—sometimes on "green sheets," tucked behind the sports pages—was considered being ahead of the curve. For an ordinary investor, just getting a report—any report, any sort of financial data—

on a blue-chip company meant a trip to a stockbroker's office. Usually incumbent in that visit (or at least the second such visit) was the investor's agreement to become a client. One couldn't go on the Web and download financial reports and news stories galore. There were no round-the-clock business cable TV shows. There was no Motley Fool Web site or CNBC.

Too, it should be remembered that mutual funds in the 1960s and 1970s were but mice to the elephantine proportions that industry has assumed today. Individual investors who wanted a piece of Wall Street generally invested in actual stocks, through stockbrokers.

So it was that Bryant's book swelled, and his position at Hayden-Stone grew more lucrative and secure, and before long he bought a home in San Marino, an upscale hamlet an easy commute to downtown Los Angeles's financial district. And Bryant had standing in Hayden-Stone—if he wasn't treated well by his bosses, he might jump ship and move to some other brokerage, and there were lots of them back then. Experience showed that the lion's share of his clients would follow him to his new home.

In many ways, perhaps even most ways, stockbrokers—not analysts or investment bankers—were the stars of the Street from the 1950s through the mid-1970s. The stockbrokers themselves put pressure on brokerages to come up with good investment selections. "Show me too many stiff deals without a good one, and I am going to take my game elsewhere," recalled Bryant. Branch managers could push brokers to meet certain goals or targets, but star brokers had clout and pretty much called their own shots.

As much as Hayden-Stone depended on the sales commissions Bryant generated, he knew how much he needed the good reports produced by the firm's research department. Sure, he got tips at the clubs, and he knew a dog as well as the next guy. But there were a lot of companies out there, and Bryant had to spend much time working with clients, or generating business. He could hardly research companies on his own. His ability to charm customers was valuable, but making money was what really counted to clients. He needed solid research, and he told his branch manager so. As Bryant put it, "Too many bombs, and you would lose them."

IN A SENSE, BRYANT AND HIS fellow stockbrokers owed their happy circumstance to a crowd of shouting, sweaty men who, back in the late eighteenth century, gathered daily in the shade of a fabled buttonwood tree in lower Manhattan to trade stocks and bonds. These traders often retreated for brews and gossip to the nearby Corres Hotel, and it was there, on May 17, 1792, that they framed what became known as the Buttonwood Tree Agreement. In part, this historic compact stated that the Buttonwooders would not trade "any kind of Public Stocks at a less rate than one-quarter of one percent commission ..." Thus enshrined, the tradition of fixed commissions became a cornerstone of the U.S. securities industry.

More directly, however, the agreeable lack of competition enjoyed by Bryant and his colleagues was a direct result of the most traumatic event in American economic history: the infamous Crash of 1929, and the following Great Depression. Scared and scarred by the economic havoc that followed the crash—in which bank failures were pandemic, stock frauds commonplace, and socialism nearly respectable—the heavily Democratic U.S. Congress transformed the nation's financial industries with extensive regulation and oversight, with the emphasis always on security and dependability. Competition took a backseat, in many regards.

The effects of the 1930s-era regulatory spasm are still being debated. But at least one consequence is undeniable: in addition to perhaps curbing the securities industry's worst excesses, Congress's Depression-era rush of economic legislation set the stage for decades of cloistered, protected prosperity in the business of brokering securities.

To begin with, the Glass-Steagall Act of 1933 barred banks and other financial institutions from the business of trading and underwriting stocks, bonds, and other securities, thus effectively clearing the field for the brokerages. It was felt that too many banks had engaged in "stock gambling," a phrase coined by U.S. Senator Carter Glass, cosponsor of the act. (This resulting balkanization of financial markets that Glass and others legislated eroded slowly over the years, but then was all but erased when the U.S. Congress passed the Financial Services Modernization Act of 1999, in October of that year. Now, for better or worse, insurance companies, banks, and securities brokerages can have at it, with whatever consequences that will entail. It is clear that the financial industry, once divided, will have fearsome unified lobbying power in the future to protect itself from re-regulation or unwanted oversight.)

The specter of competition was further eased by the Securities Acts of 1933 and 1934, which in addition to requiring brokerages to be licensed by the Securities and Exchange Commission also gave the federal government's imprimatur to the tradition of fixed trading commissions. It did this by officially sanctioning the New York Stock Exchange's practice of fixing commission rates for its member firms—a practice that effectively set commission rates for the entire industry. In short, if you wanted to buy or sell stock, you had to do it through a licensed brokerage. And they all charged the same rate. End of story.

Brokerage industry denizens, being no fools then or now, did not protest the government shackles, but rather pounced like cats on the cartel-like powers the New Deal had awarded them. Trade groups like the Securities Industry Association opened offices in Washington, D.C., to monitor legislation and make sure nothing untoward happened to the tidy little arrangements made in the fearful days of dust bowls and hobo towns.

These lobbyists did their job well. Even as brick-and-mortar WPA projects moldered into oblivion or were bulldozed by redevelopment, the financial reforms of the FDR era endured. Of course, the industry was aided by changing times. As the decades passed, and the Great Depression gave way to World War II and then to the Korean conflict and the Cold War, prosperity replaced panic. Wall Street ceased to be a cause for national concern. Only a small fraction—roughly 10 percent of the U.S. population—owned stock before 1975 anyway. (That number would grow to more than 40 percent by the latter 1990s.)[3] So it was that the brokerages were left to their own devices, with a lock on the market.

One could make piles of money trading stock for retail clients back then. In the late 1960s formulas were set, based on the number of shares and dollar size of the trade. Ordinary retail trades could cost from $100 to several hundreds of dollars. One trade in 1972 of 100,000 Northwest Industries C Preferred shares, at $98 apiece, generated a commission of $28,000, a transaction still remembered in minute detail twenty-seven years later by the stockbroker who made it for PaineWebber. That's $28,000 in early 1970s dollars, which had roughly five times the buying power of dollars in the late 1990s. Enough to live free and easy for a year, on one trade. In contrast, such a trade today would cost between $500 and $1,000, even at a full-service brokerage.

Given the protections in place before 1975, it's hardly surprising that virtually everyone made money. In a typical year, such as 1967, only one of the NYSE's 330 member firms was reported to have sustained a net loss, and even that case was unclear.[4] There was a feeling among regulators that, like banks, brokerages should not be allowed to fail. Although smaller, less-efficient firms occasionally pushed for rate increases, the steady growth of trading volume—and the resulting year-to-year increases in commission income—kept everyone more or less content.

All a brokerage had to do to make big money was to keep its stockbrokers—and their retail clients—happy. It was a sweet deal. But all things must pass.

THROUGHOUT THE 1960s, the Justice Department and the Securities and Exchange Commission made feeble efforts to raise the question of brokerage trading rate deregulation. All were easily thwarted by the industry. By the 1970s, however, even with the White House in industry-friendly Republican hands, the fight was getting tougher. The problem was that the industry was beginning to cave in to competitive pressures.

The same high trading commissions that fattened Wall Street brokerages encouraged "end-around" trading by large institutional shareholders, themselves no dummies. Fearful of the developing "third market," in which institutions traded stock off the floor of the NYSE, brokerages began cutting deals on trading commissions, awarding "give-ups," or discounts, to larger customers such as mutual funds. Of course, the NYSE and the brokerage industry also tried to outlaw the third market, but they couldn't get the SEC to go along.

Increasingly, it was only the small investor who paid full commission on Wall Street trades. As a rule, the big guys wound up paying about half the rates that little guys paid. To people outside the industry—a group that included much of the U.S. Congress—it looked suspiciously as if the small were subsidizing the large (though in fact the large trades were, on a per-share basis, cheaper to execute).

But in the end, what probably doomed the ancien régime was the lugubrious spectacle of an industry paying unstinting lip service to free enterprise and competition, but embracing for itself government-sanctioned regulated rates. How could Wall Streeters plead for protection from the very system they extolled and financed?

By 1974, with the Republicans still reeling from the effects of Watergate and President Nixon's resignation, the Democrat-controlled Congress was poised to outlaw fixed brokerage commissions. Making matters worse, anti-fixed-commission lawsuits wending their way through the federal court system were being won, and the Third Circuit Court of Appeals was prepping to strike down fixed rates. Recognizing the inevitable future, the SEC trotted to the front of the parade, announcing that effective May 1, 1975, the NYSE would no longer be allowed to regulate rates. Henceforth, competition would prevail.

Even with the courts, the legislature, and regulators against them, the brokerages didn't give up Shangri-la without a fight. Industry spokesmen warned that American free enterprise would be all but doomed if competition were allowed to be the arbiter of trading commissions. As one witness put it at an SEC hearing, "May Day is a great holiday in Russia. And Russia has said there is no need to fight democracy; it will burn itself out. Well, Commissioners, you have the candle and matches, and it will be a short fuse."

In April 1975, just two weeks before the new era was to dawn, SEC Commissioner John Evans wearily summed up the apocalyptic warnings to which he and his colleagues had been subjected:

It has been predicted that competitive rates will destroy the New York Stock Exchange as well as other exchanges in the country, create confusion and chaos in the markets for securities, destroy the greatest financial communications system the world has ever known, reduce participation of small investors in our securities markets, bring about destructive competition and thus cause a high rate of failure among broker-dealers and concentrate the securities industry into a handful of firms, lower standards in the industry, weaken desirable surveillance mechanisms that protect public investors, reduce the depth and liquidity of our markets, eliminate public markets for many securities, destroy our capital-raising mechanism, and bring about the downfall of our free enterprise system.

The dangers, needless to say, were somewhat exaggerated—although one prediction was realized: brokerages merged and merged again, becoming much larger, and the regional, cottage-industry nature of the business was obliterated.

And although it saved investors billions upon billions of dollars in reduced commissions, the switch to competitive pricing was not totally cost-free. Yes, the lucrative fixed-rate structure of the pre-1975 era was highly inefficient, soaked investors, and propped up an archaic and clubby industry infrastructure. But because of it, the retail side of the brokerage business—the little guy—mattered to the big firms. It was, after all, where they made most of their money.

A look back at the financial records of one of today's giants, Merrill Lynch, shows how important individual stockbrokers and their clients were in the era of fixed rates. In 1967, retail commissions earned by stockbrokers accounted for some 57 percent of Merrill Lynch's total revenues. Investment banking fees, by contrast, amounted to less than a tenth of that—and Merrill was a "bulge bracket" firm, with a relatively strong investment banking department. Most firms, and almost all regional firms, had much smaller banking operations or none at all.

Then came May Day. Literally overnight, what was once perhaps the most sheltered industry in the nation turned ferociously competitive.

Suddenly, the impressive-looking offices, the reassuring-sounding brokers—even the thick research reports—weren't as important to customers as they used to be. In the brave new world of competitive rates, what increasingly began to matter most was price. Why pay Merrill Lynch $300 to $400 to execute a trade when a discount broker would perform the task for just $36?

As commission rates were cut and cut again, it became tougher and tougher to turn a profit on Wall Street by simply trading stock for clients—unless, that is, you were a discount house like the increasingly ubiquitous Charles Schwab & Co., with low overhead, no individual stockbrokers, no analysts, and no oil paintings of the English countryside adorning its cheap digs.

As economists might have predicted, the lower rates meant surges in volume—although, like everything else about Wall Street in the 1980s and 1990s, the changes almost rendered the industry unrecognizable. In the late 1960s, the salad days of the old regime, a typical day on the NYSE might see a total of 10 million shares change hands. A decade later, daily volumes of 20 million to 30 million shares were considered normal; in a particularly busy session, 50 million shares might be traded.

In 1982, the NYSE saw daily volume pass the 100-million-share mark for the first time, a much-remarked-upon milestone at the time. Within a few years, such levels were considered anemic. By 1988, an ordinary trading day might eclipse 200 million shares, and by 1998 even a 900-million-share day was no big deal. On September 1, 1998, more than 1.2 billion shares changed hands, again causing some commentary. The pundits might have saved their breath. On January 4, 2001, share volume hit 2.12 billion shares on the NYSE.

And that was just on the Big Board. Since 1975, a new national securities market has grown up alongside the NYSE—the so-called over-the counter bazaar known as Nasdaq (for National Association of Securities Dealers Automatic Quotation System). From insignificant levels in the early 1970s, Nasdaq reached an average daily trading volume of 132 million shares in 1990 before ballooning to 802 million shares a day in 1998. (That same year, Nasdaq absorbed the NYSE's only other competition, the American Stock Exchange.) Daily Nasdaq volume began routinely exceeding that of the NYSE, and as of 1999, even the dollar amount of securities traded on the Nasdaq often exceeded the NYSE. In short, where 10 million shares a day might have been traded before May Day, by 2000 a 4 billion share day was doable.

The big run-up in trading volume was little more than ferocious wheel spinning from the perspective of the full-service brokerages—if not worse. New equipment had to be purchased constantly to keep up with volume.

Yet the only way they could get a piece of the new business was to cut their prices on trading, which they did again and again. Taking inflation into account, full-service brokerages slashed their rates by fully 95 percent between 1975 and 1998. And still the discount houses continued to underprice them. The full-service firms may charge just a nickel today for every dollar they charged in the days of fixed rates, but the discounters charge only a penny. And that's not even considering the trading deals available through online services, such as Ameritrade or Datek or Scottsdale Securities—the latter of which charges $7 a trade.

Their once-lavish profit margins now in tatters, the big retail-oriented firms began to go the way of the dodo, or fell into each other's arms to survive. Such once-established national names as Loeb, Rhodes and White, Weld simply disappeared, including also stockbroker Stephen Bryant's Hayden-Stone. Gone too are A. G. Becker and Mitchum, Jones, and Burnham. Stock brokerages known for generations as refuges for the slow sons of good families (or fast sons from other families) went up in smoke.

Merged firms have merged again, resulting in sprawling national empires with mouthful names, such as Salomon Smith Barney and Morgan Stanley Dean Witter. Talk about destructive competition: of the thirty largest securities firms in the country in 1971, only two have survived to this day with their names more or less intact—Merrill Lynch (one of the early consolidators) and Bear Stearns.

In this one sense, the Cassandras who warned of the living hell that deregulation would bring were proven right: competitive rates created an environment in which the smaller, less-efficient firms were

crushed by their larger, more-efficient counterparts. The largest brokerages—the so-called wire houses, such as Merrill Lynch and Salomon Smith Barney—kept growing with each wave of mergers, coming to employ thousands, even tens of thousands of brokers. By 1999,
Salmon Smith Barney employed nearly 11,000 brokers; Merrill Lynch
had some 13,400. On Wall Street today, size matters.

And many veteran brokers complain bitterly about the new role
stockbrokers have at the giants, especially Merrill Lynch. Today, the
favored form of compensation at Merrill (and, increasingly, other
firms) is "fee only," meaning the broker is not paid a commission on
trades but earns a percentage of assets under management, such as
1 percent or 2 percent of all accounts, split with the brokerage.
(Merrill keeps the trading commissions.) The Merrill strategy is to
move customers into proprietary Merrill Lynch products, such as
retirement accounts, mutual funds, checking accounts, cash management, and the like.

Experience has shown that such customers become sticky—it's a
lot harder to jump ship (and pay fees) when your whole financial plan
is being managed by Merrill Lynch. The customer relationship is with
Merrill. The broker, in this picture, follows formulas on asset allocation, touts Merrill products, and is expendable. In one generation,
stockbrokers have gone from being the stars to being glorified clerks.

Still, no matter how large and powerful a brokerage became, and
no matter how much trading volume there was, still that damnable
problem remained, farsightedly perceived by the doughty outdoor
traders who fashioned the Buttonwood Agreement back in 1792: "We
went onto Wall Street to make piles of money. How can we get rich
when rivals are charging a measly $7 a trade?"

## THE FIRST BAD SIGNS

The first industry reaction to discounted rates was to try to make
more money in underwriting—the issuing of stock and bonds, or
other investment vehicles, such as real estate limited partnerships,
which became one of the great investment debacles of the 1980s.
From post-deregulation fear, many say, the brokerage-underwritten
real estate limited partnership was born. Why?

Brokerages could effectively charge customers anywhere from 15 percent to 20 percent of the market value of a real estate partnership in underwriting fees and other deal-related commissions. A $500 million partnership (sold as "units" to investors) meant $75 million in various brokerage charges—found money for an industry reeling from price wars. The customer who put a dollar into a real estate partnership generally got back 80¢ of property, but that was pretty well smudged over in the prospectuses, which instead often touted "guaranteed returns"—interest-like dividend payments. The fact that the "returns" were often merely a portion of the investors' capital set aside for repayment was deeply embedded in nearly unintelligible disclosure statements.

The term *underwriting* refers to a stock brokerage's work on behalf of a real estate partnership, or more usually a company, that wishes to raise money by selling stock or bonds to the public. A securities firm's investment bankers and hired lawyers will write and print a prospectus for the company (similar to a business plan with financial disclosures), file it with the SEC, and then give it to the brokerage's institutional salespeople. The salespeople then give the prospectus to institutional buyers of stock, such as mutual funds, money managers, bank trust departments, and insurance companies, and try to convince them to buy the shares. Often, a "road show" is conducted, and brokerage salespeople will travel the country meeting buyers. In some cases, especially in regional brokerages or with real estate limited partnerships, ordinary stockbrokers will be enlisted to sell the stock directly to small investors. But usually—certainly with the larger brokerages, such as Morgan Stanley Dean Witter or PaineWebber (now a part of UBS Warburg)—after the initial public offering, the institutional buyers can sell their shares if they wish on the open market, where ordinary retail buyers can purchase them. Indeed, smaller investors are usually "locked out" of initial public offerings.

The late-1970s and early 1980s rush to real estate investment partnerships produced one of the more lurid industry busts. The rashness of brokerages in promoting the property partnerships was breathtaking—Prudential-Bache (now Prudential Securities) brought forth dozens of real estate deals to the investing public and later admitted to criminal, let alone civil, guilt in more than twenty of those transactions, in which investors lost 95¢ or more on the dollar. The Pru was hardly alone in concocting these shaky investments.

Some of these real estate deals, such as the VMS Mortgage Investors Fund, actually touted guaranteed income and were compared by Pru literature to an FDIC-insured certificate of deposit—before going bust less than a year after the offering date! Eventually, more than $8 billion of partnerships sold to the public by Prudential-Bache (and heartily recommended by Pru analysts) went belly-up, harming retirees, investors, and, of course, the stockbrokers who sold the investments and had to face clients thereafter. The Pru paid some fines and changed its name to Prudential Securities from Prudential-Bache. But no executives went to prison, and the SEC never even seriously suggested that the big brokerage be booted from the industry, or that its analysts have their flutes taken away.[5]

In some ways, financial memories are short, and the 1980s real estate partnership bust on Wall Street has been all but forgotten, although such partnerships have never made a comeback. But the economic forces that drove the industry to ardently seek underwriting income—and the industry's blithe tolerance for cruddy deals—are stronger than ever. That's something investors may wish to remember.

THE BROKERAGES TRIED OTHER WAYS of making money, too. For more than two decades following 1975, the brokerages increasingly, if surreptitiously, gouged the trading public by effectively realizing a sort of ersatz commission—the "spread" between the bid and asked price, especially for stocks traded on the Nasdaq, the over-the-counter (OTC) system. If the bid on an over-the-counter stock was $5 and the "asked" was $5¼ or $5½, who made the difference? After all, the spread sometimes amounted to a 10 percent commission. Brokerages, of course, made money on the spread.

Retail customers can at least take comfort that the situation is not as bad as it used to be. Prior to 1996, the ever fleet-footed SEC has alleged, the brokerage industry—including giants such as PaineWebber and Merrill Lynch—colluded for nearly twenty years to keep spreads wide on OTC stocks. The quarter-point spread mysteriously seemed to be the norm on many, many stocks. Where was the feverish competition to decrease the spreads? The SEC pushed the National Association of Securities Dealers (its ever-ready sandbags stacked for action) to strengthen market surveillance and reduce the spreads. In response to the SEC pressure and constant monitoring, most spreads since 1996 have narrowed to ⅛ or ¹⁄₁₆ instead of ¼—not perfection, but less of a gouge.

The industry hated the SEC's mandated reduction of spreads, and it hates the results. "It can't be good for us," A. B. "Buzzy" Krongard, head of the Securities Industry Association lobby and chairman and chief executive officer of brokerage Alex. Brown & Sons Inc. told *The Wall Street Journal.* "The only question is how bad is it going to be?"

Even Benjamin F. Edwards III, the A.G. Edwards chairman whose brokerage cultivates an image of old-line integrity and Midwestern responsibility to clients, was a fan of the spreads. "I think the SEC has been blind to the facts of life," said Edwards. "There is no sense trading a stock if all you can make is a sixteenth." Just as before May Day, brokerage titans said liquidity would decrease with deregulation, so Edwards warned of ominous consequences. "If firms drop stocks, it's because they think it is no longer profitable to trade them, and that could hurt liquidity."[6]

Edwards was hardly alone. Fred M. Roberts, the former chairman of the board of governors of the NASD, complained in 1996, "The public doesn't understand it. If you get rid of the spreads, other things, other services they take for granted, will cost more. They'll have to pay more in commissions."[7]

Or, he might have added, brokerages would have to figure out other ways of making money—like underwriting.

## INVESTMENT BANKING AND UNDERWRITING

Despite Roberts's prediction, the public hasn't ended up paying more in commissions. As online trading has become more and more accepted, retail commissions per trade instead have kept shrinking. The discounters are winning market share: the commission revenues of discount houses grew from $48.1 million in 1980 to $2.05 billion in 1997, a forty-three-fold hike. The mainstream brokerages have been further pushed up on their haunches to cast about for money-making ventures.

The answer? More and more, investment banking has become the profit center for the big brokerages. Although the real estate partnerships of the 1980s didn't work out, brokerages in the 1990s turned aggressively to underwriting initial public offerings (and taking lucrative pre-IPO stock), underwriting secondary or follow-on stock offerings, trading, managing private placements, handling bond offerings, and doing mergers-and-acquisitions work.

The changes have literally transfigured the industry. In the words of Jeffrey M. Schaefer, former senior vice president and director of research at the Securities Industry Association—the brokerages' own trade group—"The securities industry of the 1960s was more like the securities industry of the late 1800s than today's industry." Writing for the January 1997 SIA publication *Trends,* Schaefer continued, "[In the 1960s] industry revenues were in the single-digit billion range, with more than 60 percent coming from [trading] commissions. Today, the industry generates more than $120 billion; only 16 percent comes from commissions."[8]

As commission revenues have relatively dropped, brokerage underwriting of stock and bond issues (and attendant revenues) hasn't just shot through the roof; it's rocketed through the solar system and into deep space. In the entire 1960s, the brokerage industry underwrote a little more than $100 billion of stock and bonds. In the 1990s, the brokerage industry underwrote $700 billion to $2.23 trillion *annually,* according to Schaefer's record keeping. In the boom year 1999, brokerages underwrote $2,238 billion ($2.23 trillion) worth of corporate bonds and stock—more than *22 times* the dollar volume of underwriting that occurred in the whole 1960s combined.

Another comparison: in 1974, the year before May Day, Wall Street raised only $42 billion for American businesses. That's less than 2 percent of the 1999 level. In other words, for big brokerages, revenues from investment banking have grown roughly fiftyfold since 1974, while retail commissions have drooped to the ankles.

The underwriting boom translates into industry profit, as brokerages collect underwriting fees of between 7 percent and 9 percent of the underwriting dollar volume. Too, brokerages obtain an allotment of stock and warrants in the underwritten company and can "make a market" in the stock, earning trading commissions or even capital gains if they can sell their inventory at a profit (more easily done when the resident analyst keeps a "buy" signal on). Increasingly, a hefty profit on pre-IPO stock acquired in an earlier stage of financing completes this picture.

For students of stock market behavior, it is worth noting the special explosion in stock underwriting. For four years running—1996, 1997, 1998, and 1999—more than $150 billion of equities were underwritten each year on Wall Street. In the 1970s, the largest dollar volume of equities underwritten in any year was $10.4 billion, in 1976.

The fact that stock brokerages now commonly take private, pre-IPO stock in companies they later "take public" should not be ignored, especially when certain markets become hot, as did the telecommunications, media, and Internet stocks of the late 1990s. Huge profits can be made, if the IPO is successful and if hype or promise drives the stock price up even higher after the IPO. For example, in August 1998, the brokerage CIBC Oppenheimer (now CIBC World Markets) was lead underwriter on the initial public offering of stock in the Bermuda-based telecommunications giant Global Crossing Ltd. Before the underwriting, CIBC Oppenheimer bought $30 million of private stock. Global Crossing went public at $9.50 a share, and in trading vaulted to more than $50 a share by March 1999. According to SEC filings, CIBC Oppenheimer's stake in Global Crossing was then worth *$4.6 billion*. When a few investment bankers working on a deal can net a brokerage $4.6 billion, is it any wonder brokerages now look to investment bankers to make money, and to analysts and stockbrokers to assist?

This trend of securities brokerages taking pre-IPO stock is increasing fast in the new millennium. According to a July 2000 report in *The Wall Street Journal*, "It's beyond debate that venture investing has become more important to Wall Street. Surveys by VentureOne, a San Francisco research firm, show investment banks put money into 305 venture-backed companies last year, up from 104 in 1998. Some of the deals have been huge hits, making venture investing a significant source of profits at many banks." The *Journal* report points out that Goldman Sachs Group Inc.'s $36 million pre-IPO investment in StorageNetworks Inc., a provider of computer storage services near Boston, was valued at about $1.6 billion in 2000. Between 13 percent and 18 percent of Goldman's net income in 1999 came from "private equity" gains, primarily venture-style technology investments, compared with 4 percent to 5 percent in 1998, according to Salomon Smith Barney securities industry analyst Guy Moszkowski. At Lehman Brothers Holdings Inc., he says, such gains jumped to between 17 percent and 22 percent in the first quarter of 2000, from about 4 percent of net income for all of the preceding year; much of the increase came from a huge windfall in VerticalNet Inc., a provider of online business-to-business trading sites that Lehman invested in and then took public.

*The Wall Street Journal* raised serious ethical questions about a venture deal conducted by San Francisco–based brokerage Hambrecht & Quist (owned by Chase Manhattan Corp.). The brokerage handled the Redmond, Virginia–based Web site infrastructure outfitter Infospace Inc.'s initial public offering in 1998, took a lot of pre-IPO stock, and then had its analyst promote the stock and keep the "buy" signal on—while it sold its shares in 1999. The shares later collapsed.

By the late 1990s, a brokerage that didn't invest early in a company, taking pre-IPO stock at pennies on the eventual dollar, was looked on as a bit slow-footed. The big brokerages, such as Goldman Sachs and Donaldson, Lufkin & Jenrette Securities Corp. (now Credit Suisse First Boston), were busily forming venture capital arms—Goldman announced a $5 billion such fund in August 2000—to finance companies en route to that IPO.

When not underwriting, brokerage investment bankers are busier in mergers work than ever before, making it yet another profit center for securities firms. Again, the market hasn't just grown, it has exploded. There were 2,297 reported corporate merger deals nationwide, worth a cumulative $11.8 billion, in 1975, the year of deregulation May Day, according to Mergerstat, an arm of the Los Angeles–based investment banking house Houlihan, Lokey, Howard & Zukin. By 1985, 3,001 domestic merger deals took place, worth $179.8 billion. By 1995, there were 3,510 deals, worth $356 billion. In 1999, there were 9,278 deals, worth $1,428.1 billion (or nearly *$1.4 trillion*). Since May Day 1975, deal volume is up 120-fold in ballpark terms. Investment bankers made fees arranging many of those deals (usually the bigger ones) or underwriting stocks or bonds issued to help finance acquisitions.

Tom Weinberger, 57, president of Sutro & Co. and an industry veteran, describes alterations in the brokerage industry this way: "You could say the industry has changed. I would say it is not even the same industry. Primarily, we are a source of capital and structuring advice to major enterprises now, not just people who trade little piles of stock around."

Clearly, retail investors are no longer the major underwriting brokerage firms' most important customers. That distinction is now held by corporate clients, who can bring in big-ticket underwriting or M&A work and offer the juicy pre-IPO stock; or by big mutual funds and other institutional investors, who can buy the IPOs and the bond offerings or trade enough stock to make it worth a brokerage's while.

The implications of this shift in attention are many. Among the most significant is the built-in conflict of interest the new business focus creates for securities analysts, as shall be shown in upcoming chapters.

## MUTUAL FUNDS

That mutual funds have grown since 1975 has become a cliché, and their rise has been well covered by the financial media (well, mutual funds *are* big advertisers). Still, a quick reprise of the story is warranted, for like investment banking, mutual funds have not just grown but have also altered the character of the industry.

In 1975, total mutual equity fund assets were $37.5 billion, according to the New York–based Investment Company Institute. Hard as it is to believe today, the industry was actually shrinking then, due to the 1970s bear market. But with the bull, the situation changed, and by 1985 there was $116.9 billion managed by funds.

Again, the usual superlatives don't do justice to what happened next: By 1995, there was $1.26 trillion under management. By 1998, that figure had jumped to $2.98 trillion. By year-end 2000, $4.31 trillion worth of stock was managed by mutual stock or stock hybrid funds, with nearly 3,800 funds plying their trade on Wall Street. The equity mutual fund industry was *115 times* as large at the end of 2000 as it was in 1975. If all funds are counted, including bond and money market funds, $6.97 trillion was managed by the fund industry in year-end 2000.

Again, for the purposes of this book, the size of the funds is important in one key regard: these are brokerage customers an analyst does not want to alienate. They are major shareholders, along with other institutions such as insurance companies, bank trust departments, and money managers. When the big boys trade, it is in blocks of 10,000, or 100,000, or even millions of shares. The big institutions are the primary, often the only buyers of initial public offerings, secondary offerings, and bond offerings. And they do not want a "sell" recommendation flashing over the wires that depresses the value of a holding.

## ANOTHER LOOK AT THE OLD DAYS

It's not only stockbrokers who remember the pre-1975 era fondly. So do more than a few securities analysts. One is Stephen Koffler, a veteran of more than thirty years on Wall Street, many of them as a hired gun for a now extinct breed of securities firm—the "pure research house."

Still trim and debonair—he could satisfy a call from central casting for an investment banker—Koffler started on Wall Street in 1968 as an analyst at Auerbach, Pollak & Richardson, a research-oriented firm based in New York. "We put out two-inch-thick black binders on different industries, which we would work months and months to produce," Koffler remembers. His beat was the aerospace industry. With a Ph.D. in materials science, he was considered a natural for a field in which metallurgy played a crucial role. "People who bought our reports paid us, so to speak, by trading through us," he explains. "There was enough profit in that to support an entire research firm. We were an institutional research boutique."

After commissions were deregulated, however, the institutional customers balked at paying the relatively fat trading fees it took to support Auerbach's serious research operations. As far as the institutions were concerned, brokerage research reports simply weren't worth that much. In fact, this feeling had been growing even before May Day 1975. A 1974 study by *Institutional Investor* magazine concluded that institutional owners of stock used only 25 percent of the research they got for "free" from brokerages and would not pay for even 10 percent of it if the firms charged them hard cash.

This lack of enthusiasm may reflect the fact that no analyst, no matter how brainy, objective, or diligent, can consistently predict with meaningful accuracy where the market as a whole—or an individual stock in particular—is going. As Burton G. Malkiel argued in his 1973 classic, *A Random Walk Down Wall Street*, almost everything knowable about a stock is already reflected in its price. What that means is that future performance depends mainly on unknowables—which, in turn, means that one guess is as good as another, regardless of who is doing the guessing. That's why beating Wall Street averages, such as the Standard & Poor's 500 index, is all but impossible and why, historically, almost no mutual fund or investor outperforms the market on a consistent basis. As Malkiel concluded, perhaps a bit sacrilegiously, "God Almighty does not know the proper price/earnings multiple for a stock." (Although maybe a more southerly deity has a clue.)

Given vexing market realities, stock-owning institutions sensibly concluded that it wasn't a justifiable expense to pay for brokerage analyst "buy" and "sell" recommendations and research. Throwing darts worked as well when it came to real-world stock selection. In any event, after 1975 institutions and individual investors alike began migrating to less expensive ways to trade stock. As a result, research-oriented firms like Auerbach, Pollak & Richardson found themselves consigned to the dustbin of history. In the words of the SIA's Schaefer, "The demise of institutional research houses was swift and striking." Brokerages doing pure research—no investment banking—went the way of the dodo.

That may have been just as well, because the brave new world of unregulated commissions, with its heightened emphasis on investment banking, created a whole new—and uncomfortable—set of pressures on securities analysts, particularly the so-called sell-side analysts who work for brokerage firms. As the 1970s faded into memory, brokerage analysts found themselves less pressured by stockbrokers and their clients and instead felt the heat of the investment banking departments.

That was where the money was being made, and he who pays the piper calls the tune. And how likely would the XYZ Corp. be to give its lucrative investment-banking business to a brokerage whose research department just put out a "sell" or even a "hold" signal on its stock?

The SEC worried about the inherent conflict between the retail and the investment banking departments as long ago as 1936. Concerned that the demands of investment banking pose a conflict with a brokerage's fiduciary obligations to its retail customers, the commission even toyed with the idea of barring brokerages from underwriting new issues, noting in 1940, "The underwriter, realistically regarded, is a salesman."[9] In the end, of course, it never acted on the notion.

As a result, when "sell-side" (brokerage) analysts look over their shoulder these days, it's not the retail stockbrokers and investors they see but the investment bankers with their enormously profitable corporate clients. In addition, when they look over their other shoulder, they see huge institutional shareholders that do not want a "sell" signal put out on any stock held in their portfolio—and the institutions are the prime buyers of initial public offerings, secondary issues, and bonds, as already noted. And these institutions, such as the behemoth mutual funds, grew enormously in the 1990s, gaining clout with brokerages and often forming alliances with them.

As Koffler, who got out of securities analysis and into investment banking at just the right time, puts it, "There is more pressure on brokerage analysts today than there was pre-1975 to say good things, to not come out with 'sell' mandates, especially on stocks that have an investment-banking relationship with a brokerage. Research is supposed to be independent, but it is hard to see how it can be."

THESE FACTS OF LIFE PREVAIL even at shops once known for being heavily retail in orientation. Take A.G. Edwards, now the nation's fourth-largest brokerage, with about 6,500 stockbrokers in its ranks. For decades it has been regarded as one of Wall Street's "cleaner" firms, way above a bucket shop, and still a cut above such giant Wall Street names as Prudential or PaineWebber. Even its St. Louis base seemed to give it Midwestern value compared to those New York sharpsters. It has never been seen as an investment banking powerhouse.

As one century turned into another, Rod Essen was the managing director in A.G. Edwards's Los Angeles investment banking offices. Part of his job is to scout out growing West Coast companies that may someday wish to go public—that is, issue stock via an IPO that A.G. Edwards might manage (with attendant underwriting fees or lucrative pre-IPO stock). Essen drums up this kind of business by trying to "get in early" with such companies, usually by helping them to raise private capital prior to an IPO.

How does Essen convince a promising company to choose his firm? And how does he persuade institutional investors to participate in a private placement? Essen has a pretty good pitch. He tells entrepreneurs and institutional investors that when the company in question goes public, he can more or less assure that A.G. Edwards's research department will cover it—that is, assign an analyst to follow its progress and periodically issue reports and recommendations on its stock.

This is a powerful promise, for the vast majority of the more than 8,000 publicly traded companies in the United States today are not covered by recognized Wall Street analysts. And coverage is crucial. Like the tree falling in the forest with no one to hear it, a company without coverage might as well not exist. Unless some analyst is willing to assess and report on its prospects, even good-quality small-cap companies generally trade at far lower price/earnings ratios than the well-followed blue chips. By the year 2000, such companies were so common that the term "orphan stocks" had been coined to describe them.

Thus Essen's promise not only tells the company's founders that their efforts will be noticed (and presumably rewarded) by the marketplace, it also provides an "exit strategy" for institutional investors who participate in pre-IPO private placements. When A.G. Edwards takes the company public, the early institutional investors can sell their stock in the IPO, usually at huge multiples of their original price—"ten-baggers" is investment-bankingese for a return of 1,000 percent, based on baseball-influenced lingo that a "single" is 100 percent and a "home run," 400 percent.

Of course, this puts the analyst in something of a bind. What if his or her analysis reveals that the company being herded to an IPO isn't as great as everyone wants to believe? A research report to that effect could torpedo the IPO, costing the firm millions of dollars in fees and lost time and effort by the investment bankers, not to mention the losses incurred by the pre-IPO institutional investors and outrage on the part of the company's founders.

Even Benjamin Edwards III, scion of the A.G. Edwards empire, hems and haws a bit when talking about this dilemma. "An analyst has a hard time being objective if the client is important," he concedes. "They always want us to be optimistic and bullish."

As a result, he says, for all his firm's vaunted probity, if an Edwards analyst balks in this kind of situation, the miscreant will often be asked to explain just what he or she is doing. "Our analysts work with our investment bankers," Edwards explains. "We usually have a meeting, and we question the analyst, 'Are you sure you are not just sore at somebody?'"

As the chapters that follow reveal, this intrusive reality obtains throughout the securities industry. Even at an old-line firm like A.G. Edwards, it's the investment bankers who are in the driver's seat, while the stockbrokers—the old customers' men—are merely along for the ride. So, too, are the securities analysts, who are increasingly pushed into a role that has less to do with clear-eyed evaluation than it does with bright-eyed salesmanship.

# 3

# COMPROMISED RELATIONSHIPS

For years, these [brokerage securities] analysts toiled in relative obscurity, writing reports on companies or industries, making earnings forecasts and recommending which stocks investors should buy or sell.

All that has changed in the 1990s. The boom on Wall Street—as securities firms advise corporate America in record numbers on mergers and initial public stock offerings—has transformed many analysts' roles. Instead of simply assessing stocks, analysts increasingly promote them. The lure is great: If analysts aggressively tout a company's stock, their firm stands a greater chance at snaring an advisory role, and the fat fees that follow. Now, analysts can be stars, receiving bonuses of several hundred thousand dollars for big underwriting deals. Bash a stock, and your firm could be shut out.

The upshot: Many analysts now focus on helping bring in investment-banking deals. Independent stock picking is out the window. This evolution has picked up steam in recent years because when stocks seem only to rise, the value of fundamental analysis falls. And so, marketing stocks, where analysts help investment bankers be cheerleaders for companies their firms want to do business with, is where the action is.

—THE WALL STREET JOURNAL

May 18, 1998

IT IS ONE OF THE GREAT MODERN ironies of Wall Street: just as analysts toss down the green eyeshades and pick up the flutes to accompany their investment banking departments, they also become more celebrated, more widely quoted, much more highly paid—and much more aggressively courted for their coverage by publicly traded companies, or companies that want to become publicly traded.

In one telling sign of the times, Bloomberg News, the business-oriented news wire service, went beyond merely assigning a single reporter to cover analyst reports and projections. Instead, it has established an entire group of reporters to carefully monitor and report on analyst advisories. Bloomberg's move reflected the blunt facts of life in the go-go markets of the late 1990s: growth companies, Internet start-ups, and wanna-be IPOs all wanted—sometimes demanded—the tip of a hat from Wall Street's new huzzah kings. Existing companies want coverage initiated with the "buy" signal on, and already covered companies want earnings estimates freshened, with a positive word or two stuck in. With the wire services flashing analysts' latest touts as news, with all-finance cable news anchors tilting their hairdos in recognition, and with the World Wide Web disseminating their projections almost instantly to millions of investors, brokerage analysts have found themselves enjoying a kind of clout they could have hardly imagined just a few years earlier.

Bloomberg, with its team of dedicated analyst reporters, was also acknowledging another financial reality of the 1990s: brokerage analysts, with their allied trading departments, with their hordes of stockbrokers in tow—and with connections to powerful institutional traders, such as mutual funds—have real power to move a stock, at least for a while. Even before a "buy" recommendation hits the wires, the mutual funds have typically been tipped off to the pending tout, and they often assemble blocks of stock in front of the recommendation. Likewise, a brokerage firm's trading department will accumulate a particular stock in advance of a well-regarded analyst's tout, a practice legal, immensely profitable (like shooting fish in a barrel, really), and rationalized as assembling product to service pending customer demand. Like it or not, an analyst's call can be news.

"You know that the mutual funds are tipped off," says Mark Hulbert,

*New York Times* columnist and founder of the Alexandria, Virginia–based *Hulbert's Financial Digest,* a stock market newsletter rating service, "because a stock tends to creep up before a big 'buy' recommendation, and it is large blocks that are traded. It's a market event. It's news."[1]

## THE NEW BREED

The dynamics of Wall Street A-Go-Go set in motion in the late 1990s are well illustrated by the stories of Wall Street's then hottest Internet stock analysts, Henry Blodget of Merrill Lynch and Mary Meeker of Morgan Stanley Dean Witter. These two thirtysomething number crunchers—or perhaps dream weavers is a more apt description—were widely credited with possessing an almost talismanic power to point and levitate a stock north. And as John Cassidy put it in *The New Yorker,* both analysts had the ability (fleeting, as it turned out) to help a heavily vested entrepreneur take that "big step toward billionairedom" in an initial public offering. Yet neither Blodget nor Meeker professed to believe in the underlying value of many of the companies whose fortunes they boosted.

A history major at Yale, Henry Blodget got his undergraduate degree in 1988, then spent a year teaching English in Japan and a half-year after that trying unsuccessfully to interest publishers in a book he had written about the experience, which he evidently thought was momentous. Floundering about, he put in a few months as a reporter for CNN Business News (excellent training, as it would turn out) before signing onto the corporate-finance training program at Prudential Securities in 1994, a program for budding investment bankers. In 1996, with a couple of years on the Street, he joined CIBC Oppenheimer—as an analyst. He'd never run an operating company, he'd never managed a money fund. He wasn't a CPA, and he doesn't have an MBA. He had never been an analyst in a bear market, or even an investor. The bull is all Blodget had ever known.

It hardly mattered. Like many of the new breed on Wall Street, Blodget was not shy about dealing with the media, and CIBC Oppenheimer gave him a solid platform. The firm may not have been top tier, but neither was it a runt on Wall Street; it ran a respectable investment banking operation and employed more than 630 stockbrokers. As one of its most articulate and engaging young analysts, Blodget appeared on financial television talk shows virtually every week, lifted his flute for this or that stock, and chatted with reporters almost every day. That's the perfect new job description of a successful analyst.

Blodget's big break came in December 1998, when he was covering the hottest of the era's hot stocks, Amazon.com, the groundbreaking online bookseller. At the time, Amazon was just beginning to implement its long-term strategy of branching out into other forms of e-commerce, which some suspected was an implicit admission that the company wasn't able to make money in its original business, which was selling books online.

Although Amazon had never earned a penny of profit—and according to even the most optimistic analysts, wouldn't for at least another five years—the company's stock was nonetheless trading in the stratosphere at $243 a share, giving the fledgling Web company a market capitalization of $27.3 billion (shares outstanding times share price, or the value of the company as perceived by investors). That market cap figure hardly raised an eyebrow on the Wall Street of the late 1990s, though in many regards it was a stupendous set of digits. Amazon was a company that in 1998 reported a loss of $124.5 million on revenues of $610 million. Amazon was trading for 45 times revenues, forget net income. (That meant that Amazon's market capitalization of $27.3 billion was 45 times the level of its annual revenues. Most "Old Economy" companies trade at multiples of *earnings*, such as 15 times earnings.)

Against this backdrop, virtually no one was expecting Blodget to say what he did when he got on the horn with his colleagues on December 16, 1998, as part of the daily ritual known as the "morning call." With CIBC Oppenheimer's New York brokers gathered in the firm's downtown auditorium (and those based elsewhere around the country listening in on "squawk boxes"), Blodget announced to his stunned colleagues that he expected Amazon stock to be trading at more than $400 a share within the next year. This wasn't the lilt of a flute—it was a riff from a rock guitar, speakers on max.

Stockbrokers can be a blasé lot, particularly when it comes to the predictions they hear on morning calls. Veteran brokers have heard thousands of such predictions, and the ones who last—at least in the old days—are the ones who understand such forecasts are taken with a grain of salt.

But this was different. Only two months earlier, Blodget had pegged Amazon's target price at $150. Now he was predicting a level nearly three times higher than that—in other words, that the company would reach a market cap of $45 billion while still twenty calendar quarters or more away from netting a red cent. "My God, that's aggressive," a broker in the CIBC auditorium was heard to gasp. (By way of comparison, the Ford Motor Co., the second-largest maker of cars and trucks in the world—which was enjoying a terrific 1990s and which reported net income of $6.1 billion on revenues of $144.4 billion in 1998—had a market cap of about $72 billion at the time of Blodget's forecast.)

Within two hours of the now-famed Blodget morning call, the major financial wires sizzled with accounts of Blodget's prognosis, and Web chat rooms lit up with commentary. Over the course of the day that followed, Blodget logged more than 100 telephone inquiries, a third of them from brokers, the rest from clients and the media— among them, the business news cable network CNNfn, which put him on the air live.

Almost immediately, Amazon stock started surging. Nothing could hold it back, not even a statement Blodget issued making it clear that he expected Amazon to hit $400 within twelve months, not twelve hours. By the closing bell, the stock had reached $301.75, a nearly 25 percent jump in a single day. Some $6.6 billion of new market capitalization had been created for the shareholders of Amazon.com. Not because of anything the company had done, not on the fundamentals or a material event, but almost exclusively as a result of Henry Blodget's bullishness. For a day, Blodget was a $6 billion man.

That's not to say everyone shared Blodget's enthusiasm for Amazon's prospects. One prominent skeptic was Jonathan Cohen, the chief Internet analyst at the international brokerage and money management empire Merrill Lynch. When it came to this particular stock, Cohen was considerably more old school in his approach. What he was looking for, he liked to say, was some sign of black ink, some real indication of viability on Amazon's part.

In Cohen's view, a chimera of profits in five years could easily turn into a nightmare—a lot can happen in a half-decade. Back in the late 1970s, for example, when crude oil prices were blasting past $40 a barrel, there were serious people predicting petroleum would trade at $100 a barrel by the 1990s. But instead, by the 1990s the world was awash in oil, and black gold was selling for as little as $10 a barrel (although in the late 1990s and into 2000, oil again edged up).

Then remember the investor hysteria the television shop-at-home craze stirred in the 1980s, sucking in even finance-pop-cult luminaries such as Diane Von Furstenberg and Barry Diller. There was heady talk that Americans would buy piles of goods—perhaps even the majority of nonfood items—while shopping from home, casting aside concerns about quality because such respected brands or names as Von Furstenberg would be backing the product. The best-laid plans of mice and men, as they say.

To Cohen's skeptical eye, Amazon.com was pricey at $50 a share, let alone $150 or $300. As a result, while Blodget was telling the world the sky was the limit, Cohen was repeating his recommendation that investors "reduce" their holdings—a rating of "reduce" being as close as most brokerage analysts ever tread even to the edges of that radioactive word "sell."

In fact, Cohen and Blodget weren't as far apart in their views as it might seem. Certainly, Blodget did not dispute Cohen's argument that as a business Amazon was nowhere close to proving itself. By traditional yardsticks, Blodget told *Fortune* magazine editor-at-large Joseph Nocera in a May 1999 interview, Amazon.com was probably worth only about $30 a share. But unlike Cohen, Blodget didn't think that fact had much relevance. As the wavy-haired, blond Blodget told Nocera, "Stocks don't go up or down because they have a specific 'value.' They go up and down because investors decide to buy or sell."

And Blodget, with the power of a major brokerage behind him, with its hundreds of billions of dollars under management, its vast trading department, and its ties to the giant mutual funds, had some influence over what investors decided to buy or sell.

To Nocera, Blodget's analysis was sadly "threadbare," typical of the shallowness of much of what passed for insight on Wall Street in the dot-com frenzy of the late 1990s. "When you listen closely," Nocera wrote, "what you hear from Blodget is that the main reason you should be buying Internet stocks is because other people buy them. Which is to say, his analysis is itself part of the bubble."

Perhaps, and probably, and maybe even certainly. But as people on the Street like to say, Blodget did call the move. Incredibly, Amazon was destined to reach $400 a share.

History—or at least "History: The Lite Version"—vindicated Blodget, and more rapidly than even Blodget had imagined. On January 6, 1999, just three weeks after he made his bullish call, the price of Amazon stock (adjusted for a three-to-one split) sailed past $400, ending the day at $138 a share—or $414 at pre-split prices. The cyberized bookseller was closing in on a market cap of $50 billion. Who says Americans don't read books? Not Wall Street.

Wall Street doesn't like a naysayer, and if naysayers are ever wrong, they are "pasteurized" (sent out to pasture). After Amazon's epic three-week ascent, Merrill Lynch quickly sacked Cohen as its chief Internet analyst. His successor? Henry Blodget.

Why did Merrill Lynch hire Blodget? There's no denying he had made the right call. Maybe Amazon stock violated the laws of investor physics, but a fact was a fact. Blodget's prediction was closer to the mark than Cohen's—and at least in the short run, that's what counts on Wall Street. And on Wall Street today, one good siren call—loud and compelling enough to rally investors—can make a career, at least for a while.

Blodget's Amazon call elevated his standing in the financial community even more than it raised Amazon's stock. Not only was his gutsy forecast proved right with phenomenal speed, but it proved he had the moxie, the timing, the oomph to move a stock—even with the smaller CIBC Oppenheimer as his brokerage. Imagine what he could do at a really big house like Merrill Lynch!

So it was that Blodget became a Wall Street superstar, one of the hottest Internet analysts in the business. Suddenly, an aggressive buy recommendation bearing his name could move an Internet stock. He

had influence, clout, muscle, the big flute—precisely what investment bankers need to dangle in front of prospective Internet corporate clients. There is little more important to a company about to
float a new issue than an underwriter's ability to arrange for coverage
from an analyst, who has the charm in his flute—the ability to make
stocks rise serpentine, uninhibited by grubby earthly concerns, like
earnings. That was what Merrill Lynch was really after when it hired
Blodget.

There was another reason Merrill grabbed Blodget. Big Merrill
needed someone to set sail against Morgan Stanley Dean Witter,
which had been ruling the Internet high seas with its star analyst,
Mary Meeker. Morgan Stanley was winning underwriting business
Merrill wanted.

A FEW YEARS OLDER THAN BLODGET, who was thirty-three when he
jumped to Merrill Lynch, Mary Meeker began her Wall Street career
as a junior computer-industry analyst at Salomon Bros. in 1986. After
a short stint with Cowen & Co., she joined Morgan Stanley in 1991.
An early enthusiast of the Web, Meeker was predicting that the
Internet would reach into millions of American homes and businesses back when Microsoft's Bill Gates was dismissing it as a new toy for
the ham-radio crowd. An early report of hers on the future of the
Internet, hundreds of pages long—a length common enough among
stock researchers pre-1975, but now regarded as truly heroic—is still
talked about reverentially by investors in the business. By the mid-
1990s she was, hands down, the most powerful Internet analyst on
Wall Street.

Meeker has never denied the fundamental absurdity of Internet
stock prices. Indeed, in January 1999, she put out a report containing
some cautionary comments on the subject. In response, the market
quavered for a couple of weeks—not good for IPOs, and not good for
clients who owned stock in IPOs Morgan Stanley had underwritten.
She has stuck with "buy" recommendations ever since—like Blodget,
citing the logic that the intense demand for Internet stocks means
they must go up. "A stock can go up or down based on money flows

at a much more rapid clip than it can on the fundamentals," she said.[2] Translation: "I've got the stockbrokers, I have the connections with money managers to move the market. I am just as much an authority as anybody. If I say buy, then the stock will go up."

Not surprisingly, with Meeker rapidly waving "buy" signals on the Internet sector, Morgan Stanley became the premier underwriter of Web-related stocks, handling a dozen such endeavors by mid-1999, with many more on the boards. Morgan Stanley was the hot underwriter for Internet stocks, and the Internet was the hottest sector. That's brokerage nirvana, 1990s style.

And Morgan Stanley investment bankers knew their formidable dominance lay in part, maybe in large part, in their alliance with Meeker. To companies entering the equity markets, the prospect of having an influential analyst like Meeker "on your side" was hard to beat. Take the Priceline.com offering. Late in 1998, the Connecticut-based online retailer and purveyor of cheap goods and services, knowing that it offered precisely the kind of business that made Wall Street foam at the mouth, organized a "beauty contest" among brokerages. First prize was the lucrative assignment of taking the company public.

In the old days, securities analysts would have been far removed from this sort of high-skirted maneuvering. Winning corporate chieftains as clients was the bailiwick of the investment bankers, who won business on their reputations for structuring successful stock and bond offerings. Analysts weren't part of the equation. Even as recently as the 1980s, people in the brokerage community still kept a straight face when extolling the "Chinese wall" that separated research departments from the investment bankers and the salesmen.

But that was then. Now, what Priceline was looking for was favorable analyst coverage, and no analyst mattered more to it than Mary Meeker. Indeed, when Priceline's backers first approached Morgan Stanley to discuss financing in the summer of 1998, they did so not by contacting the firm's investment banking department but by telephoning Meeker!

And in the end, when Morgan Stanley won the investment banking beauty contest, Priceline made clear why it awarded the brokerage the "10." It wasn't Morgan Stanley's venerable lineage that made the difference, but its hot Internet analyst Meeker. "We just think Mary is the best," Priceline CEO Richard Braddock said. "That was the distinguishing reason we chose Morgan."

Braddock's faith in Meeker was justified (at least for a while). Priceline.com went public at $16 a share, selling 10 million shares, or 7 percent of the company's stock outstanding. In the first few trades, the stock hit $85. On the first day of trading, Priceline.com reached a market capitalization of $11 billion. It had been operating for less than a year, in which it had lost $114 million on revenues of $35 million, and it operated in a medium that was wide open to competition. Meeker put out a "buy" signal on the stock after about one month of trading, and by mid-1999, Priceline stock soared toward $170 a share, for a market cap of $22 billion or so. The company still hadn't made any money, and hadn't into the year 2001, either.

## FADDISH IMITATION

American consumers know the gag of commercial imitation well, learning in their preteens that if a certain type of jeans becomes hot, there will be knockoff brands that mimic the original, or if a movie such as *Gladiator* hits, then soon there will be chintzy-looking, but supremely gory and lusty, sword-and-sandal flicks invading the made-for-television film cable network market.

Wall Street by the late 1990s began to show Hollywood and the fashion houses a thing or two: lesser analysts, at second-tier brokerages, also started tub-thumping for Internet stocks their brokerages had underwritten, trotting down the footpath blazed by Blodget and Meeker.

So it was in April 2000, when Thomas Bock, a twenty-eight-year-old former cable telephone installer then employed as an Internet analyst for brokerage SG Cowen, made a prediction that QXL.com, a London-based company taken public by SG Cowen, would hit $333 a share in two years. Before Bock made public his divinations on QXL.com's future, it had been trading on the low $20s.

The Bock call was a thing to admire, if only for its spectacular efficacy: the stock promptly soared to more than $117 a share in the first day of trading after the Bock call, before heavy selling drove it back down to $52 a share. Bock was influential, to say the least, as there was no major news about QXL.com that day.

There were other aspects about Bock worth mentioning. The Amherst college political science major had worked at SG Cowen for one month, and it was his first recommendation. Bock professed that QXL.com would become the eBay (the U.S.-based online auction house) of Europe. "We're not focusing right now on earnings or even revenues," Bock told *The Wall Street Journal.* "We're looking at the size of the market and their defensible position in it." At the time of the Bock call, QXL.com had revenue of $2.5 million in its latest reported quarter, and pretax losses of $61.4 million. Profitability would have to wait until 2003, Bock estimated, and that was if everything went just right. Bock pointed to his own "extensive" twenty-eight-page analysis of QXL.com as proof of the pudding; after all, eBay had a market cap of $25 billion, so why shouldn't QXL.com?

*The Wall Street Journal* did note that "Some folks were especially overjoyed by [QXL.com's] run-up: QXL's original investors. Next week these investors, including venture-capital firms, will be able to sell QXL shares under terms of the company's 'lock-up' agreement related to its initial public offering...."

Scott Sipperelle, cofounder of Midtown Research in New York, told the *Journal,* "Aggressive price targets get attention and sometimes can be self-fulfilling.... The question is why investors listen."

## LIVE AND DIE BY THE STAR

Of course, the star system of investment banking can sometimes backfire. It's not enough for a brokerage merely to promise a corporate client the kind of market-influencing coverage that can shoot a stock to the moon. The analyst has to deliver—or else.

Consider what happened to Morgan Stanley in May 1999, when it was in the midst of a $65 million IPO for Nextcard Inc., a hot Internet company that issues online credit cards. Just days before the brokerage was to take Nextcard's management team on the obligatory "road show," in which company executives crisscross the country presenting their business plan to potential investors, Morgan Stanley was unceremoniously dumped as Nextcard's lead underwriter; Donaldson, Lufkin & Jenrette Securities Corp. was selected instead to lead Nextcard to the IPO altar. The reason wasn't that Morgan Stanley's investment bankers were unpersuasive, nor that its pricing of the stock was wrong, nor that its fees seemed excessive. There was nothing wrong with the Morgan Stanley investment bankers.

The reason Morgan Stanley got dumped was that Nextcard didn't feel that Mary Meeker was sufficiently involved in the process. She missed meetings, the complaint went; she seemed out of the loop. "Morgan didn't deliver on the level of service it was promising," is how one source at the company put it to a reporter at the time. Fat underwriting fees were lost, and extra-fat pre-IPO stock went down the drain, for Morgan Stanley.[3]

The message Nextcard's tantrum sent to the brokerage industry— aside from the jab in the eye that underwriters could be switched like taxicabs—was unmistakable: If you want to be the one to take us public, you'd better make sure your analyst is prepared to give us lots of attention and lots of positive coverage.


TO BE SURE, WALL STREET IS HARDLY a place where only the brokerages get shoved around, while investors get mugged. Occasionally, maybe usually, the brokerages have the upper hand—and when they do, they slap by the same tough rules of the Street. As noted earlier, brokerage research departments follow only a small fraction of the thousands of publicly traded companies clamoring for attention in the nation's equity markets. The vast majority, most of them small-cap companies (in today's superheated market, companies with a market capitalization of less than $350 million or so, although some now place that figure as high as $1 billion), are absolutely bereft of coverage—or, if they are lucky, are covered erratically by a single analyst.

This is a real problem, for on Wall Street, ignorance is not bliss. If you've never heard of a company, it's not likely you will invest in it. And ordinary investors almost never hear of small-cap companies in general, much less those whose stock no analyst covers.

Professional money managers and mutual fund chieftains, who

have their own research departments, shy away from small caps for a different reason: a lack of liquidity. When you're running, say, a $10 billion fund, you tend to buy stock in sizable blocks; rarely, if ever, will you execute a trade involving much less than $20 million worth of a particular issue. The problem is, that much stock is bound to represent a significant chunk of a small cap's total equity (or shares outstanding). At the very least, a trade of that magnitude will send the price of a small-cap stock reeling; at worst, it can make a money manager (usually diffident sorts) a controlling shareholder, with far more responsibility for the company than he or she probably wants.

So with both individual investors and huge funds eschewing small-cap stocks, managers of smaller companies face an ongoing challenge: they must get coverage to have the stock appreciate.

This, of course, is much easier said than done, for precious few small caps have what piques the interest of brokerage analysts these days—namely, a need for the kind of investment banking work that can generate outsize fees for a brokerage firm. After all, the company is already public, so it can't offer the possibility of a lucrative IPO. And being a small cap, it's probably too small to justify a major secondary offering, meaning there aren't likely to be any lucrative underwritings to manage. So it is that when a small-cap company approaches a brokerage seeking coverage, it is almost always turned down. As Los Angeles investment banker Fred Roberts puts it, "Basically you are told, 'No deal, no coverage.'"

A former chairman of the board of the National Association of Securities Dealers, Roberts earned a reputation in the 1990s for engineering deals for small-cap companies that substantially increased shareholder value. But to do that, he almost always had to arrange for his small-cap clients to be merged into larger companies.

What he learned in the process was that without the prospect of investment banking fees, brokerage analysts generally can't be bothered to pay attention to even the most promising of small caps. "I had one client who was absolutely terrific," he says, "a terrific company. Every brokerage was the same: 'If you have a deal to do, then we can get you coverage.'" Unfortunately, his client didn't—so despite its prospects, it was ignored. A merger was arranged.

The coverage that brokerage analysts extend to large caps but in general not to small caps seemed to be playing a role in a growing—and otherwise inexplicable—dichotomy seen on Wall Street in the 1990s, which extends forth to this day. Blue chips have surged, as measured by the Standard & Poor's 500 (a broad index of blue chips), while the Russell 2000 (the 2,000 stocks below the largest 1,000) has not kept up. From 1990 through 1999, based on the annual average of the S&P 500 index, blue chips advanced 345 percent. (It should be also noted that in 1998, 1999, and into 2000, the price/earnings ratio on the S&P 500 index was above thirty. The index has never before sported such a high P/E ratio on a sustained basis.) In contrast, in the 1990s the Russell 2000 advanced only 232 percent in the same time frame.

Viewed from another perspective, in the ten-year period ended mid-August 2000, the largest 200 U.S. stocks (by market capitalization) had appreciated an annual compounded average of 18.49 percent, versus only 13.59 percent for the stocks in the Russell 2000 index.

Much of the surge in blue chips is almost certainly due to incessant buying of big-cap stocks by burgeoning mutual funds, which by necessity need to deploy hundreds of millions of dollars with each investment decision. It would be too expensive to perform due diligence on dozens or even hundreds of small-cap stocks, given the tens of billions of dollars many mutual funds now have to invest—platoons of researchers would have to be employed, even though the recommendations issued forth probably wouldn't beat the market averages. And anyway, why research small caps when blue chips marched ahead effortlessly?

It is more than whimsy to deduce that brokerage analysts, in alliance with their investment banking departments and trading departments, have entered into a symbiosis with the mutual funds and institutional investors, each hand helping the other to keep prices plumped and send IPOs off with a bang.

THE MID-CAP AND LARGE-CAP companies with ongoing investment banking needs, in contrast to small caps, often find themselves called upon regularly by investment bankers, who now are proactive in seeking business. "It's not enough to answer the phone," says Mark Lanigan, managing director in the corporate finance department of Donaldson, Lufkin & Jenrette (now part of Credit Suisse First Boston). "You have to contact corporate management, propose to them acquisitions or opportunities for financings. If you don't, some other banker will."[4]

These in-favor companies not only attract the attention of Wall Street's pied pipers, but they help write the scores the analysts play by. To say that blue chips and Internet hotshots began to feel their oats in the 1990s is to put it mildly. As brokerage firms competed ever more furiously for their business, such companies became intolerant of anything but glowing analyst reports—and increasingly willing to retaliate against firms they felt were overly critical.

This counterpunching became almost routine in the 1990s, with such run-of-the-mill cases as Bell South, for example. In 1994 Bell South made a point of not hiring Salomon Bros. (now Salomon Smith Barney) as lead manager for a large bond issue—a role the giant firm had traditionally played—after a Salomon analyst described the company as one of the worst-run of the seven so-called Baby Bells. Similarly, in 1991 after an analyst at Kidder Peabody reiterated an ultrarare "sell" recommendation for Nationsbank stock, the giant bank holding company instructed its trust officers to stop trading stocks and bonds through the firm.

In a few cases, however, aggrieved company officials went even further. Perhaps the most famous such incident involved Marvin Roffman, a respected securities analyst and self-described stock market junkie who made the mistake of crossing Donald Trump.

Back in 1990, Roffman was following the gaming industry for Janney Montgomery Scott, a well-known regional brokerage based in Philadelphia. Then fifty, Roffman had worked at Janney Montgomery for sixteen years and been in the industry for three decades. Among the companies he followed was Donald Trump's money-losing Atlantic City casino, the Taj Mahal.

Roffman became a human punching bag after he issued a report on "The Taj," as it was known, in which he concluded that the seaside wagering emporium was too risky a bet—if not for crapshooters, then certainly for investors. The mercurial Trump, livid at being called to account by an obscure figure at a regional brokerage, responded to Roffman's findings by demanding that Janney Montgomery fire its insufficiently respectful analyst. The Trump also threatened litigation.

Janney Montgomery mulled matters for a few days and then sent Roffman packing. Evidently, sixteen years of service counted for little. After he was fired, Roffman worried in print about paying for his medical insurance, and reminisced about how he had read financial papers as a boy with his mom and had always wanted to be an analyst. Now he was middle-aged and out of work, and evidently radioactive on Wall Street. As it happened, Roffman's skepticism was justified. Gushing red ink, the Taj sought Chapter 11 bankruptcy protection the following year. Roffman got canned for being right.

Roffman, meanwhile, became something of an everyman-type folk hero among investors and Wall Street insiders who knew something of the pressures on analysts. Both he and the editors of financial publications that covered the incident received hundreds of admiring letters. "We should never let the absolutely incredible actions taken by Janney Montgomery Scott slip from our memories," read a typical missive (this one published in *Barron's*).

Fortunately for Roffman, being vindicated by events was not his only reward. He sued Trump for defamation and settled for an undisclosed sum. He also went after Janney Montgomery, which eventually was ordered by a New York Stock Exchange arbitration panel to pay him $750,000 in damages. Given that such industry panels tend to favor brokerages, Roffman's award was doubly meaningful.

Nonetheless, he never worked for a major or regional brokerage again. Eventually he started up his own boutique investment shop, Roffman Miller Associates. Through the 1990s and into the new era, pressures on brokerage analysts have only gotten worse, Roffman said. "Research departments are not profit centers. Money is being made in investment banking and corporate finance. An analyst can't get in the way of that," commented Roffman.[5]

Too, increasing concentration among brokerages means there are fewer big-time analyst slots open, even in boom times. "With all the mergers on Wall Street, there are less positions for analysts. Even in good times, analyst jobs are decreasing. Look at the proposed buyout [in August 2000] of Donaldson, Lufkin & Jenrette by Credit Suisse First Boston," said Roffman. "They are not going to need all those Donaldson analysts after the merger."

The trend to financial conglomerates—mergers among banks, securities firms, and insurance companies—makes conflicts of interest rife, said Roffman. An analyst's "sell" signal might rile a commercial bank's client, and that client could decide to take business elsewhere. If that commercial bank owns a securities firm, it is probably a safe bet no "sell" signals will be issued on its banking clients.

Roffman termed the situation for honest analysis in 2000 "worse than ever. And it was already pretty bad." Roffman has moved into managing money, about $150 million worth. "Now I can tell the truth," he said.

The Roffman-Trump trials were not lost on other securities analysts, but just in case anyone missed the point, a mere two years after the Trump tantrum another stubbornly straightforward analyst, Richard Lilly of JW Charles Securities in Boca Raton, Florida, found himself taken to the same woodshed, for many of the same reasons. If anything, Lilly displayed even greater perspicacity than Roffman. In fact, he unearthed a fraud, employing the sort of gumshoe work no longer much associated with his profession, most of whose members appear to be spoon-fed information by company officials.

In 1992, Lilly was taking a second look at a stock he had previously recommended: Cascade International Inc., a women's clothing chain. Over the previous two years, Cascade had been a highflier, rising from $2 a share in 1990 to $11 a share in fall 1991. For the most part, the impressive run-up was the result of three factors: the company's good earnings reports, Lilly's "buy" recommendation, and JW Charles's 500 brokers (who, based on their colleague's endorsement, began talking up the stock to anyone who would listen).

By June 1991, however, Lilly was growing uneasy about Cascade. The sort of analyst (increasingly rare) who likes to talk to corporate employees below the management level, he was beginning to hear things that made him question the company's integrity. The biggest problem: Cascade claimed to have 181 stores around the country, but Lilly could find only 81. Working with David Brown, an analyst with Overpriced Stock Services, a San Francisco research firm, Lilly telephoned every area code in the United States, vainly searching for the missing 100 stores. In the end, Lilly was convinced that Cascade had deliberately inflated the figures. Incensed, he prepared a "sell" report that detailed the company's fraud.

Lilly was well aware of the risks connected with blowing the whistle. "You yell 'fraud' and you're wrong, you're out of business for life," he said at the time. "You could have a criminal record. If I represented that something was a fraud, it drove the stock down, and it turned out to be wrong? There could be enormous liabilities...." Nonetheless, he was determined to proceed.

Alerted to what Lilly was planning, Cascade contacted JW Charles and vowed to file a $50 million lawsuit if the analyst circulated his report. The threat worked—at least up to a point. The brokerage did order Lilly to keep his findings to himself, but Lilly refused to be muzzled. Convinced the public was being deceived, he defied his bosses and sent letters detailing his allegations to the media and Cascade investors. JW Charles responded by firing him.

Shortly thereafter, Cascade's founder disappeared, and the company collapsed. Like Roffman, Lilly did not get his job back. Still, he seemed content with the turn of events. "At some point in life," he told reporters, "you have to put ethics ahead of everything else."

Other cases, not so clear-cut, abound in analyst circles. Tom Brown was the banking analyst for Donaldson, Lufkin & Jenrette in the mid-1990s. In 1997, with institutional clients in tow, he actually visited the headquarters of San Francisco–based Wells Fargo, the banking giant. In a rare effort, he wanted to get behind the numbers and get a feel for management. It turned out to be a fiasco.

Brown was aghast at what he perceived as a very feeble, almost dismissive presentation made to him by company officials—in a word, Brown was snubbed, and in front of his clients, no less. He had been worrying about Wells Fargo's ability to digest its recent acquisition of First Interstate, another banking giant, formerly based in Los Angeles. His questions about indigestion, and many other questions, went unanswered, or worse, were treated as irrelevant, Brown decided. He was all but humiliated in front of clients. He told associates that Wells Fargo seemed like a rudderless ship, or one in which too many deckhands were missing.

Returning untriumphant to New York, Brown did not issue a "sell" recommendation—he didn't want to base a recommendation on somewhat personal resentments—but he did write a letter to clients that his confidence in Wells Fargo was weakened. In fact, Brown's worries about earnings were justified, and Wells Fargo floundered in subsequent quarters.

Again, being right was no defense. Brown had bad-mouthed a major bank, a major client, and he was seen by some inside DLJ as being in a "tiff" with Wells Fargo. The spirited tone of the letter he sent to clients didn't help. In 1998, he left DLJ to join the money management shop Tiger Management in New York, and he later surfaced working for Second Curve Capital, a hedge fund. There, he told reporters that while he worked at DLJ, a banking analyst could earn a $250,000 bonus for bringing in a $10 billion, midsized bank as a brokerage investment banking client.[6]

Fooling around with "buy" and "sell" signals on banks is indeed a tricky business, as George Salem, a banking analyst formerly with Prudential Securities and then with brokerage Gerard Klauer Mattison & Co. in New York, found out before retiring in 1999. He was regarded as an "analyst's analyst," and other analysts often altered their recommendations or outlook in deference to him. Salem wrote a series of negative reports on Citicorp in 1992, and suddenly Prudential couldn't lead-manage any more Citicorp bond offerings. The bank told Prudential it was because of Salem. Undaunted, Salem next dared to lower his rating on Banc One, the big Columbus, Ohio, banking company. Banc One then cut back its trading of bonds through Prudential. Thereafter, Salem left Prudential, and he told *The Wall Street Journal* that the pressure was extreme on analysts who cover banks. "Let's face it," he said, "a bank is a much more intimidating company to research than the trucking industry. It has a lot more clout."

But perhaps Salem said that only because he had never covered the industrial side of the fence. Consider the case of David Snyder.

Also an analyst for DLJ in the late 1990s, Snyder was covering Agco Corp., a manufacturer of farm equipment. Agco was going through hard times. Ever since embarking on an overseas sales push in 1996, it had been wallowing in mediocre numbers, consistently missing earnings estimates. As a result, the company's stock was hurting. In the first half of 1998, it lost nearly one-third of its value.

Not liking what he was seeing, Snyder removed Agco from DLJ's "recommended" list on May 30 of that year. Given Agco's history, he wrote, "investors are not likely to be very patient with any disappointments." Adding insult to injury, Snyder went on to apologize to clients for having previously recommended the company to them, noting "we have been terribly wrong on Agco's stock over the past two years."

Admission of error is hardly part of Wall Street's ethos. Neither is telling the world that an investment banking client is a loser as an investment. In each of the previous two years, the firm had co-managed underwritings for the company. And what of institutional investors who had bought on DLJ's say-so? How would they liquidate their positions? Shortly after Snyder issued his critical report, his career at DLJ ended.

In the new millennium, analysts hardly turned over a new leaf, although the financial press was beginning to ask itself aloud about analyst ethics and whether analysts are worthwhile "quote fodder." In one sensationally brutal story, which ran on the cover of *Bloomberg Markets* magazine in July 2000, Stephen Balog, former research director at Lehman Bros. and Furman Selz, told reporter Faith Keenan, "An analyst is just a banker who writes reports…. No one makes a pretense that it's independent."

Even more blunt were the comments of Sean Ryan, former banking analyst with Bear Stearns. He told *Bloomberg Markets* magazine that while with Bear Stearns in 1999 he recommended the Alpharetta, Georgia–based Internet bank NetBank even though he thought it was a crummy company. "I put a buy on it because they paid for it," he said.

Bear Stearns had handled two equity and one debt underwriting for NetBank, worth $307 million—read fees in the $25 million range, even before potential profits on warrants, options, or other equity kickers and those made by the trading department. Ryan kept the green light on for ordinary investors but called his large institutional clients and told them what he really thought. "I said, 'We just launched coverage on NetBank because they bought it fair and square with two offerings.'"

Too bad for regular investors, who thought a buy recommendation from the analyst of a major brokerage like Bear Stearns might be more than concentrated essence of horse manure. NetBank stock crumbled from a hyped-up $78 a share in April 1999 to $9.80 a share in early 2001.

SUCH CAUTIONARY TALES NO LONGER surprise veteran analysts. Charles "Chuck" Hill, for example, considers it par for the course on present-day Wall Street. With more than thirty years under his belt as an analyst at such firms as Kidder Peabody and Bache Securities (which was long ago merged into Prudential Securities), Hill recalls the 1970s and early 1980s, when the Chinese wall protecting the independence of research departments at major brokerages was more than a fiction. "I can tell you, I was never pressured," says Hill.

Now the director of research for First Call/Thomson Financial, the widely quoted Boston-based agency that tracks analyst projections, Hill doesn't hesitate when asked how things have changed. "These days, to justify the cost of doing research, you've got to help the investment banking side of the business," he says flatly. "Unquestionably, there is a rising tendency for analysts to worry about investment banking or corporate clients."

But what does this mean in practice? Okay, so analysts are expected to help the brokerage generate investment banking fees. But analysts are, for the most part, professionals with stellar educations. Perhaps they can "thread the needle"—keep investment bankers appeased while truly touting only solid prospects. Unfortunately, the numbers say otherwise. In fact, as a group, analyst earnings forecasts have been too optimistic, and their "buy" recommendations have underperformed the market, consistently and over many years. It is a damning indictment.

## THE DREMAN STUDY AND OTHERS

Probably the largest and most comprehensive review of analyst performance ever undertaken was carried out in the mid-1990s by well-known Wall Street contrarian and financial columnist David Dreman (author of the 1980 book *Contrarian Investment Strategies: The Psychology of Stock Market Success*), with the assistance of Michael Berry, a professor of business at James Madison University. A preliminary account of their work—in which they reviewed some 94,251 analyst forecasts, involving more than 1,500 NYSE, Amex, and Nasdaq stocks, between 1971 and 1996—was first published in 1995 in *The Financial Analysts Journal,* a respected industry semimonthly. Dreman updated the data in his 1998 book, *Contrarian Investment Strategies: The Next Generation.* His report was not very reassuring. As Dreman put it, "The results are startling—analyst projections were sharply and consistently off the mark."

Specifically, what he and Berry had found—by looking at forecasts over a period long enough to wash out the impact of any number of clearly unpredictable events, such as a Presidential resignation or a Gulf War—was that the typical analyst forecast of corporate earnings missed the target (that is, varied from the actual result) by 42 percent.

Today's analysts, of course, have far better tools—and more of them—with which to read their tea leaves than did their counterparts in the 1970s and 1980s. Thanks to the Internet and a plethora of continuously updated proprietary databases, analysts can now access other forecasters' projections almost instantly—not to mention a cornucopia of financial reports, corporate announcements, economic statistics, and news articles, all of which can be instantly downloaded and run through brokerage firms' sophisticated computer models. When it comes to available information, the contrast between now and the pre-1975 era is nothing short of astounding, for analysts and even for ordinary individual investors.

Nonetheless, analysts are no better at predicting future performance today than they were twenty-five years ago. Quite the contrary. As Dreman noted in his book, "in spite of the information revolution, estimates seem to have gotten worse, not better...." Specifically, while the average error over the twenty-five-year period Dreman and

Berry studied was 42 percent, in the last eight years they looked at (i.e., 1989 through 1996), analyst forecasts missed the target by an average of 50 percent.

To be sure, one could argue that this figure sounds worse than it really is. Many companies report quarterly earnings of only a few cents per share. Being just one penny off on a forecast for a company that earns, say, 5¢ a share amounts to an error of 20 percent. With this in mind, Dreman and Berry "cleaned" their data, weeding out forecasts involving all companies that reported earnings (or losses) of less than 10¢ a share. This improved the results, but only somewhat: over the 1971–1996 period, the average analyst forecast still missed the mark by fully 23 percent.

There was, however, something more striking—and disconcerting—than the size of the typical error: its direction. When analysts guessed wrong, Dreman and Berry found, they usually guessed wrong on the high side—that is, by a 3-to-1 margin, their projections tended to be overly optimistic rather than unduly pessimistic.

In reality, the upside bias of securities analysts may be even stronger than those figures suggest. Since the early 1990s, it has been common practice for high-tech and blue-chip companies to try to persuade (or "prep") analysts to issue earnings projections that are slightly below what the company is actually preparing to report—a long-running gag at Microsoft, a company forever "beating" earnings projections. The idea is to present to the world a company just so white-hot that waves of business are pouring across the transom, even more than predicted by optimistic soothsayers. If it weren't for this prepping practice, the predilection of analysts to overestimate earnings would be even worse.

In any case, Dreman and Berry's data are absolutely consistent with the worrisome trends on Wall Street of growing pressures on analysts to cater to their firms' powerful investment banking departments, and to not damage an institutional investor's holding of a favorite stock. In such an environment, one would expect to see an overall decline in accuracy, with a growing preponderance of misses on the upside—and that is *precisely* what Dreman and Berry found.

Dreman concludes that the best way to invest is to actually go against the analysts—to be a contrarian. Investors should select good-quality, out-of-favor stocks not being touted by analysts and hold onto them for the long run, advises Dreman (among much other advice).

While Dreman's study is admirably herculean in its scope, it is hardly the only academic look at Wall Street analysts, although all serious studies draw similar conclusions. A study released in February 1999 by Roni Michaely of Cornell and Kent Womack of Dartmouth explored several issues, such as the fact that "It is common for a significant portion of the research analyst's compensation to be determined by the analyst's 'helpfulness' to the corporate finance professional and their financing efforts." The study also cites an internal Morgan Stanley memo from 1992, which stated, "Our objective ... is to adopt a policy, fully understood by the entire firm, including the Research Department, that we do not make negative or controversial comments about our clients as a matter of sound business practice."

Entitled "Conflict of Interest and the Credibility of Underwriter Analyst Recommendations," the study goes on to note, "In the past, the corporate finance arm of the investment bank was more likely to perform due diligence on an issuer using its own staff and not analysts in the equity research department. Only after an offering was completed would the underwriting firm assign an equity research analyst to cover the stock. The trend in the last two decades, however, has been to use equity research analysts directly in the marketing and due diligence processes."

In the language favored by careful academics, Womack and Michaely finish by stating, "We conclude that the recommendations by underwriter analysts show significant evidence of bias. We show also that the market does not recognize the full extent of this bias. The results suggest a potential conflict of interest in the different functions that investment bankers perform."

Among other findings, Womack and Michaely found that buy recommendations issued by underwriting analysts did fluff up target stocks for between several days and five months—long enough to let big institutional clients profit, and perhaps sell out. A funny thing happened after six months: the flute music lost its enchanting effect, and the stocks stopped floating above average market returns, and instead dropped below average and began tracking worse and worse through twelve months, never to beat the market again. All of this is consistent with the concept that brokerage analyst "buy" recommendations—put into effect by leagues of stockbrokers advising retail clients to buy, and leaked to institutional clients before hitting the wires—can elevate a stock for a while, through sheer buying power. Then selling pressure mounts, and the fundamentals begin to sink in. Analysts, meanwhile, have moved their attention to the next deal, the next IPO to be flogged, the next hot stock in which the brokerage trading department has amassed a big stake.

Yet another academic treatise, a working paper issued by the Harvard Business School in 1997 entitled "The Relation Between Analysts' Long-Term Earnings Forecasts and Stock Price Performance Following Equity Offerings," found that earnings estimates of underwriters' analysts are significantly more optimistic than those of unaffiliated analysts, and the stocks that were most overpriced compared to fundamentals were those covered by brokerage analysts whose firm had been the underwriter.

And one more serious study, "Why So Much Error in Analysts' Earnings Forecasts?" published by the *Journal of Financial Analysis* in November/December 1998, found that brokerage analysts, even in the healthy economy of the 1990s, on average overestimated annual earnings per share by about 12 percent when predicting current year's earnings near the start of the year. The author, Vijay Kumar Chopra, suggested the accuracy of the projections would have been worse, but the unexpectedly and sustained strong 1990s economy—the best perhaps in the whole of the postwar era—provided a good backbeat for the optimistic songs played by analysts. But they still projected too high.

OKAY, SO BROKERAGE ANALYSTS CAN'T project earnings, and they are too optimistic, probably due to conflicts raised by investment banking and other relationships. Who cares? More important are the "buy" or "sell" recommendations; that's what counts to investors. When you boil it down, really that's all that counts. This is the money question:

Can individual investors buy according to brokerage analyst recommendations and beat the market?

Sadly (but not surprisingly), analysts crap out in stock picking, too, according to the indefatigable researcher Dreman. Rummaging through dozens of surveys, from *The Wall Street Journal*'s annual canvasses (in which Hemant Shah had been singled out as a star) to the Cowles polls of 1929–1932, the celebrated contrarian Dreman found that when analysts picked their own favorite stocks for the year ahead, they wound up underperforming the market a whopping 75 *percent* of the time.

In contrast, "Throwing darts at the stock pages, or flipping a coin, would give you a 50-50 chance of beating the market," Dreman noted. Given the generally random and unpredictable nature of stock price behavior looking forward (remember Burton Malkiel's "random walk"), for analysts to consistently underperform the market is a remarkable feat. It is as challenging, in its own way, as beating the market regularly. It should be as hard to assemble a portfolio of losers as winners. Somehow analysts do it, however.

In his book, Dreman summed up the situation by quoting former UBS securities analyst Peter Siris. "There's a game out there," Siris observed. "Most people aren't fooled by what analysts have to say … because they know in a lot of cases they are shills. But the poor [small] investors—somebody ought to tell them."

The sustained skunky record compiled by analysts over the years, although chronicled by academics and known to exist empirically, has not yet yielded to an elegant theory, even in academic literature. In a roughly perfect market, it should not happen.

One explanation, which may merit research and which is consistent both with the empirical observation and with industry practice, is as follows: Analysts first tell their trading departments and large institutional clients that they will issue a "buy" recommendation—of course, this is taken for granted following an initial public offering of stock. The "inside" buyers accumulate stock, causing a bulge in the price leading up to the date when the recommendation is made public—a pattern that industry experts and academics have in fact observed.

But of course, since everything relevant is already known about the stock, this bulge is artificial, a product of genteel manipulation, and the stock, at the moment the "buy" signal is released, is actually somewhat overpriced, other things being equal. The stock thereafter lifts a little further, as brokerage stockbrokers bring retail customers into the issue and the analysts sing the stock's virtues in the financial media. After all the early action subsides, however, the stock drifts back down to its proper level, or—the somewhat more cynical explanation—the brokerage trading departments and institutions exit the stock, dumping their shares on retail buyers.

Without as strong an institutional base, the stock sags. The analysts' buy recommendations, good for a few months, are bad a year later (when compared to market averages). This is absolutely consistent with the data as presented by Michaely and Womack. It is also the pattern attested to by market professionals, who know if they speak on the record about such a topic, they will be unemployed.

Another survey: Zacks Investment Research polled brokerage analysts for their "best picks" for 1998 and 1999. In the period measured in 1998, analysts' picks fell 11.5 percent, compared to a smaller 8.2 percent decrease in the Russell 2000, an index of small-cap stocks. In 1999, the analysts tripped and fell another 12 percent, while the Russell 2000 rose 7.6 percent. Meanwhile, the S&P 500 index rose 28 percent in 1998, and another 21 percent in 1999. Any investor in a garden-variety index fund of blue chips would have easily outperformed Wall Street's "best picks" for the periods measured by Zacks.

In study after study, the results are the same: Analyst recommendations underperform the market as a whole. Investors armed with darts will beat brokerage analysts and their flutes almost every time.

## LET'S GET SERIOUS

Even as sober a watchdog as Federal Reserve chairman Alan Greenspan—the inflation hawk who in 1996 scolded Wall Street for what he called its "irrational exuberance"—seemed at times entranced by analysts' carnival-barker enthusiasm. On May 5, 1999, speaking at a conference organized by the Federal Reserve Bank of Chicago, Greenspan held up bullish corporate-earnings projections of securities analysts as a meaningful indicator that inflation may be well whipped. Given that analysts "presumably are knowledgeable about the companies they follow," he intoned, their increasingly optimistic forecasts could be read only one way: corporate productivity was "accelerating," and that meant inflation was hamstrung.

(Greenspan's exact language was considerably more convoluted. "There appears little reason to doubt that analysts' continuous upwards revisions reflect what companies are reporting to them about improved cost control, which on a consolidated basis for the economy overall, adds up to accelerating productivity," he said. Because "companies are apparently conveying to analysts that, to date, they see no diminution of expectations of productivity expansion," he concluded, inflation was not the threat it might be otherwise.)

Perhaps a better interpretation of analysts' ever-hiking earnings forecasts was that the market was trading at roughly thirty times earnings—about double long-term historical averages—and that it was getting hard to entice investors to jump in without some real histrionics.

It was a little reassuring that later in 1999, the Fed chief authorized two rate increases, and he didn't mention analyst forecasts again as figuring in his economic outlook. One can only hope that Greenspan, in his mid-seventies and a Wall Streeter almost the whole of his adult life, was for a Midwestern day in May nostalgic for the era of two-inch-thick industry reports and analysts as resident brokerage academics, free of investment banking imperatives. Let's say that in that frame of mind, he reflected on analyst earnings projections. Most likely, Greenspan woke up on his return home to Manhattan.

## "ONCE AGAIN, RETAIL INVESTORS ARE LEFT HOLDING THE BAG"

Of course, the chickens did come home to roost in 2000, for the Henry Blodgets and Mary Meekers of the world, for the Internet stocks they had praised so lyrically, and for the investors who followed their siren songs. In a spectacular spring-cleaning on Wall Street in February, March, and April, Internet stocks of all varieties lost half, three-quarters, or all of their value. By the time baseball fans tuned in to the All Star game in July, an index of Internet stocks was nearly cut in half from its early year peak. Investors by mid-2000 began to worry whether the e-stocks could ever make money.

In a sign of the times, a satire-drenched all-news site called www. fuckedcompany.com became popular—even profitable, ironically enough—featuring graphics that mimicked some better-known Internet business magazines. The site basically (if crudely and maliciously) tolled the bell daily for dot-com bombs in the tech wreck that had become Wall Street. It was a lot of work; each day seemed to bring five to ten dot-com burials, with abundant use of the f-word to describe what happened to investors, or the abilities and sincerity of dot-com management and original sponsors (read brokerages that took such companies public).

The picture for e-stocks was so bad by summer 2000 that the fabled prince of Web land, the handsome Henry Blodget, downgraded eleven of the twenty-nine e-stocks he covered in the first week of August. Maybe he waited until everybody else in New York had left on vacation, and it would be hard to blame him for choosing the dog days to admit error. Such stocks as Pets.com and Buy.com had lost 90 percent of their value, while eToys.com had plummeted 95 percent from its high. Amazon.com, the stock that had made Blodget what he was, was down 71.1 percent from its high. And iVillage, an e-site where women could hold cyber hands, was down 87.5 percent from its frenzied high.

Eventually, Blodget cracked under the relentless fall of e-stocks. All through the first seven months of 2000, he had called those e-stocks, and twenty-five others, "buys." In July 2000 Blodget told the world he had reservations about the twenty-nine Web stocks. He didn't put sell signals out. But he did lower a number of ratings, as noted above, and even put out two "hold" ratings. (One joke going around was that they were no longer e-stocks, but "f-stocks.")

It should be stated that Blodget wasn't alone. In particular, one of Meeker's stocks, the aforementioned Priceline.com, which had soared to nearly $170 under Meeker's prodding in 1999—it was her firm, Morgan Stanley Dean Witter, as was stated, that had taken it public—tumbled from that ethereal level in mid-1999 to hit just $25 by August 2000. Meeker's other picks suffered similarly.

And let's not forget Thomas Bock, the twenty-eight-year-old wunderkind whose tout on QXL.com, that London-based online auction house (think the eBay of the Old World) had shot the stock from the low $20s to $117 for part of a day. By early 2001, QXL.com was worth not Bock's predicted $333 but $3 a share. Bock was off by about 99 percent, although to be fair, he had eighteen months left on his two-year prediction.

In any event, was Blodget, the titular head of the Internet star-analyst crowd, a tad late in warning investors? "From a pure stock-performance basis, sure," Blodget blithely told *The Wall Street Journal*. "We could presumably have downgraded at the beginning of the year." Oh, really.

But maybe Blodget's comments weren't the most galling made on Wall Street by an analyst that summer. Another Internet analyst, Lise Buyer, formerly with Credit Suisse First Boston, told *Fortune* in June 2000 that she "can't remember the last time I read a 10Q thoroughly." Why not? "Nobody cared," she answered.

In Buyer's defense, she had quit CSFB to join a venture capital firm in Silicon Valley, and she was grousing about the lack of integrity among brokerage analysts and the pressure on analysts to provide lusty mood music for investment bankers. What had her analyst job really been about? "It was about who can make the biggest noise," Buyer answered.

# 4

# THE PIED PIPERS
# WITH GOLDEN FLUTES

I t is hardly worth noting anymore, so accepted has the mundane reality become: securities analysts scarcely ever utter the word "sell." Of 33,169 "buy," "sell," and "hold" recommendations made by brokerage analysts in 1999, only 125 were pure sells. That means just 0.3 percent of recommendations were "sells," according to data put together by Zacks Investment Research. There were another 224 recommendations, or 0.7 percent, that could be interpreted as "sells," such as rankings with such tepid language as "market underperformer."

To be sure, the year 1999 was another in the run of the bull. But there must have been more than 1 percent of stocks deserving of a "sell" recommendation. There must have been a number of stocks that had soared in price yet whose fundamentals had remained roughly the same, or whose prices had surpassed the targets set for them by analysts. And surely there were a few companies that just went to the dogs.

But no. As the track records of star Internet analysts Mary Meeker and Henry Blodget make clear, if a stock inflates wildly, beyond all expectations rational or otherwise, then the fundamentals are tossed overboard and "buy" signals left on. "Almost everybody is in a 'buy' or 'hold' mode," says Bruce Mandel, who oversees a $220 million pool of stock in Los Angeles. "They will never say 'sell.' If they do, they will never talk to a company's management again." Or maybe to their own investment banking departments. Or their big institutional clients. Or their own trading departments.

Analysts, in other words, must forever entrance the buying public with lyrical tales of higher and then higher share prices ahead and the resulting easy, fat capital gains. Their role is not to critique the players on the field but to attract and mesmerize investors, to keep them coming back for more, laying their money down again, to get another chance at the millennial jackpot named Wall Street. The sort of carnival barkers one finds outside chintzier Vegas casinos come to mind.

In recent years, with the flood of initial public offerings and the bulge in price/earnings ratios on Wall Street, analysts have played faster and more enchantingly than ever before. Now IPOs are usually posited not just as profitable enterprises selling shares to the public but as multibillion-dollar bonanzas in the making, with concepts that can be duplicated worldwide, or reach everywhere through the Internet.

Planet Hollywood, the restaurant chain, was cast from this mold. Planet Hollywood was hardly Wall Street's biggest bomb ever. Indeed, Planet Hollywood's status as a dud is being freshly challenged by candidates emerging from the Internet meltdown, such as Pets.com and eToys.com.

Nonetheless, Planet Hollywood did vie with certain film fiascos—*Waterworld* and *Ishtar* come to mind—as a stupendously grand financial bust. It also makes for entertaining reading. Unless, of course, you happen to be one of the unlucky investors who bought on the Wall Street hoopla.

## PLANET HOLLYWOOD, BABY

At first blush, the idea behind the Planet Hollywood restaurant chain didn't seem so half-baked. With movies and television becoming the touchstone for a culture hollowed out by the imperatives of modern life, the nation—indeed the world—seems to have a growing, insatiable appetite for all things Hollywood. So, in the theme-oriented nuttiness of the dining-out trade of the mid-1990s, why not a restaurant based on celluloid? Why not a nationwide chain of outsized, movie-themed restaurants, most of them large enough to serve 600 people at one seating? Would not the masses, starved for some connection to the glamour of Tinseltown, pay real money to dine—and buy souvenirs—in a faux "Hollywood experience"?

Actually, even a halfhearted amount of investigation and truth-telling would have given potential investors—and real analysts—indigestion. For one thing, people seem to like to eat in theme restaurants just once, maybe twice—a death knell for most themed restaurants. As a result, what are known as same-store sales—that is, sales at existing branches (as opposed to newly opened ones)—tend to decline over time at themed dining establishments. For another, only a handful of tourist cities worldwide could profitably support the huge dining emporiums that were constructed by Planet Hollywood.

These conceptual problems plagued Planet Hollywood almost from the start—but they were smothered by the hype and buzz that accompanied the chain's launch in 1992. Stirring the PR pot were Planet Hollywood's chairman and founder, movie producer Keith Barish, and its CEO, Robert Earl, a former top executive at the successful Hard Rock Cafe restaurant chain. As a result of their expert drumbeating, Planet Hollywood looked to be a financially sexy proposition, at least during the first course.

To be sure, the restaurants were very lively—an uncharitable person might say they were loud—the result of music systems turned high, the clank of cutlery, and the dull roar of waitresses and patrons shouting to be heard. Some call this "eater-tainment." Planet Hollywood described it as a "high-energy environment."

The walls of every Planet Hollywood restaurant were drenched with movie and TV memorabilia: a film poster from the 1940s, Sharon Stone's ice pick from *Basic Instinct,* the actual sailor's cap Bob Denver wore on the *Gilligan's Island* television series. Video monitors hung hither and yon screened snippets from old movies, often musicals, their sound tracks competing with (and often drowned out by) the high-energy house music.

Then there were the house celebrities. In an effort to attract an A-list crowd, most trendy restaurants "comp" recognizable actors, actresses, and other well-known figures. Chairman Barish adopted the comp policy and put it on steroids: he enticed two dozen Hollywood stars to invest in the chain even before the IPO. The likes of Arnold Schwarzenegger, Whoopi Goldberg, Sylvester Stallone, Bruce Willis, Demi Moore, and Cindy Crawford bought a cumulative

18 percent of the stock—which was offered to them at discount prices, in return for their agreement to show up at the grand openings of new Planet Hollywood outlets. It was a brilliant ploy. Not only did the assembled star power reinforce the chain's image as a Hollywood hangout, it also ensured that the media coverage for openings was terrific, bordering on slavish, giving each new location the kind of free advertising for which most restaurateurs would endure ptomaine poisoning.

All this cost money, of course—and plenty of it. The Planet Hollywood prospectus outlined that public relations costs were far higher than industry norms—including both in-house and hired publicists—and restaurant staffing levels richer than cheesecake. Most diners noticed the food was a bit pricey—and it was, as they were paying for a lot of overhead. As a private company (before going public), the Planet Hollywood chain borrowed more than $126 million to get rolling and spent millions more raised through private equity (pre-IPO sales of private stock).

In its first three years, the chain generated a steady flow of red ink. It finally poked its head into the black in calendar 1995, earning a reported $20.7 million on revenues of $270.6 million. That was the zenith for the Planet Hollywood chain—and as later financial reports revealed, management either knew it or should have.

For one thing, same-store sales were sinking like a popped soufflé—they would be down nearly 5 percent in 1996 (and fully 40 percent over the following three years). For another, although there were thirty Planet Hollywood restaurants around the world at the time the chain sold stock to the public, nearly half of the chain's revenues were being generated by just four spots (Orlando, Las Vegas, Paris, and London). In other words, the remaining twenty-six Planet Hollywood restaurants were nearly deadweight, or worse.

Especially worrisome, the chain was already in all the best markets—meaning that adding more spots would almost certainly prove but a dead-end strategy, for future expansion would by definition be restricted to less-profitable secondary markets. Unlike Denny's or McDonald's outlets, which can be sprinkled throughout a city, theme restaurants like Planet Hollywood are so big and expensive that they are a one-to-a-big-city proposition—a fact mentioned in Planet Hollywood disclosure statements. But the good cities were already tapped out.

So faced with declining same-store sales, glutted markets, an expensive business model, and new restaurants that burned the bottom line, what did Barish and Earl decide to do?

What else? They decided to take Planet Hollywood public. Hire securities brokerage Bear Stearns & Co. to sell the chain to the public, and get your pre-IPO investors squared away.

IN THE PRE-INTERNET DAYS OF 1996, the Planet Hollywood IPO was considered hot stuff. With the long-established Bear Stearns & Co. as the lead underwriter, Planet Hollywood generated big buzz with its glitzy connections and promise of global reach.

"It will certainly be the spotlight stock for 1996," enthused David Menlow, president of the IPO Financial Network Corp. "It's going to be huge as far as investor reception." [1]

"It will go into orbit," echoed then analyst Linda Killian of Renaissance Capital Corp. "It's the name that will carry it." [2]

Perhaps more tellingly than he realized, Manish Shah, the editor and publisher of the newsletter *IPO Maven,* added, "Planet Hollywood is going to be an extremely successful offering because a lot of retail investors will be interested." [3]

In a curious sort of symbiosis, Greg Novello, a portfolio manager for the Smith Barney Special Equities Fund—Smith Barney being one of the co-underwriters of the Planet Hollywood IPO—told *The New York Times* a few weeks before the offering that he planned to add the stock to his portfolio. "Obviously, it's going to be a deal that gets a lot of press attention and publicity," he explained. The "buzz," he added, was bound to make the issue a winner. [4]

It must be nice for underwriting brokerages when they can get semi-captive money managers to tout their upcoming IPOs and then buy the stock. Now, that's buzz millennial-style on Wall Street. It's hard to tell who was craftier at PR on Planet Hollywood: chairman Barish and his Tinseltown troops, or Planet Hollywood's underwriters, led by Bear Stearns.

The Planet Hollywood IPO prospectus oozed confidence about conquering such sexy cities as Tel Aviv, Boston, Tokyo, Bangkok, Seattle, San Antonio, Sydney, Taipei, Singapore, Shanghai, Berlin, Amsterdam, and Oberhausen, Germany, in the future—a nice, snazzy jet-set angle. In addition, Planet Hollywood executives spoke of launching yet another "eater-tainment" chain, the sports-oriented Official All-Star Cafe, which would garnish its walls with jerseys and basketballs and other athletic accoutrements. Athletes, not actors, would be the celeb hosts and investors. They also talked about basing a chain on Marvel comic books, to be called Marvel Mania.

By the time Planet Hollywood went public on April 22, 1996, the market had reached a boiling point, fired by smart public relations, friendly quotes from fund managers (many of whom worked for the underwriters), and a terrific road show conducted by Bear Stearns. (Michael Tarnopol, senior managing director and chairman of Bear Stearns's investment banking division, would ultimately take a Planet Hollywood board seat.)

The IPO price was first set at $15 a share. Then, just before the offering, it was nudged up to $18. But that was small potatoes. On the very first trade, Planet Hollywood stock popped and hit the gong at $31 a share. As it would turn out, that was the zenith. What sort of investor was willing to pay a 72 percent premium over the IPO price without knowing what the market's reaction to the stock would be? Bear Stearns, which handled the trade, says it doesn't know who the buyer was.

Tellingly, institutions began selling their shares almost immediately that first day and continued doing so until the close. The stock wound up finishing its initial session at $26.875—down noticeably from its high, but still a sizzling 50 percent higher than the offering price (in the pre-Internet days, considered very spicy stuff). Volume was very heavy, with 22.6 million shares changing hands that first day—at the time, a record for an IPO on the Nasdaq. It was also a sure sign the institutions were selling, since only institutions can lock up IPO stock in a hot underwriting. If the stock was trading in huge volume, by definition, the institutions were dumping.

Gauged in terms of fundamentals, Planet Hollywood shares were trading at about 140 times trailing (the previous year's) earnings and roughly 70 times estimated earnings for 1996. That translated to a market capitalization of $2.9 billion, or a staggering $100 million or so for each of the thirty Planet Hollywood restaurants then in business. It had cost Planet Hollywood an average of $7.3 million to build and open each of its outlets, considered record-breaking sums at the time. In the initial public offering materials, Bear Stearns had posited to the investing world that each Planet Hollywood was worth $66 million, or ten times what it cost to build. Now, at the close of the first day of trading for the new shares, Wall Street said each one was worth $100 million.

That was certainly sweet desserts for the Hollywood stars who had acquired pre-IPO stock. Their cumulative equity stake in Planet Hollywood became worth $537 million—a confection to tickle the blabbermeisters on the talk-show circuit for several moons.

The IPO was also rewarding to Planet Hollywood's early institutional backers, for it allowed many of them to get out of the company at a substantial gain. Of the $197 million that the IPO brought in, $66 million went to pay off a note held by a director of the company, while another $60 million went to pay off senior debt held by institutions. Additionally, institutional holders of pre-IPO Planet Hollywood stock such as Lincoln National Life Insurance, First Britannia Mezzanine Capital NV, Planetco Ventures Ltd., and Electra Investment Trust PLC sold their private shares into the IPO, reaping enormous profits as they bailed.

Many institutional investors, who locked up the stock at the $18 IPO price, were out of the stock in the time it takes to boil an egg. A spokesman for Boston-based Numeric Investors conceded to reporters his firm had sold its block of Planet Hollywood shares so quickly it was "almost a flip."

THE SEC MANDATES A "QUIET PERIOD" for twenty-five days before and after an IPO. During this time, public statements by company officials or underwriter employees—including analysts—that could be interpreted as hyping a stock are prohibited. So, under rule of law, analysts were kept quiet. But once the timer hit twenty-five days, the analysts leapt onto center stage with trumpets blaring.

On May 14, 1996, four brokerages—all of which had managed or were lead syndicators in the Planet Hollywood IPO—issued "buy," "outperform," or "attractive" ratings on the stock. It was the analysts' equivalent of the big-band sound. Smith Barney (now Salomon Smith Barney), Montgomery Securities (now merged into Banc of America Securities), Schroder Wertheim & Co., and, of course, lead underwriter Bear Stearns & Co. fell all over each other singing the praises of glamorous Planet Hollywood stock and its in-the-know CEO, Robert Earl.

First to lift his flute and begin piping was Joseph T. Buckley, Bear Stearns's top research analyst for restaurants. His panegyric for the company was subtitled in part, "Planet Hollywood: A High-Volume Growth Machine."[5] At the time Buckley issued his nineteen-page report, Planet Hollywood was trading at $26 a share. That's 51 percent higher than its IPO price—the $18 initial public offering price that was ostensibly the "fair" one for shareholders and management, as deduced by investment bankers and accountants.

Nonetheless, Buckley rated the stock "attractive" (the equivalent of a "buy" recommendation). He touted Planet Hollywood's ability to market not just food but merchandise, the sales of which Buckley predicted would reach fully half of total revenues "within the next few years." No other restaurant chain had ever sold so much in apparel and knick-knacks, but Buckley predicted it anyway.

Although Buckley acknowledged that the theme-restaurant business as a whole was fading as fast as yesterday's hits, in his score Planet Hollywood would crescendo and drown out the trend. "Planet Hollywood will show greater staying power than most newer entrants," he wrote. "Its themes have broad, universal appeal. Movies and sports are a firmly established part of American pop culture, and their popularity shows no signs of fading. Also, since star power is a big part of Planet Hollywood and All-Star's attraction, we think celebrity ownership in the company will help ensure the longevity of Planet Hollywood's brand-name success...."

Among the reasons Buckley cited to justify plunking down $26 or more for a share of Planet Hollywood were more than a few chimeras. "[Planet Hollywood] is also working on a Chefs of the World theme restaurant, which could ultimately serve as a springboard for other business ventures (e.g., a tie-in television show or gourmet cookware product line)," he noted. "In the future, we expect management to start a licensing business as a cost-effective way to create additional high-return revenue streams. We think these licensing efforts offer solid growth potential, as they require little capital and help to reinforce brand identity."

This was a parroting of Earl's ill-defined vision of a populace buying many, many different kinds of Planet Hollywood branded products, as consumers came to identify with a restaurant-chain-inspired lifestyle. Just why consumers would buy Planet Hollywood cooking tongs or expensive leather jackets instead of ones bearing a recognized culinary or apparel label was never explained.

But Buckley knew there was trouble in paradise. On page seven of his report, he noted that same-store sales "were down 4.6 percent in the first quarter of 1996." One would expect an astute analyst to regard declining same-store sales as a sign that maybe it was time to push back from the table and consider what was being served. Indeed, a flinty analyst might have written something like, "These shares are already up 50 percent from the price at which we underwrote them just a few weeks back, with no real change in the fundamentals. Now same-store sales are coming in very soft; in fact, they are down. Maybe it's time to wait and see on Planet Hollywood."

But not Buckley. Instead, he attributed the weakening sales to "bad weather." How bad weather could affect a chain operating in thirty different cities on several continents he did not say. (In fact, the "bad weather" excuse originated with Planet Hollywood management, which maintained that unusual meteorological conditions were hurting business in enough locations to harm the whole.)

Buckley apparently consulted a very long-range crystal ball when peering into Planet Hollywood's future. Despite the fact that the chain had constructed only one All-Star Cafe—which Buckley called crucial to its growth plans—he went on to predict that Planet Hollywood earnings would be up by 83 percent in 1996, followed by a 57 percent jump in 1997, after which they would settle down to 30 to 35 percent annual growth into the distant horizon.

In essence, Buckley's report amounted to hardly more than a saccharin-laced, fast-food version of the IPO prospectus Planet Hollywood and Bear Stearns underwriters had filed with the SEC. (Managements of publicly held companies cannot indulge in such starry-eyed projections, under civil law and SEC guidelines. It is a curious feature of extant SEC law that analysts, now so closely aligned with their investment banking departments, are still cloaked in protective regulations—a safe harbor granted in the days when analysts were separated from corporate finance by a Chinese wall.)

Buckley's report evinced no digging behind the numbers, no observations suggesting that management was too optimistic about this or that trend or event, no sign of any firsthand research. If Buckley actually went and ate at any Planet Hollywood restaurants and paid for it with his own money, he did not say so.

Conspicuously absent from Buckley's report was any recognition of the fact that Planet Hollywood restaurants, with their large staffs, relentless public relations, expensive furnishings, and busy Tinseltown wall decor, cost considerably more to operate than similar-sized competing restaurants. This too was revealed in the prospectus. Nor did Buckley mention that some large pre-IPO investors had exited Planet Hollywood in the IPO, or that most of the money raised in the IPO had gone to repay debts. And Buckley didn't mention that heavy first-day trading in Planet Hollywood stock meant that many institutions had already exited the stock.

In a curious way, however, Buckley's report did underline the fragile nature of Planet Hollywood from the investor's viewpoint. Deep in his report, Buckley almost nonchalantly stated that the earnings projections he made for Planet Hollywood assumed a successful and profitable launch of the All-Star Cafe chain. (Oh, is that all?) In other words, the primary driver of earnings growth would be not the Planet Hollywood restaurants—Buckley conceded that—but an almost completely untested commercial concept.

Buckley was hardly alone in his ringing praise of his brokerage's newest client. Analyst John J. Rohs, then of comanaging firm

Schroder Wertheim & Co., also initiated coverage with a positive recommendation (in his case, an "outperform" rating), citing the same
roll call of supposed virtues trundled out by Buckley. Rohs even
seemed to borrow Buckley's crystal ball, predicting long-term annual
earnings growth of 35 percent for the restaurant chain. Where this
magic figure came from remains a mystery. It was as if Buckley and
Rohs had looked each other in the eyes and then lifted their flutes
skyward in frenzied unison.

Struggling heroically to find some way to justify Planet Hollywood's enormous price/earning ratio—it was trading at 60 times estimated annual earnings when he issued his ten-page report on May 22,
1996—Rohs likened the fledgling, struggling restaurant chain to such
retailing titans as Home Depot, PetsMart, and Bed, Bath and Beyond. But these so-called category killers, the most dominant brand
names in American retailing at the time, were then trading at an average of 46 times earnings—very hefty indeed, but even they couldn't
match Planet Hollywood's awesome multiples.[6]

Like Buckley, Rohs did acknowledge that Planet Hollywood was
actually posting falling sales in restaurants open more than eighteen
months. But also like Buckley, he attributed the decline to "bad
weather."

As investors were about to discover, there soon would be rainy days
and nights all over the world, all the time, for Planet Hollywood.


WHAT WAS IT ABOUT PLANET HOLLYWOOD that made the analysts blow
their fifes so furiously? For some, it may have been their brokerages'
investment banking relationships with the newly public company.
Others whose firms lacked such obvious ties may have been angling
for future banking business, or were helping their large institutional
trading clients exit the stock, or even may simply have been a bit
starstruck.

Certainly, CEO Earl made deft use of his expanding stable of stars,
trotting them out not only to wow the press at restaurant openings
but also to woo analysts at financial briefings. One such gathering
took place on a hot June day in 1996 in Las Vegas, where no less a

megastar than Arnold Schwarzenegger appeared before a group of industry analysts to extol the virtues of restaurants decorated with movie bric-a-brac. Evidently the analysts were impressed with what they saw, and shortly thereafter, Salomon Bros., PaineWebber, and Cowen & Co. all initiated coverage of Planet Hollywood with "buy" signals.

But there was more to the analysts' interest than Arnold's manly charms. The fact was, there was much to be gained by currying favor with Planet Hollywood management. Were Planet Hollywood to expand, it would probably need to arrange new financing—meaning there would be more stock to be issued, more bonds to be sold, and perhaps even some lucrative mergers-and-acquisitions work. And if the chain foundered, there would be the opportunity to earn fees for work-outs or bond offerings.

Over the months that followed the IPO, Earl and the analysts—perhaps sensing they may have waded in a bit too deep, given the frothy multiples—began to reposition Planet Hollywood. No longer was it just a restaurant chain. Now it was a builder of a hot brand that would click with consumers for years to come. Suddenly, there was talk of a Planet Hollywood lifestyle. Of course, that would take time to build.

In this new spin, the future tense was always emphasized, along with the fact that merchandise sales made up roughly 40 percent of the chain's total revenues. "We see ourselves as building a trademark," Earl said, describing plans to sell T-shirts, ice cream, board games, and perfume. Others speculated about co-branded Visa bankcards and a *Planet Hollywood Squares* television game show.[7]

Although it was obvious that more Planet Hollywoods weren't the solution—the most-lucrative cities had already been blessed, and the business model didn't work in the vast majority of locations—the chain kept building, zombielike in its dedication to blueprints drawn in headier days. By October 1996, the chain had forty-five restaurants up and running. While the new money holes were being built—and Morris the Cat's food bowl acquired for the Chicago location—Planet Hollywood officials skittered across the business landscape in search of more-profitable ventures. The stock got a short-term boost when

Planet Hollywood announced (with suitable fanfare) plans to build a 3,200-room hotel and casino on a thirty-four-acre site adjoining ITT's Desert Inn casino on the Las Vegas Strip and a smaller, 1,000-room gambling resort on the boardwalk in Atlantic City. ITT would be the business buddy in these ventures. "It's more than food and drink," Earl said. "It's about making our trademark famous."[8]

It wasn't hard to see why there was so little talk by management about Planet Hollywood's core business—selling food in restaurants, remember? In a nutshell, the basic business was rancid. While revenues in the second quarter of 1996 were up—rising to $85.4 million from $65.8 million a year earlier—earnings had plummeted, falling to $721,000 from $9.2 million. To be fair, Planet Hollywood's second-quarter results did include an unintelligible one-time charge of $10 million. Skeptics regarded this as mere financial fancy dancing, but even if the charge were accepted at face value, the best one could say was that earnings were flat, and declining as a fraction of revenues. More restaurants didn't mean more profit. (One corporate insider claimed that "the numbers were managed" in Planet Hollywood's first few quarters, to try to keep up appearances. In this regard, the insider claimed that expenses were postponed and revenues forwarded into the first few quarters. This, of course, allowed major institutional buyers of IPO stock a chance to exit their positions.)[9]

Even more significant—and, sadly, far less noticed by most investors—same-store sales kept on sinking. Also shrinking was the percentage of total revenues generated by merchandise sales.

One would think these figures suggesting decline—disclosed in the company's SEC-required 10Q report just a few months after the IPO—should have raised some questions by analysts, such as "Why are restaurant sales declining?" Or, "I thought merchandise sales would make Planet Hollywood different from other chains. Why are they dropping?" But one would be wrong to think those questions would be asked, at least by analysts working for the underwriters. They more or less ignored the numbers, assenting to management's view that Planet Hollywood openings were so spectacular that some decline had to be expected in the first year, although it would someday level off. "Buy" signals were left on by Buckley and Rohs.

Analysts seemed mesmerized by Earl's talk of opening "hundreds" of "Cool Planet" ice cream parlors and "Sound Republic" live music venues, and they relayed Earl's pitches to investors. In December 1996, Earl told *Fortune* magazine he believed the company could sustain earnings growth of 40 percent per year. Although this was higher even than the 35 percent annual earnings growth the most enthusiastic analysts were predicting, no one on the Street blinked an eye.

For shareholders, there was a problem with grand plans and grandiose predictions: none of the plans jelled, while the basic business was spoiling fast.

With money disappearing down the Planet Hollywood sinkhole, there was no money to launch casino hotels, no Official All-Star Cafe chain to spin off, no diners based on Marvel comic books. There was no line of PH cutlery or cooking utensils, or "Chefs of the World" restaurants. There were no Planet Hollywood movie complexes, no Cool Planet shops selling Planet Hollywood–brand ice cream. There was nary a peep from the Sound Republic idea, which at one point was blueprinted to have 100 locations. There was no board game, no *Planet Hollywood Squares* TV show. Big investor buddies, such as ITT Corp., seemed always to get cold feet about joint ventures with Planet Hollywood. No Planet Hollywood casinos were built.

But what was hurting investors the most was that Planet Hollywood restaurant sales stunk. After an initial visit, customers stayed away in droves. Same-store sales fell by 11 percent in 1997, followed by another 18 percent nosedive in 1998. Merchandise sales shriveled, falling to just one-fifth of total revenues in 1998, as customers snubbed the $400 PH leather jackets.

By late 1998, one analyst, it should be acknowledged, had had enough. Too late to help most investors, SG Cowen's Paul Marsh threw down his pom-poms in October 1998. In a stinging report, he called Planet Hollywood the "anti-brand," noting: "This is a story of bad food. And the stars never come out after grand opening." Maybe they didn't want to be mistaken for part of the decor. In any event, Marsh added that his earlier "buy" recommendation on Planet Hollywood had been his "career" worst call.[10]

After 1998, the bottom just plain fell out. In the first quarter of

1999, the company reported a stunning 22 percent drop in same-store sales from the lousy year-earlier quarter. By then, the typical Planet Hollywood restaurant (if it was still open) attracted about 60 percent of the patrons it had served in 1995. By this time, Planet Hollywood had built eighty-seven restaurants, a truly bewildering endeavor, given that the recipe had proven unprofitable almost everywhere except huge tourist towns. Planet Hollywoods showed up in places like Gurnee Mills, Illinois, and the Mall of America, near Minneapolis.

Investors would need strong stomachs to digest their next serving: finishing up 1998, Planet Hollywood reported a net loss of nearly $238 million on revenues of $387 million in March 1999.

For ordinary investors who bought stock after the IPO, Planet Hollywood was an unmitigated disaster. Virtually the only profit takers were the private, preoffering investors who sold into the IPO and the institutions that were able to buy stock at the IPO price and then liquidate their positions in the first-day run-up. From then on, the stock sank in unusually consistent fashion for three straight years, with only a murmur of resistance here and there, usually following some talk about new casinos.

On January 22, 1999, with the stock trading at $3 a share, Bear Stearns's Buckley finally tucked away his flute, slunk off the stage, and downgraded Planet Hollywood from a "buy" to a "neutral." Even that call was wrong, for the stock sank to less than $1 shortly thereafter. Anyway, would you be neutral on the stock of a company arguably headed for bankruptcy? In the real world, that's called a "sell." In any event, the chain later in 1999 declared Chapter 11 and went belly-up. At last glimpse, creditors were fighting over the carcass.

## PLAYBOY, BABY

The "pump-and-dump"—the hyping of a stock by brokerages and institutional investors, so that retail customers will buy it, letting insiders and big traders get out—is not limited only to initial public offerings. Sometimes out-of-favor stocks are dragged back into the limelight—usually following propitious news, such as oil stocks after a spurt in oil prices—and flogged. Analysts will tip their largest clients of an impending report, the funds will start buying—giving a self-fulfilling prophecy to the analysts' projection that a stock is about to go up—and then the analysts will begin to play to the media, hyping the stock in question. After a nice run, the big boys head for the exits.

The business of hyping an existing stock reaches its fullest expression in the case of secondary offerings (also called follow-on offerings), which is a public issue of stock in a company that is already traded on the Nasdaq or NYSE. A prime example of the "secondary shuffle" was the May 1999 offering of 2.875 million shares in Playboy Enterprises Inc., the Chicago-based soft-core sin-and-skin empire.

*Playboy* magazine, as most middle-aged (and older) American men know better than they are wont to admit, was hot stuff back in the 1950s and early 1960s. Founder, publisher, and editor Hugh Hefner broke barriers that today seem puritanical, and he did it in a way then seen as suave.

But by the 1970s, *Playboy* was waning in circulation. The company slogged through the 1980s. In 1988 father Hef passed the leadership reins over not to new blood but to his daughter, Christie, bred of a Playboy bunny. Profits did nothing under Christie, Wall Street was unimpressed, and the stock traded flat as a board in the 1990s, never straying too far from $10 a share. Why would shareholders endure such mediocrity, not for years but decades? As we shall explore more closely later, the senior Hefner had the majority of company voting stock in bondage such that minority shareholders could do nothing but watch.

In any event, after nearly a generation of obscurity on the Big Board, suddenly Playboy Enterprises stock began to show some interesting curves—upward for a change, in late 1998 and early 1999. Why? Brokerages Credit Suisse First Boston and ING Barings Furman Selz LLC began pushing the stock before their May 11 underwriting of 2.875 million shares for the rabbit. Hef needed some money and had decided to cut a fraction of his hoard loose. Just a fraction, not a controlling stake.

Through the first four months of 1999, minus any positives in the fundamentals, Playboy stock rose. There was (curiously) a persistent rumor that when Hef—at 73, proudly popping Viagra and nearly quadruple the age of some of his "friends"—dies and his estate sells his block of stock, a real management change would take place.

The Playboy secondary offering went off with a bang, at a thumping $30 a share on May 11, about triple where the stock had been a year earlier and way higher than it had ever been before. Credit Suisse First Boston wasn't shy about taking credit for the stock spike. Before the secondary offering, CSFB troops toured the country, extolling the virtues of Playboy to institutional investors and high-end stockbrokers. "The combination of [our] twelve-day road show to sixteen cities and the public float of 2.875 million shares has sparked new interest in the Playboy story," wrote CSFB analyst Steven Barlow on May 24, 1999, as he put a "strong buy" rating on Playboy stock, then at nearly $31 a share. The title of his forty-four-page ode to the land of the well-endowed was "Playboy—Leveraging the Only Global Multimedia Men's Brand Name to Accelerate Cash Flow and Asset Value."[11]

At co-underwriter and brokerage ING Barings, analyst Stewart Halpern hopped into the love session with his fifteen-page report featuring a "strong buy" recommendation. Halpern called Playboy in his May 12, 1999, report "An ideal 21st Century Entertainment Content Investment Opportunity" and a "rare, near-pure play on the global growth of digital entertainment."[12]

What the Credit Suisse and ING Barings road-show warriors told institutional clients and brokerage stockbrokers at the sixteen dog-and-pony shows was that the underwriters were high on the stock, and that their analysts liked the stock, too—in other words, after this underwriting, we are going to flog the stock, and our network of stockbrokers will tell their retail clients to buy the stock, too. That's called "institutional sponsorship" in Wall Streetese.

Institutions bought some Playboy stock even before the secondary underwriting, including, among others, Fidelity Research & Management, Alliance Capital Management, and Wanger Asset Management, according to filings with the SEC. Fidelity was particularly aggressive, with a 12.97 percent stake in Playboy. The institutions also bought into the secondary offering, and sold heavily in the next few days. Trading volume in Playboy stock after the secondary offering was at all-time records—almost a sure sign the institutions were moving out a lot of their Playboy inventory. No analyst mentioned that.

BUT LIKE SO MANY STOCKS UNDERWRITTEN in 1999, it was hard to like Playboy on the fundamentals—in fact, the selling of Playboy stock seems positively sinful if one takes a look at the underlying numbers.

Playboy's revenues had been lackluster for years, and profit soft to nonexistent. In 1998, the company reported modest net income of $4.3 million on revenues of $317.7 million, a profit level all the more lamentable when compared to the $13 million the company earned on sales of $363 million—in 1980! That's eighteen years of sickly sideways drift while the Hefner family controlled the voting stock and ran the business.

At the May 1999 secondary offering price of $30 a share, Playboy was selling at about 100 times estimated 1999 earnings of 31¢ a share (an earnings estimate made by friendly analysts, no less). That's 100 times earnings for a company whose dated main product—soft-core photos of nude women—was being replicated by untold thousands of Web sites, in historically unmatched profundity, and in video stores nationwide. In 1999, hard-core in America was probably easier to find than the carefully edited soft-core offered by *Playboy* and a few other purveyors of "clean smut." It was also 100 times earnings for a company that made less money in 1999 than in 1980. One has to give credit to Credit Suisse First Boston and ING Barings for robust sales work, if nothing else.

But at the time of the secondary offering, was there an upside explosion in Playboy earnings pending? Although analysts Barlow of CSFB and Halpern of ING Barings put their best face on matters—with a lot of conditional, "if this works, then ..." in their analyses—they estimated Playboy would earn only about 38¢ a share in 2000. That meant Playboy in 2000, if its secondary price of $30 held, would be trading at 80 times earnings—still far above even the historically high S&P 500 range of about 30 times earnings in 1999. In general, in ordinary times, run-of-the-mill stocks trade between 10 and 15 times earnings. A company like Playboy, tepid on Wall Street for years, should arguably sell for less than a run-of-the-mill stock.

Still, the $30 secondary price was small compared to what was said to be awaiting under the covers: CSFB analyst Barlow put a "target price" of $50 on Playboy stock, within twelve months—meaning that Playboy would be trading at *138 times* estimated year 2000 earnings per share, if it hit Barlow's target. Remember: Playboy was not a new company, or a growth company, and in fact it had been stagnant for nearly two decades.

Even more inexplicably, Barlow and Halpern were making these moon-shot estimates while Playboy's flagship product—its magazine—was struggling financially, if not sinking. Although it had 3.15 million readers in mid-1999, *Playboy*'s cost of delivery had been soaring, due to consolidation and resultant price gouging among wholesale distributors. Paper costs were up, and ad revenues in 1999 had barely budged from 1998 or 1997—even in a good economy. The magazine, unlike other adult glossies, actually spent money on editorial product and talented photographers, which made the publication twice as expensive per page to produce as rival skin mags.

Worse for *Playboy*, the Publisher's Clearing House subscription service, the magazine's main source of new subscribers (the "You, John Doe, Have Won $10 Million!" folks), cut back its mailings in 1998 and raised prices sharply. So what would drive this lust for Playboy stock predicted by Halpern and Barlow?

Not the magazine. Barlow and Halpern conceded that, although they touted it as upholding the Playboy banner. The best that could be hoped was that *Playboy* would scale back its subscription base and raise subscription prices in sort of a rear-guard action, they said.

Instead, the analysts proffered that Playboy had a bright future in adult cable television, and—what else in the late 1990s?—on the Internet. Too, Playboy had just opened a casino on the Greek island of Rhodes (don't mention that Playboy casino in Atlantic City in the 1980s, long since defunct).

In cable-television land, Playboy TV in 1998 purchased the Spice and the Spice Hot nudie cable-TV outfits, something of an industry roll-up for adult fare for wired homes. Sensibly enough, the analysts argued that the greater distribution wouldn't increase production costs. Fatter margins should result, they opined.

What the analysts ignored is that far more "sexplicit" videos than Playboy's TV shows are available for rent or purchase all across America, often for $1 a night (there is such an outpouring of porn that some video stores give away old titles with new rentals). Also, streaming porno video is clogging up the Internet and promises to grow in the future. The underwriting analysts argued that Playboy, with its brand name associated with "nice" porn, would stand out in the crowd. Maybe so, but in 1999, the porn world was a crowded stage, and Playboy was a rather mild presence. For example, in 1998, the online porn industry was a $1 billion business, reports Mark Hardie, of Forrester Research Inc. Playboy Online revenues for the first six months of 1999 were $3.1 million, including product sales.

There are some unintentional moments of low comedy in Barlow's report as he rattles off the virtues of Playboy Online. In one lugubrious look into Playboy's cyber customers, he writes, "Playboy Cyberclub currently has 30,000 paid subscribers that pay $60 per year for access to photo archives, live chat sessions, and interactive videos." Live chat sessions? Interactive videos? Images of lonely men in Indiana winters, sitting in front of their personal computers hooked up online, come to mind. This was the stuff of a Big Board company selling for 138 times earnings?

The real story was that after nearly five years of effort in the cyber world, Playboy had only 30,000 subscribers. That figure was less than 1 percent of the number of magazines it sold most months. Playboy wasn't scoring in cyberspace, not after five years. Why would it start now? The analysts couldn't say.

In adult television, Playboy might have had a better shot. Many cable companies do not want to carry fare more raunchy than that offered by Playboy. So tame is Playboy by today's standards that the Pentagon in the late 1990s issued an edict that Playboy materials could be sold in PXes on base without violating sexual harassment laws. It's sort of government-sanctioned T&A. Indeed, in 1999, Playboy sold the Spice Hot cable show it had just bought because it was too raw—although here again, there is a little unintended humor in

Barlow's report. Playboy didn't sell Spice Hot for cash—rather, it sold it for "noncompete payments" in the future. That sounds a lot like royalties with a standoffish name, but what the heck. A publicly held company can't exactly be seen as a retailer of hard-core smut—even if that is where the porn profits are.

BUT WHAT THE ANALYSTS MOST EXPLICITLY FAILED TO MENTION was that although Playboy was Chicago-based, the real power behind the throne remains firmly ensconced in Los Angeles, in the inimitable form of Hugh Hefner, 70 percent shareholder of the company's voting stock and titular editor-in-chief of the company's signature product, *Playboy* magazine. And for shareholders in Playboy, that's the rub. Hefner doesn't seem to care much about profits. Indeed, while Playboy reported net income of $4.3 million in 1998, the empire spent an identical amount maintaining the famed Playboy Mansion, where Hefner resides with the help of a staff of seventy and a small bevy of beauties.

In short, Playboy could double its reported net income simply by selling the manse and leaving Hef to scrape by on his annual compensation of $868,916, at latest count. That would mean, all things being equal, a doubling of Playboy's stock. Minority shareholders have said as much at annual meetings.

Making matters worse for minority shareholders, The Hef in June 1999 informed *The New Yorker* magazine that the thrust behind Playboy "has little to do with money." It is a business he runs "from the heart," he said. With his daughter, Christie, 47, installed as chairwoman and chief executive—despite a cruddy record of no growth spanning more than a decade—it would appear that Hef is true not only to his principles but to his word.

But how about those persistent rumors that someday, perhaps not so far off, the senior Hefner would pass on? The story line was this: The estate would sell the controlling block of stock, and the aging Christie—what woman would want to run Playboy in her fifties, after all?—would gracefully retreat, plenty rich to enjoy life without having to look at pictures of younger, nubile maidens all day. Under aggressive new management—and perhaps relieved of the Playboy mansion—the old Playboy name would regain virility, the rumor went. A neat little rumor right before the secondary offering went pop.

*The New Yorker* floated the idea that the stock could *quadruple* under new leadership—and named Rupert Murdoch of the News Corp. as possibly the guy who could do it. But with the secondary offering completed—into which Hefner sold 2 million shares, or $60 million worth—the Hef not only announced he will leave his shares to his two sons (also born to a Playmate), aged nine and seven, but also that in perpetuity his estate will support daughter Christie as chairwoman and CEO of Playboy.

It appears Playboy, with its struggling magazine, its meager, tame presence in the cyber world, its soft-porn cable television fare—and let's not forget that casino in Greek waters—will be run by Christie and then her half-brothers for at least the next fifty years, if they so chose.

As if to underline the situation, Playboy in August 1999—mere months after the glowing buy recommendations from friendly analysts—reported a net loss of $3 million on revenues of $78.1 million, versus a net profit of $2.1 million on revenues of $77.8 million in the year-earlier period. In other words, revenues were going almost nowhere, and black had turned to red.

Not surprisingly, investors began to wonder what Wall Street had ever seen in the aging Playboy rabbit. True, the Hef had made a minor splash in media circles in early 1999, showing up at the Cannes Film Festival with four beauties in tow, getting some coverage (also causing some to wonder if the cumulative age of Hefner's quartet exceeded his). The entertainment media (even larger than the financial media), with their huge news hole to fill every day, did some stories on Hef and this or that newish Hollywood star visiting the Playboy mansion. But hype isn't profits.

By September 1999, Playboy stock had tumbled to $20. The CSFB analyst Barlow did not give up the fight, or at least the charade. He issued a report that sounded like a musician responding to a bad review: "At $20, we are pressed to find a better cable and satellite television play than Playboy," he wrote. "We believe the sell-off is unjustified, and $20 represents unbelievable value."

Barlow was right about one thing: Playboy was an unbelievable value at $20, as it turned out. But Barlow was wrong about the latitude. The stock was unbelievably high. As quarter after quarter of losses were reported, and as the Internet strategy failed to make any money, Playboy stock became increasingly flaccid, hitting $11.61 a share by early 2001. It looked to be heading back to the $10-a-share range it had inhabited for decades on Wall Street, before Credit Suisse and ING Barings decided to give it a boost.

Wall Street—even the Wall Street of the 1990s and turn of the millennium, which believed in the bull, in Internet stocks hitting the moon, in blue-chip stocks at record multiples—found Playboy a dry story. But not before the brokerages made good money on the secondary offering, and mutual funds jacked up the price of Playboy stock on the day of the offering, before exiting.

### JACK GRUBMAN

No one charms them like Jack Grubman. Among analysts and stockbrokers, Salomon Smith Barney telecom stock picker Grubman is a titan, spoken of in hushed tones. "The guy made $25 *million* in one year," says a stockbroker with Salomon. "He has made some bad picks, but evidently he is doing something very valuable for the firm, or they wouldn't pay him that way."

In 1998, the year of his stupendous salary, what did Grubman do? Was his stock picking superlative? Did he call that year's summer slump and Far East meltdown? Did he save Solly from underwriting a dog?

No. "Grubman gets the big bucks because he is among Wall Street's hottest 'superanalysts,' high-ranked analysts who also bring in lots of investment banking business," wrote *BusinessWeek*. He *brings in the business*. That's what analysts are for on Wall Street today.

Indeed, the only question is should Grubman be referred to as the highest-paid analyst or as a middling-paid investment banker. Grubman is widely credited with bringing deals to Solly, and big ones, and then helping fabricate the deals—all the while wearing an analyst hat for the investing public.

His friendship with WorldCom president and chief executive officer Bernard C. Ebbers is said to have landed Salomon Smith Barney the WorldCom-MCI merger, a $35 billion whopper, which resulted in, of course, MCI WorldCom. And Grubman was in the picture in getting advisory business on SBC Communications' $62 billion planned merger with Ameritech, and also Bell Atlantic's $53 billion deal for GTE Corp. Some say Salomon earned $200 million in fees on those deals, let alone future business or trading commissions, and Grubman figured heavily in winning the business.

Grubman doesn't just get close to Solly's investment bankers, he actually participates in the deal-making process—so much so that he earned the moniker "research-analyst-cum-investment-banker" from *The New York Times*. In May 1999, Grubman was apoplectic about a busted deal between MCI WorldCom and Nextel Communications. Grubman evidently had a part in the negotiations. Somebody leaked information, probably at Nextel, and the deal broke apart. Grubman took it personally, seemingly as an affront. "If the other side had kept their trap shut, this would have been a normal process," Grubman complained to a reporter.[13] Grubman thought a deal could have been done.

When another analyst deigned to have an opinion on the merger, Grubman went on the warpath. The offender? Walter Piecyk, a former Nextel employee and analyst at PaineWebber, mused publicly that the busted deal might be glued back together. "It is dead," Grubman told the *Times*, before insulting Piecyk's intelligence and dismissing his comments. Grubman bluntly told the *Times* that he, Grubman, had been in the talks, and not Piecyk.

So much had Wall Street changed in the 1990s that even money managers no longer batted an eye at Grubman's dual investment banker/analyst status. "He's accessible, knowledgeable, and I don't think he is unduly influenced by investment banking," Brian Hayward, manager of the Invesco Funds Group, told *BusinessWeek*. "All the big-name analysts have investment banking ties, and those of us on the other side have to keep that in the back of our minds."[14] Other money managers were equally blasé. Grubman is very "bank-oriented," Eric Efron, portfolio manager at USAA Aggressive Growth Fund, told *The Wall Street Journal*. "Whenever he picks up a company [covers it], I think the presumption is that there is a banking deal in the works." But what's the big deal? Many analysts do it, said Efron.

But not only is Grubman good at getting deals, he is great at media relations—probably worth $25 million a year just in advertising to Salomon Smith Barney. How do you put a price tag on Grubman being the featured guest on the popular Louis Rukeyser's *Wall Street Week* television show? Grubman was the star analyst in June 1998 and told Rukeyser that he was a bit soft, in general, on telecom stocks— so much fresh competition, you know. Stocks he liked?

"I would buy WorldCom all day long," Grubman told Rukeyser. His pal's company, and a Solly client. Ordinary investors at home might be forgiven for assuming that the immensely charismatic Rukeyser had a reason for putting Grubman on the air. And probably that reason was that Grubman was very good—why bother putting somebody on the air who wasn't good?

But is Grubman really such a good analyst?

Later, on the same show, Grubman told Rukeyser and millions of viewers that the burgeoning world market for wireless phones would be immense, so a company named Iridium LLC "will be the way." Those were his only two recommendations on the show. Rukeyser did not point out that both companies recommended were Salomon clients.

Iridium was a company, at the time, in the middle of an ambitious program to launch sixty-six satellites to provide cell-phone service around the globe, particularly in underserviced remote regions. Like most start-up telecom ventures, Iridium ate money. Laying down cable, launching satellites, hiring squadrons of engineers to design and build, hiring teams of lawyers to protect turf and negotiate rights with private property owners and with governments—the telecom business needs a lot of financing. That means bond underwritings and stock offerings. Wall Street is alert to that. Of course, Salomon had taken Iridium public, in 1997.

But Grubman's TV tout on Iridium, made when the company was trading at $60 a share, turned out to be bad advice; about a year later, the satellite launching enterprise had declared bankruptcy. It turned out—which many people in the industry knew—that customers didn't like the bulky Iridium telephones, which didn't work well indoors, or the large and complicated bills. Instead of signing up 50,000 customers a month, Iridium signed up fewer than 10,000.

After declaring Chapter 11 in mid-August 1999, Iridium stock fell to $3 a share, presumably because investors didn't understand that in most bankruptcy settlements, shareholders get zero. Grubman had kept the "buy" signal on for Iridium almost until the bitter end. In April 1999, well after problems emerged and the stock had sunk to a sliver of $60, Grubman put a "neutral" on the stock. Not a "sell."

Other questions have been raised about the timing and purpose of Grubman's buy recommendations. On February 18, 1999, Grubman put out a buy recommendation on a publicly held fiber-optic cable company named Level 3 Communications Inc. and raised his target price to $70 from $54. The *same day,* the company announced a secondary stock offering of 20 million shares (about $1 billion at then-current market prices). It was also announced that Salomon Smith Barney, Grubman's employer, would be the lead underwriter.

Four days later, Grubman issued a forty-page report on Level 3, describing the company as perfectly placed for the brave new world of international Internet transmissions and possessed of a low-cost way to transmit data. Whether due to Grubman's flute work or not, ensuing demand was robust, and the secondary offering was jacked up 25 million shares and went out the door on March 4 at $54 each. Just like that, $1.35 billion was raised. Grubman deserved his share of credit. At first, Grubman's music was enchantingly accurate—indeed Grubman if anything could have used a little more forte on his notes. Level 3 skyrocketed after the secondary offering, smashing through Grubman's $70-a-share target price and racing all the way to $100 a share—a $36 billion market cap for a company that hardly existed in 1998!

What Grubman, and investors, seemed to forget is that Level 3 Communications not only loses money by the bushel, it also needs to raise gobs of lucre to finance an ambitious effort to lay down 24,000 miles of fiber-optic cable worldwide, to carry voice, data, and yes, Internet transmissions. By mid-1999—when Grubman was telling clients to buy—it had laid 1,400 miles of cable. That's less than 6 percent of the projected total. Purportedly, Level 3's cable system is cheaper but carries more traffic than rival outfits. By the company's own projections, it will consume $8 billion to $10 billion—read, absorb $8 billion to $10 billion in losses—building the network. A lot of junk bonds and stock was, and will be, sold to pay for that. Salomon Smith Barney can expect its share of underwriting income.

The build-out must be financed through at least 2003, and no profit is on the horizon until 2005 or later—a longer wait for profits than even Amazon.com shareholders are told they must endure. In any event, Level 3 wasn't worried. In 1999 it was building a $70 million corporate campus near Denver. But some argued there is a lot to worry about—with telecom corporate pockets bulging with money, fiber-optic or other networks are sprouting up all over the world. The companies Qwest, IXC, Frontier Communications, GTE, and Williams are all building and nearing completion of fiber-optic networks. The oligarchs, AT&T and MCI WorldCom, also have networks, though older, which they are upgrading.

*Barron's* reported in June 1999, "Much of this fiber lies 'unlit' [unused] in conduits, stockpiled for future demand." Oh, really.

The sobering reality of Level 3's speculative business perhaps began to hit home in the second half of 1999. The company, despite unrelated profitable operations in mining and investing, lost $183 million on $106 million in revenues in the second quarter, ended June 30.

A consensus of analyst projections was that the company would lose $1.87 a share in 1998, followed by another loss of $2.82 a share in 1999. By summer, the stock had slid all the way back to less than $45 a share and was still falling. The same institutions and mutual funds that had bought into the secondary offering and watched as Grubman's projections and the buzz had run the stock up largely flipped out of the stock when it threatened to breach $100. Probably about when retail buyers began to believe the run-up was real and had legs.

Of course, the jury is still out on Level 3. The stock was trading around $60 a share in summer 2000; it had dropped to around $50 in early 2001. It may emerge as a profitable cable company midway through this decade. If all goes well, it will be better than most rivals in carrying Internet transmissions, and even voice over the Internet. Moreover, recent history seems to suggest that estimates about telecommunications traffic are usually conservative—greater capacity usually begets greater traffic, such as cable-hogging graphics. People may "rent" videos over the Internet, or talk to each other through 3-D graphics interfaces. Or, of course, another company could buy Level 3 out, a likely scenario if it can't honor debt payments—and a situation rife with investment banking opportunities.

But one must wonder about Grubman, who estimated Level 3 to be worth $25 billion, even though it wouldn't see black ink for six years, in a highly competitive field.

As questionable as his performance on Level 3 has been, Grubman did even worse on a Los Angeles–based telephone calling card company named SmarTalk Teleservices Inc., which Salomon took public in August 1996. Again, the advantages for corporate finance were abundantly clear for SmarTalk—it planned to, and did, go on a nationwide buying spree, acquiring all manner of calling card companies, running up fees galore for investment bankers who proffered M&A services. A Solly-led $150 million convertible bond offering was sold in 1997. The company had numerous contracts with retailers and hotel chains to sell its cards.

Grubman liked the stock and recommended it. But something was funny about SmarTalk, chiefly that it never made money, even as it rampaged across the country, buying left and right. Perhaps not surprisingly—rapid-fire roll-ups very often buy doggy companies—much of what it bought wasn't worth it. By April 1998, things began to smell funny at SmarTalk. The company announced that first quarter earnings were in red ink, due to "higher costs" and "delay of new product." The stock fell $8.69 to close at $22.44 a share. Grubman lowered his earnings estimates but kept his "buy" signal on. Problems mounted for SmarTalk, and in October 1998, it put out a release to the effect it would be re-stating earnings. Finally, SmarTalk declared Chapter 11 bankruptcy in January 1999.

Despite his penchant for backing corporate finance clients of Salomon Smith Barney's, even ones headed for oblivion, Grubman is consistently ranked high by *Institutional Investor* magazine—although it is interesting to examine why. The *Institutional Investor* survey annually asks big money managers which analysts they like the most, based not just on stock-picking ability but also on industry knowledge, accessibility, and other criteria. Grubman's industry knowledge is legendary—not only a star analyst since 1987, he worked in the industry before that. He has friends in high places and personally sits in on the deal-making process. You can't get much more knowledgeable than that. And for that, he is on *Institutional Investor*'s first team, year after year.

But a careful reading of the magazine's 1998 list reveals that Grubman's name is absent from the lists of best stock pickers, best at earnings estimates, and best useful or timely calls. So why is Grubman ranked so highly? Sure, one might say, analysts may not care that much about retail clients anymore. But surely they don't want to blithely issue "buy" recommendations when institutional clients are putting down millions on the advice. After all, don't institutional clients want good advice? Aren't they big clients, who generate trading commissions, who buy those initial public offerings that make so much money?

The answer: It's not about accuracy. It's about customer service. More and more, the pressure from institutional clients is to maintain the "buy" recommendations—or at least keep any "sell" signals private, before a public downgrade is issued, if there has to be a downgrade.

"When one young telecom analyst at a top-tier firm downgraded a popular company, a fund manager with a huge position in the stock gave this message to an institutional salesman: 'Tell your analyst he's an idiot,'" reported *Institutional Investor* in its 1998 annual survey story. The gist of the article was that only "young" analysts put out sell recommendations, because older ones know better. "Even in a relatively healthy stock market, inexperienced analysts are at a distinct disadvantage. They may not realize, for example, that it can be career suicide to pronounce doom and gloom for a popular stock," reported *Institutional Investor*.

Because the institutions have taken such large stakes in the

*Fortune* 1000 companies today, they find themselves more and more vulnerable to public sell recommendations. It is hard to unwind large positions, and if one tries to in the wake of a sell recommendation, it is harder yet to accomplish without taking a haircut. Yet such stocks, on average, walk on stilts at 30 times earnings, ready for toppling by bad news of any sort or analyst sell signals. A sell signal from a brokerage analyst only depresses the value of a holding of many large institutional traders. The best analysts, brokerages and mutual funds agree, are those who keep the buy signals on. At least until large clients have exited the stock.

## PANCAKE MAKEUP

Within the industry, it is called "flipping," or "the flip." The flip is when the large institutional buyers, who lock up all or most of an initial public offering, then "flip out" of the stock, sometimes within hours of the stock's going public—à la Planet Hollywood. Flipping became a prevalent, perhaps even a dominant feature of IPOs in the 1990s, certainly of the red-hot Internet IPOs, or even popular secondary offerings. Too, flipping occurs when a buzz develops about a stock or a sector. Oftentimes the institutions have moved into stocks ahead of brokerage analysts' buy recommendations, or at least by the time when the recommendations are made public.

Importantly, the practice of flipping answers a basic question about brokerage analysts and brokerages: If brokerage analysis is so self-serving, then why do institutions, empowered with their own analysts and resources, buy the IPOs?

Answer: The big institutions intend to flip out of the IPOs and sell the new issues either to lesser institutions who think there is some run in the stock or to individuals, who—entranced by analyst touts, sensational media coverage, and a dazzling run-up in IPO price—don't ever seem to catch on that they are getting a pig in a poke.

The difference in returns between institutions and individual investors, who have to wait until the big boys push away from the table—indeed, have to buy what the big boys are willing to sell—is disheartening, if you don't happen to be running a big money fund. According to a study conducted by the Web site Worldfinancenet

.com and cited on the Red Herring Web site page in July 1999, "As
the first half of 1999 came to a close, a record-setting ninety-nine
Internet ventures had gone public, and the few lucky investors who
got in at the offering price made a killing. But everybody else was left
with high-priced shares that tanked."

The institutional investors, with their financial muscle—brokerages don't dare anger a Fidelity, Magellan, or Vanguard—made an
average of 86 percent returns on investments in Internet-related initial public offerings in the first half of 1999, according to Irv DeGraw,
research director for Worldfinancenet.com. Obviously, such institutions are happy to keep buying what brokerages are offering.

But individuals? Those who had to buy once trading had commenced on an IPO? They *lost an average of 9 percent on their IPO
Internet stock purchases,* since they could not buy at the offering
price but had to pay subsequent trading prices. The study is based on
all Internet stocks that went public in the first six months of 1999 and
their closing prices on June 30 of that year.

Nor did individual investors who shied away from Internet IPOs do
much better. IPOs as a whole are bad investments. In the first half of
1999, "Despite all the media hype, only 4.5 percent of [all IPO] offerings were big hits [i.e., had aftermarket returns of more than 60 per-
cent] for ordinary investors. So only 9 of the 201 offerings were big
hits. That's about average for the IPO market. But investment disas-
ters were far more common, despite the reassuring words of analysts
who try to buttress every offering." On the other hand, 70 percent [of
IPO offerings] had returns of breakeven or less.... More than 22 percent of the IPOs lost more than 30 percent, and several lost more
than 70 percent," according to DeGraw.

By the way, even if ordinary investors can buy into an IPO, they are
usually constrained from flipping out—a typical practice in second-
tier regional brokerage firms that are taking a company public without the sponsorship of large institutions, such as mutual funds or bank
trust departments. Stockbrokers typically lose their commissions if an
individual client flips out of an IPO, and the client can be—in fact,
usually is—barred from shares in upcoming IPOs. In short, retail
clients are there to provide stability to IPO offerings, a backstop so

that institutional investors have a clear field and can do their flipping without competition.

Academia is aware of the flipping phenomenon and even has concluded that the stocks that institutions flip out of are, in fact, the dog stocks. A 1998 study, entitled "The Persistence of IPO Mispricing and the Predictive Power of Flipping," released by the Amos Tuck School at Dartmouth, concluded that institutions flip out of stocks that will perform poorly, and that brokerages "underprice" IPOs so that institutions will buy them. According to the study, institutions tend to hold onto the IPO stocks that will do better in the long run. Interestingly, the study found that the worst investments for individuals were the stocks that were the "hottest" on IPO day (although it should be pointed out that the study covers 1,232 larger IPOs from January 1973 through May 1995, largely before the Internet craze).

Stocks that rose 60 percent or more on IPO day turned out to be weak performers subsequently, and one year after the offering were typically down about 6.8 percent—very close to the finding of Worldfinancenet.com that individuals lost about 9 percent buying Internet IPOs if they bought "retail," or on the open market, after trading commenced. But for retail investors, the siren song is incredibly alluring—who *wouldn't* be interested in a stock that doubled on day one of trading?

That big investors tend to flip out of hot IPOs is almost beyond dispute. The Amos Tuck–Dartmouth study found that on "hot" IPOs (those rising more than 60 percent on the first day of trading), a hefty 52 percent of trading volume takes place in the first hour. In that first hour, it is only institutions that have stock to sell. The first two hours account for 72 percent of trading volume; again, almost by definition, the institutions flip out, although perhaps some day traders have moved in and out after 120 minutes of trading. On "hot" IPOs, an average of 70 percent of the total float is traded on the first day, according to the study. The inescapable conclusion is that the big institutions are flipping out of IPOs, and regularly. *They buy wholesale and sell retail.* For individual investors, it should be remembered how hard it is to make money both buying and selling retail.

There is another take on bad IPO performance, this one presented by the Anderson School of Business at UCLA in late 1997. "Researchers had previously uncovered that IPOs are, on the average, poor performers, with many filing for bankruptcy within a couple of years. Those that survive offer a return of about 5 to 10 percent per year less than comparable firms, or the market overall," said the study, entitled "Earnings Management and the Long-Term Market Performance of Initial Public Offerings," conducted by UCLA finance professor Ivo Welch.

The reason for the bad performance? "[I]ssuers frequently manipulate their reported earnings to look as good as possible to induce potential share buyers ... under SEC regulations, it is perfectly legal to 're-state' past earnings so as to show earnings growth," wrote Welch. In other words, the investment bankers are juicing the figures, and analysts are telling investors how great it looks. Does this sound like Planet Hollywood? Welch advises investors to steer clear of IPOs "without doing some serious homework."

Given that the lion's share of profit on an IPO is taken by those who get in at the offering price, one must wonder at brokerage-analyst "buy" recommendations that inevitably appear twenty-five days after an IPO is issued (the waiting period mandated by the SEC). In general, those retail investors who buy on the analyst's belated buy signal will lose money—even as they help provide an exit strategy for institutions.

Once again, the financial media deserve a C-, this time for their IPO coverage. Just as the media herald winners of state lotteries or give lots of ink to victims of sensational crimes or accidents, so the unusual winners in the financial world—the spectacular IPO home runs—get the lion's share of ink. But studies showing that crime is down or that IPO investing in general is a losing proposition show up in the dark inner cracks of the newspaper, if at all.

AS SEEMS ABUNDANTLY CLEAR, ANALYSTS have really gotten into the swing of helping their brokerages sell stocks and bonds and cement relations with investment banking clients. But what this book has looked at so far is just the first team, so to speak. Just as there is Playboy and then there are sordid skin mags, so there are major underwriters like Bear Stearns and then there are boiler-room happy, hard-selling, smaller brokerages—"bucket shops"—although, as will be shown, it is getting harder to tell the difference between the legitimate, the edgy, and the truly sleazy.

5

# THE PIED PIPERS
## (brass flute versions)

I n the mid-1980s, Peter Butler was a highly regarded chemical-
industry analyst at the major New York–based brokerage
PaineWebber, having placed second in his sector for two years
running in *Institutional Investor* magazine's annual ranking of Wall
Street securities analysts. "Eye-Eye," as the glossy magazine is called,
is considered the industry bible. Its annual rankings make and break
careers. Unfortunately for investors, as discussed in Chapter 4 as
well, a gold star from *Institutional Investor* is no guarantee that the
recipient is playing the game straight.

Certainly the SEC thought Butler wasn't. At the time, he was particularly fond of a Stamford, Connecticut–based company named
Memory Metals Inc. The company's key product was a line of copper
alloys that after being bent or otherwise pushed out of shape would
revert to their original position when heated. The idea was certainly
novel, but it had little commercial use, and the practical application
of such alloys remains rare to this day.

Whatever his reasons, in 1985 Butler began touting the small company to friends, money managers, and PaineWebber's stockbrokers—
who, in turn, persuaded many of their clients to buy the stock. To say
that Butler "recommended" Memory Metals is to understate the case.
According to the SEC, Butler told people "this was the stock they
would retire on, and that the stock's price was likely to hit 200 within
five years."

At the time, Memory Metals was trading at less than $10 a share.
In other words, Butler was predicting a 2,000 percent return over the

next five years for the maker of metal novelties. Evidently, this was the stuff of a champion forecaster, at least according to *Institutional Investor.* The SEC took a different view, however. In a civil suit it brought against Butler in 1988, the commission said he should have known "that such statements were materially false or misleading."

But, as often happens, the SEC moved too late. In 1985 and 1986, while Butler was doing his thing, Memory Metals stock rose like a cobra enchanted and hit a high of $16.625 in 1986. Although that was still a long way from the $200 a share Butler had promised, it nonetheless represented an impressive 66 percent increase in a single year. Before the Internet frenzy of the late 1990s, a run-up like that was considered pretty hot stuff.

However, as the SEC would belatedly charge, Butler's efforts on behalf of Memory Metals were not disinterested. As he touted the company, he was also buying its shares for his own portfolio. This can be an obvious conflict of interest, if analysts engage in so-called front running—buying a stock and then too obviously plumping for it.

But in general, analysts at major brokerages are free to buy stocks, even stocks on their "buy" lists. Selling is a lot harder, and usually requires permission from brokerage compliance departments. In Wall Street's heavy webs of conflicted interests, the fact that analysts are allowed to trade, preferably own, the stocks they cover represents a minor strand—yet investors can get caught on it as easily as on any other.

At least one cannot fault Butler for halfhearted efforts. According to the SEC, among other activities, he threatened to withhold advice from anyone who sold Memory Metals stock, and he requested compensation from Memory Metals in implicit exchange for flogging its stock. Butler also organized a "short squeeze"—that is, he prompted a buy-in of Memory Metals stock with the intent of driving the price up, according to the SEC. Short traders (who were ultimately vindicated) had to either "cover their positions" or buy Memory Metal shares on the open market to return to lenders. (Butler's short-squeeze activities are particularly interesting, as will be described in a later chapter.)

But perhaps the worst thing Butler is said to have done was alleged by Tom Barton, a partner in the short-trading outfit famed in the 1980s, the Feshbach Brothers. In a deposition under oath, Barton told the SEC that in the summer of 1986 he furnished Butler with clear evidence that specific contracts Memory Metals claimed to have were nonexistent or otherwise bogus.

At that point, the SEC charged, Butler bailed out of Memory Metals, selling his stock in the company. He got himself out, and perhaps his better clients as well. But he kept recommending the stock to others, according to court records.

Butler's move was nifty, if only for himself. In late 1986, Memory Metals' stock tanked after the company issued "clarifying" statements about previous announcements regarding contracts with larger concerns. Actually, the contracts didn't exist, as Feshbach testified. By 1991, the company had been rechristened Memry Corp., its stock was trading at a minuscule 37.5¢ a share, and no analyst would touch it.[1] Meanwhile, ordinary investors who had listened to PaineWebber's analyst Butler got bent, and no matter how hot they got, they couldn't straighten out.[2]

AS IT HAPPENS, THE MEMORY METALS scam didn't begin and end with Butler. In fact, he may have been merely the tip of the iceberg.

There is a kind of low comedy that pervades the lesser ranks of Wall Street, those second-tier regional firms or single-branch outfits that underwrite small-cap or microcap companies and try to sell penny stocks (defined now as a stock worth $5 per share or less) to smaller institutions, medium-sized pension funds (sometimes led by corrupt portfolio managers), and a retail crowd that never seems to get smart, generation after generation.

This is not to say that all regional or even single-branch brokerages are less competent or more corrupt than the big boys. But the polish, and much of the always-dubious power of compliance departments, usually diminishes the further one gets from the major wire houses, such as Merrill Lynch or Morgan Stanley Dean Witter. (It is the job of a brokerage's compliance department, often a single individual with multiple responsibilities at a smaller brokerage, to make sure business conduct is kosher.) Off Wall Street Major, the flutes tend to be made out of brass, not gold, and the beat is heavy, not subtle.

One of the most pervasive games played regularly on Wall Street Minor is the "pump-and-dump." The pump-and-dump is when a group of traders artificially boosts the share price of a selected stock, usually a small-cap issue, and then sells out before reality hits and the stock plummets. They usually do this by coordinating timed purchases with a wildly positive public relations campaign, the centerpiece of which is generally a highly favorable analyst's report—the enthusiastic analyst being a hired accomplice who is often paid in stock for his efforts.

On Wall Street Minor it is small-cap stocks that are targeted, for three main reasons. First, small-cap stocks rarely receive analyst coverage from major brokerages—meaning that anyone who puts out "research" about a small-cap stock has an open field and becomes the de facto expert on the stock. Second, small caps are generally ignored by the media. True, newspapers are hardly the muckrakers of yesteryear, and broadcast reporters rarely read past a press release, but even so, a hype job is easier if nobody from the media even knows or cares. Which they don't. There are more than 8,000 small-cap stocks in America, and the major financial media resolutely ignore the vast majority.

The third reason is that small-cap companies, by definition, have smaller floats, in terms of market capitalization. As a result, even a small amount of buying pressure—artificially induced or otherwise—can send small-cap stocks soaring. Then the pumpers can dump.

The nearly incessant bull markets of the past two decades have made things easy for pump-and-dumpers. The newly ascendant business media have been, until relatively recently, awash with stories of Internet IPOs doubling and doubling again, of newly christened dot-com companies with the flimsiest of business plans becoming white-hot investments overnight. Even legitimate publications have been rife with stories of investors, or even secretaries, who accepted stock in a Web start-up only to become millionaires (even if only on paper).

The atmosphere this creates tends to leave many people feeling they haven't been invited to the ball—but wanting to get in and dance to the music. The combination can be a dangerous one. At a Tulsa, Oklahoma, town meeting in 1998 about small-cap investing, then SEC chairman Arthur Levitt told investors, "It's like a tinder and match. As SEC chairman, I've seen too many people's life savings go up in smoke."

The pump-and-dump is big business. In 1996, largely before Internet mania drove Wall Street to previously undreamed-of heights—and opened the doors for even more dubious stock schemes—state securities regulators reported that Americans lost $6 billion a year as a result of small-cap frauds, a figure they estimated was 25 percent higher in 1997. And that was just in cases that regulators knew about. (Although a cynic might comment, "Big deal. Retail investors lost $2.9 billion on Planet Hollywood alone.")[3] In any event, almost certainly a far larger sum than $6 billion is being lost annually in scams that never blip on government radar screens, or are so murky that no one can tell whether investors' woes are due to brokerage incompetence, cruddy corporate management, or manipulation.

But manipulation abounds.

BARRY DAVIS WAS A SELF-DESCRIBED Robin Hood who told federal regulators and the press that sure, he manipulated stocks, but so did everybody else in the business. Although memories of Davis have faded, he is still an interesting case study, timelessly exemplary: as long as there is a Wall Street (and feeble enforcement by the SEC and NASD), there will be the Barry Davises of the brokerage industry.

Back in 1989 and 1990, Davis ran a New Jersey financial public-relations firm called Princeton Financial Services. At the time, financial public relations was considered one of the hottest growth industries in America. It still is. There is no end of obscure small-cap companies across the country that believe, or want to believe, that their stock is being unfairly ignored and undervalued. These companies are not always self-deluded. With more than 8,000 publicly traded companies competing for attention—and the big institutional funds almost necessarily limited to investing in blue-chip stocks—it's a real challenge for small-cap outfits to get noticed.

One way they can do so is by hiring a financial PR firm to organize and mount an informational campaign on their behalf. The standard strategy involves sending out a string of letters, reports, and other literature to brokerages, stockbrokers, smaller money managers, anybody who might buy a small cap. At the same time, the PR firm will try to plant positive stories in financial publications and broadcasts.

To improve the odds, some financial PR people are not above cutting ethical and legal corners. This is particularly true at the smaller shops that tend to get paid not in cash but in a client company's stock. In fact, a lot of target-company stock can be splashed around, giving stockbrokers, money managers, financial advisers, and even an occasional wayward news reporter a stake in the upward ascent of the stock. Barry Davis's Princeton Financial Services knew about using stock to hype a stock.

Barry Davis had a colorful history even before he went into financial PR. In the late 1960s and early 1970s, when he was still doing business under his earlier name of Barry Sutz, he ran a Valley Stream, New York, stock brokerage named Sutz & Ross. According to the SEC, the firm failed to meet capital requirements, and Sutz himself was accused of "converting [clients'] funds for his own use." Some call that stealing.

Whatever the terminology, the SEC wanted no part of him, and in 1971 it barred him from the securities industry. Bloodied but unbowed, Sutz opened an insurance agency. That lasted only a few years before state regulators, alarmed by hundreds of client complaints and missing funds, closed him down in 1975.[4] So Barry Sutz became Barry Davis, and Barry Davis went into financial public relations, an even less regulated corner of the securities world than the alcove inhabited by brokerage analysts.

Naturally skillful at PR—Davis bragged openly that his "best weapon was my mouth"—and perhaps a little more than mildly knowledgeable about the actions and skills of regulators, Davis thrived. He made money by manipulating stocks. He did this by employing what *Barron's,* the national financial weekly newspaper, called the "basic tools" of small-cap stock manipulation. These included:

➢ Parking, in which an accomplice agrees to buy a stock in order to create a trade and then to "park" it in his brokerage account so that it will be ready to sell when needed. This protects the identity of the true manipulator.

➢ False accounts, in which a brokerage account is actually controlled by someone other than the person whose name is on it. Again, identities are obscured.

➢ Matching orders, a practice in which brokers or brokerages agree to trade stock with each other—often merely passing the same shares back and forth—at what are recorded as higher and higher prices, though no money actually changes hands, ostensibly in response to a "news" event or positive financial reports. For those not in on the gag, it is hard not to believe in a stock that keeps trading up.

But, of course, the basics of stock manipulation are usually simple: Get a lot of stockbrokers at regional firms to start hyping the target stock to their clients. The buying pressure pushes the stock up. The stockbrokers don't let the clients sell until insiders have sold out.

And that is what Davis did. To help carry out his schemes, he recruited more than 100 willing accomplices—for the most part, traders and stockbrokers lured by the prospect of quick and easy money. In some cases, they received straight cash payments; in others, the guarantee of a role in future schemes; still others were promised reciprocity (that is, Davis pledged he would help them out in some future swindle of theirs). Of course, they knew in advance which stock to buy, which was going to be given an artificial boost. It is interesting to note that not one of Davis's 100-plus accomplices spilled the beans until after federal prosecutors started throwing their weight around. As we shall see, fear may have played a role here. In at least one case, there was a dark hint of mob reprisal.

Typically, Davis underwrote what federal prosecutors call "boxed" IPOs. Shares were sold only to friendly brokers who would put their clients into the stock and more or less box them in for the duration of the pump phase of the pump-and-dump scheme. In addition to cooperating brokerages, Davis pumped stock with his Traders and Investors Alert telephone hotline (remember, this is pre-Internet), and other hot lines, that touted stocks to callers. Davis's flute work, at least initially, showed even the pros on Wall Street how to carry a tune and set standards that were matched only by the Internet-stock moon shots of the late 1990s.

The stocks Davis touted surged, creating something of a self-fulfilling prophecy. As a stock went up, more investors would become convinced that Davis was onto something. They would then buy, pushing the stock even higher. So it was that the price of shares in such Davis-backed companies as Vista Capital Inc., Bellatrix Corp., and Castleton Investors Corp. soared by anywhere from 400 to 1,000 percent within a month or two of Davis's sounding his flute. Davis worked hand in glove with the now-defunct Fort Lauderdale–based Sheffield Securities, which handled initial public offerings for Vista and Bellatrix.

Unfortunately, investors who traded through Davis found that buying was a lot easier than selling. An associate of Davis's named Eric Wynn was caught on tape by the FBI telling a fellow broker that the stocks they pushed were "like a roach motel"—investors could get in, but they couldn't get out. This is typical of pump-and-dump schemes, in which stockbrokers are instructed to resist customers' efforts to sell. They do this in all manner of ways, including trying to talk them out of their decision, not answering the phone, threatening to cut off relations—or simply telling the customer that the stock has been sold, even if it hasn't been.

The lack of an easy exit was characteristic of Davis's scams in general. Once a broker got involved with one of his pump-and-dump operations, he usually found it difficult, if not impossible, to change his mind and back out. According to federal prosecutors, Davis's associate Eric Wynn was tight with Frank Coppa, whom the feds identified as a captain in the Bonanno organized-crime family. On at least one occasion, Wynn brought Coppa to a diner in Fort Lee, New Jersey, to meet a stockbroker who wanted to sell his clients out of one of Davis's pump-and-dump stocks. After meeting with Coppa and looking around the diner in Fort Lee, the stockbroker decided maybe it wasn't such a good idea for his clients to sell the Davis stocks.

In the end, of course, any outsider who bought stock in one of Davis's deals wound up a loser. After the pump stage, the stocks always dumped, after the insiders sold out. While the full extent of investor losses may never be known, in 1991 Davis pleaded guilty to organizing five separate stock scams involving five publicly traded companies that were said to have bilked investors out of some $5 million.

Of course, that is a mere drop in the oceans of money gushing across Wall Street these days. Davis himself, or the 100-plus stockbrokers who helped him, are by themselves not all that important—what is important is that such scams have proliferated on Wall Street for generations, and investors should be aware of them. There seems little will on Wall Street to rid the industry of its seamier side.

## PETER BUTLER REDUX

But there is more to the Davis-Wynn story. According to federal prosecutors—who ultimately put Davis and Wynn behind bars—one of the stocks manipulated by the Davis-Wynn tribe was Memory Metals. The very same Memory Metals so fiercely championed by Peter Butler, the erstwhile PaineWebber star chemical industry analyst. (The SEC never charged that Butler knew about the origin of Memory Metals. One might wonder why an analyst would tout a microcap without checking its underwriters, however.)

Among the several defendants in the Davis-Wynn case was a Pericles "Perry" Constantinou. Then 60, he had amassed a long record with federal securities industry regulators, extending back to at least 1973, when a federal court in New York permanently enjoined Constantinou from further violations of securities laws. Another federal court in 1975 ruled that Constantinou was part of what *Barron's* later called a "massive securities fraud scheme" perpetrated in part by Robert Vesco (the old Richard Nixon campaign contributor and one-time international fugitive). Also in 1975 Constantinou was barred from the industry by the SEC, finding that he manipulated stock prices, particularly for a company named Fantastic Fudge Inc.[5]

Constantinou popped up again in 1985, as a financial consultant to Memory Metals, which went public that year. The brokerage that took Memory Metals public was Securities First Inc., a small over-the-counter underwriter, at Constantinou's behest. Constantinou explained his operation in federal court this way: "I am not a broker, but deals come to me, companies to be underwritten, and I bring them to certain brokerage houses to underwrite. I get a fee for that ... sort of a finder's fee."

Just as the Davis-Wynn team manipulated stocks, so did the Constantinou organization. Large blocks of stock in companies going public would be acquired prior to the IPO or as part of the initial public offering, and there was extensive use of phony accounts and stock swapping (at inflated prices) by cooperating brokerages—all to drive the price of Memory Metals up, said fed officials.

Constantinou even managed to take private stock in companies prior to an IPO—just like major Wall Street brokerages do today, making Constantinou something of a trendsetter. Through a company in New York City named World Wide Capital, Constantinou would provide "bridge financing" to private companies, to see them through the going-public process. In exchange, World Wide Capital would take pre-IPO, unregistered stock.

Federal prosecutors charged that Constantinou provided bridge financing to Memory Metals in exchange for 360,000 shares of company stock—worth $10 each when the stock was touted by Butler in 1985, and worth more than $16 each at the peak, or nearly $6 million. Memory Metals was a Constantinou stock.

It has never been determined, at least publicly, why Butler, at a major brokerage such as PaineWebber, was touting Memory Metals. None of the SEC charges seem to have mattered much to First Boston (now Credit Suisse First Boston), which hired him from PaineWebber.

Butler left the industry in 1992, a full six years after his role in the Memory Metals flop was exposed, but only after the SEC had him sign a consent decree in which he neither admitted nor denied he had violated the law, but which barred him from the industry for six months. He also was ordered to return ill-gotten profits of $37,249. The extent of investor losses was in the tens of millions of dollars.

The bad news is that the role of pump-and-dump brokerages and the Mob on Wall Street appears to be increasing, not diminishing. On June 17, 1999, federal prosecutors in the Eastern District of New York threw RICO (Racketeer Influenced and Corrupt Organizations act) charges at eighty-five stockbrokers in nine firms, alleging they had manipulated stocks and burned investors to the tune of $100 million and counting—using the usual pump-and-dump modus operandi.

The rip-offs were directed by the Colombo organized crime family and new Russian crime syndicates, said fed officials. Such crime families had "controlled" New York City's trash-hauling, concrete, and construction industries through the 1980s, but as a result of prosecutions, they had moved into securities instead. "We have detected increased attempts by organized crime groups to become involved in the manipulation of stocks and securities," Lewis Schliro, then FBI assistant director, told reporters.[6] It's nice to know that as the investment-crazy 1990s closed, even the Mob was getting out of the dirty-fingernail businesses and into the securities game.

But as the century turned, there seemed no end to stock frauds, whether connected to the Mob or freelance. On July 8, 1999, the New York State District Attorney for Manhattan, Robert Morganthau, filed charges that the Naples, Florida–based brokerage A. S. Goldmen and thirty-three of its employees or accessories had cheated investors out of $100 million in known frauds. Examples of real-life pain were legion: One seventy-three-year-old man lost his life savings and had to return to work as a bus driver. Another woman lost $25,000 she had saved to make her daughter's wedding a real event. The A. S. Goldmen trial began in New York in February 2001, and defense lawyers vowed a vigorous defense.

A. S. Goldmen's chief financial officer at the time the alleged frauds took place was Stuart Winkler, a former National Association of Securities Dealers (the industry-financed self-regulatory body, often called the NASD) official, one of several over the years who have popped up at questionable brokerages. Morganthau said Winkler knew many ways to hide A. S. Goldmen's wrongdoings. It was a curious feature of the A. S. Goldmen case that it took a New York state official—the D.A. Morganthau—to pursue the case. The NASD, and the SEC, were not carrying much, if any, weight in this case.

In yet another curious feature of the A. S. Goldmen case, internal
NASD documents pertaining to the investigation somehow ended up
in Winkler's possession—in short, almost certainly someone within
the NASD had leaked documents to Winkler. The NASD never found
out who did the leaking. At one point, the NASD considered a $1 mil-
lion fine against A. S. Goldmen (about 1 percent of investor losses),
but an NASD appeal panel later dropped the fine to $150,000, at the
suggestion of A. S. Goldmen lawyers.

The NASD, ever fierce in its defense of small investors, eventually fined Winkler $36,000 and suspended him from the industry for
two whole years. One might well wonder what a fellow had to do to
be permanently barred.[7]

As comically pathetic as the NASD actions against A. S. Goldmen
might have been (except, of course, to the investors who had been
burned), that does not mean Winkler got off easy. Evidently, Winkler
was on a steep downhill path as of August 2000. By then, Winkler was
in jail, where District Attorney Morganthau had put him. In early
August, Winkler had planned to fly to the Cayman Islands, and
Morganthau became alarmed about the flight plans. The D.A.'s office
requested in state court that the terms of Winkler's $1 million bail be
toughened, a request granted by Judge Leslie Crocker Snyder of the
Manhattan State Supreme Court. Winkler couldn't meet bail and was
incarcerated. Evidently angered by the judge's decision, Winkler
allegedly contacted a hit man and "described the security arrangements near the judge's courtroom and provided details such as when
the judge would be in town or on vacation." Winkler was subsequently found guilty of conspiracy to commit murder. Winkler's
lawyer said he was "set up" by a cellmate and vowed to appeal.[8]

## THE OLD-FASHIONED STOCK PROMOTER

And then on Wall Street Minor are those affable characters who are
not part of the Mob, or a pump-and-dump crew, or even a hustling
Boca Raton regional brokerage. There is on Wall Street a hardy breed
of unabashed stock promoters, who treat stock like cars or personal
computers or houses, a product to be sold by whatever sales pitch
seems to work, no harm intended. Alan Stone is a stock promoter.

A graduate of the University of Pennsylvania's famed Wharton School, with an MBA in finance and investments from New York University as well, Stone started out in the 1980s as an analyst for Merrill Lynch Asset Management, looking at stocks and high-yield bonds in New York. He also worked for Prudential-Bache (now Prudential Securities) on private placements, the industry lingo for investments not registered with the SEC.

In the early 1990s, Stone moved to Los Angeles, where he began hosting "corporate focus luncheons" for the American Stock Exchange. Those monthly powwows were held at swanky spots such as the Jonathan Club downtown or the Regent Beverly Wilshire Hotel in Beverly Hills. Their purpose was to spotlight a selected Amex firm before the southern California investment community of brokers, money managers, and pension-fund executives.

Stone was well qualified for financial-relations work. Because of his background as an analyst, he could think from the buyer's perspective. Not bad with a pen, he could also talk the talk. As a result, some companies featured at the luncheons he hosted were impressed enough with him to retain his services afterwards. By 1993, he had opened Alan Stone & Co. and was working full-time as an investor-relations consultant and publicist for small publicly traded companies, almost always compensated in cash and stock.

Unlike a Davis or a Butler, Stone has a record that's as clean as a whistle. He does nothing illegal and has never been sanctioned by the SEC or any other government agency. Yet the first thing one notices about Stone is that he can sling hyperbole without the slightest embarrassment, and somehow never stray past the boundaries of the stretched truth. Take, for example, the brochure he uses to promote his firm. Inside, it features a photograph of a major, architecturally significant West Los Angeles office building. The photo caption reads, "Alan Stone & Co., Corporate Offices, Los Angeles, California."

A potential client might conclude the whole building was the headquarters of a vast and powerful Alan Stone & Co. empire. In fact, as Stone will casually concede, he merely rents an office in the building. Actually, he doesn't even rent—he takes space in an executive suite on the building's sixteenth floor. The executive suite company does the actual renting; Stone is a customer, not truly a tenant. The executive suite consists of a conference room and several well-used-looking offices, adorned with what looks like motel-room art and out-of-date law books. The offices encircle a common receptionist's desk. No office is Stone's alone; like other customers of the executive suite, he just uses whichever one happens to be free.

"This is one of the premier executive suites in the city," says Stone, seemingly oblivious to the fact that he lacks even a door with his name on it. "One of the best law firms in the city used to be on the floors above us," he adds. "But they needed more space and moved out."

Although Alan Stone & Co. is essentially a one-man shop, Stone bills himself as its managing director, and the cover of his promotional brochure features a snazzy corporate jet in mid-takeoff—bearing the letters "ASC" on its tail. But even though he has no corporate jet, Stone is no phony. After more than twenty-five years on Wall Street, he knows his way around a balance sheet. He knows what investors want to hear, and how to write a digestible, three-page report on a company, which is his specialty. He also knows how to disseminate the report to the right brokers, the right money managers, the right financial advisers. In short, he knows how to get the price of a small-cap stock to jump, at least for a while.

A KEY FEATURE OF STONE'S SERVICE to clients—publicly traded companies looking for a "higher profile" on Wall Street—is what he describes as "enhancing shareholder value." For the most part, he claims to do this by "arranging leading analyst coverage through research reports prepared by experienced CPAs."

In fact, Stone pays a single analyst—whom he identifies as Joseph E. Jones of the firm Wall Street Research—to write three-page research reports on his clients. According to Stone, Jones's résumé includes stints at Standard & Poor's and Brown Brothers Harriman as well as the American Stock Exchange, where he was director of research. When pressed to produce him in the flesh, Stone explains that Jones takes four extended sea cruises every year and, as a result, is not often available for interviews. Despite his seasonal sea campaigns, however, Jones does finds time to write reports (invariably favorable ones) on Stone's clients.

Stone reproduces Jones's reports in the form of glossy four-page pamphlets, which he distributes to between 2,000 and 5,000 brokers and money managers. He also posts them on the Internet. Working mainly with thinly traded microcap issues, most of which are penny stocks, Stone says this strategy can be enormously effective. "We can often get a stock to double or triple after a company becomes our client," he claims, and he has records to prove many cases. Like all stock promoters, Stone jumps on stock trends or fads. If energy is hot, he will sell a company as an energy play. If the Internet is hot, he will advise a client to add a dot-com to its name and launch a Web site.

It is only mildly surprising to learn that Stone *owns* Wall Street Research, but he says he does not regard this as a conflict of interest. "I don't feel conflicted, even though I get paid [by client firms] for the research," he says. "If I ever felt a stock was not good, we would take it off our buy list." Stone concedes this has never happened. And, he says, the fact that client companies pay him to be covered by Wall Street Research gets "adequate and proper disclosure" in the literature he prepares. Or as he puts it, "We give the caveat emptor, so to speak, to the public."

Nonetheless, there are busts. For all of Stone's enthusiasm, the fundamentals have a way of coming back to haunt investors. The story of Stone's client LifePoint Inc. may be typical. Based in Rancho Cucamonga, California, LifePoint markets medical testing devices. Its first product was billed as a rapid, on-site test that could determine whether alcohol and drugs had been used or abused by a motorist, employee, or patient. LifePoint claimed it had a way of detecting many drugs in saliva (as opposed to blood or urine), thus enabling it to offer a quick, non-invasive, and relatively inexpensive way to get results. Stone took LifePoint under his wing in 1998. Shortly thereafter, he put out one of his Wall Street Research reports on the company, recommending it as a buy at $1.03 a share. Before very long, the stock had ramped up to $6 a share—a home run by anybody's measure.

By June 1999, however, the stock had fallen all the way back down to $1 a share. "There was a large amount of convertible stock out there, and it converted into common, and that drove the price down," says Stone. Of course, the company wasn't making money either. For some reason, the existence of the convertible stock hadn't been mentioned in Stone's first Wall Street Research report. No matter, says Stone. "At this price, I think it is a really good buy. It is a good company with a good product." Maybe so. The stock by early 2001 had vaulted back to more than $5 a share.

Stone even handles IPOs, just like the big brokerages. "From time to time we get involved in an IPO. We are always looking for a really good company to take public. Most recently, we took New Frontier Media public."

As it turns out, the Boulder, Colorado–based New Frontier Media provides adult entertainment to cable television subscribers. It grew quite a bit in 1999 but was still losing money. Borrowing a page from Playboy's book, New Frontier in 1999 bought an Internet porn provider, which, among other services, features purported eighteen-year-olds taking their clothes off for paying Web site customers who can direct the action online. Maybe New Frontier is a cut cruder than Playboy's chat rooms also featuring naked women, but money has to be made one way or another. Except New Frontier isn't making money—it reported a loss of $7.6 million on revenues of $9.5 million in fiscal 1999.

For investors, the results have been appropriately torpid. After going public at $4 a share in 1998, the stock touched both a bottom of 63¢ a share and a top of $10.69 a share in 1999. By early 2001, it was trading in the mid-$3-a-share range. At least it was doing better than Playboy's secondary offering.

Stone sees little contrast between his practices and those of the major brokerages. "The only way a brokerage will get involved with a company is for an economic reason," he says. "They tend to have conflicts, they have stock, they have warrants. The buy side"—that is, the money managers and the big investment funds—"know this, they know there is a conflict."

Of course, there is an element of truth in Stone's self-image. Sure, there are differences between Stone's shop and Bear Stearns with its Planet Hollywood, or Credit Suisse First Boston and Playboy, but the differences are ones of size and degree and not type. Although Stone inhabits Wall Street Minor—in that regard, a lot like Hemant Shah, of anti-Biovail fame—he is a walking microcosm of the same conflicts and biases found on Wall Street Major. Again, the Alan Stone story by itself is not so important. What is important is the fact that there are hundreds if not thousands of Alan Stones splashed across the face of financial America. Investors beware.

## THE WORLD WIDE WEB

As with so much else in this world, the World Wide Web is a double-edged sword. Amid the bonanza of information it offers lurks a danger: Web touts. With its slick graphics and curtain of anonymity, the Internet offers a powerful platform to all manner of swindlers and con artists.

By all accounts, fraud on the Web is rampant. In a single crackdown on online fraudsters in October 1998, the SEC accused forty-four companies and individuals of manipulating the prices of no fewer than 235 stocks.[9] True, they were mostly small-cap stocks, but the scale of the con was breathtaking nevertheless. An ethically challenged analyst such as Hemant Shah or Barry Davis or Peter Butler might want to knock a stock here, boost a stock there—but 235 stocks?

Typically, the online fraud artists had an equity stake in the companies being touted—a cyber-world variation of the pump-and-dump. For example, according to the SEC, Jeffrey C. Bruss of West Chicago, Illinois, recommended about twenty-five microcap stocks to more than 100,000 subscribers of his Future Superstocks Web site. Just like the big brokerages, Bruss provided "analysis" on selected issues. And just like the big brokerages, Bruss received money or profits from clients—in his case, cash and stock worth some $3 million from the companies in question. Unlike the brokerages, however, Bruss didn't disclose his financial interest to investors. He simply told them the stocks would double or triple in price over the following month. (A lawyer for Bruss said the SEC charges provide only the SEC's version of events.) As of early 2001, the SEC case against Bruss was pending.[10]

Online scamsters employ a number of basic tactics to con online investors. Among them:

➤ Spamming, in which the tout sends messages extolling the virtues of a particular stock to hundreds of thousands or even millions of e-mail addresses. If only a tiny percentage of the recipients are hoodwinked into investing, the returns are substantial, and the action in the stock hot.

➤ Phony Web sites, which are created to make a company seem more substantial than it really is or to masquerade as a source of "independent" judgment.

➤ Ersatz postings, in which touts conceal their identities and circulate disinformation in stock market chat rooms, such as those hosted by Yahoo! or the Silicon Investor.

By 1998, online stock fraud had become so rampant that the SEC established a special Office of Internet Enforcement to pursue Web cases. To many experts, however, the SEC was the wrong agency for the job. The problem is that the SEC is empowered to bring only civil—and not criminal—charges against malefactors. In other words, no jail time. Unfortunately, as director Richard Walker of the SEC's enforcement division said in 1999, "the prospect of a prison sentence is apt to deter more fraud than anything the SEC can do, such as imposing a financial penalty or barring a rogue broker."[11] It's hard not to conclude that the SEC is essentially waving paperwork at a bunch of hardened cons hiding in the cyber bushes.

Moreover, the Web has amplified the reach of boiler-room "analysts" to heights never previously dreamed of. According to the SEC, in one night a New York financial PR firm sent out no fewer than 6 *million* e-mails touting two small-cap companies. Assuming one minute per call, an eight-hour day, and a five-day week, it would take fifty telemarketers a year to call that many people. The e-mailing PR firm did it in one sundown to sunrise.

Cunningly, many Web fraudsters set themselves up as being in public relations or in the "analysis" business, not as brokers. Thus, they are not subject to the SEC's regulatory authority and cannot be expelled from the industry. As wrong as it may seem, many touts—"analysts"— can structure their activities so that they are perfectly legal.

The SEC can wield the big stick of criminal charges by coordinating its efforts with the U.S. Department of Justice. A dedicated U.S. Attorney can put a crook behind bars. But that's extremely time-consuming and probably not very practical, given the voluminous number of cases. The fact is, the Justice Department is simply not equipped to pursue hundreds—probably even thousands—of Web fraud cases, many involving losses of less than $1 million. Privately, many U.S. attorneys admit they have a loss "threshold" below which they won't chase a case, as there are too many cases anyway. Someone stung in a $500,000 scam probably can't look for the U.S. cavalry to come to the rescue.

As will be described in Chapter 8, feeble enforcement is the rule on Wall Street, not the exception. The pied pipers, the cheerleaders, the pump-and-dumpers simply overwhelm existing enforcement agencies, and have for decades. Lamentably, Wall Street Major has never called on Congress, or the SEC, or the NASD, or the U.S. Attorney's Office, to radically beef up efforts to rid the industry of fraud and miscreants. Indeed, for decades some major Wall Street brokerages, most notably Bear Stearns & Co., have actively helped even known pump-and-dump shops clear trades.

## FINE BY US

The reaction of Wall Street Major to the pump-and-dump shops and to possible Mob influence is lamentable. There has been no industry outcry that bucket shops need to be driven from the industry. On the contrary. For generations, dubious brokerages such as A. G. Baron, A. S. Goldmen (of Stuart Winkler fame), Blinder Robertson, and Sterling Foster have executed their trades through major brokerages, most particularly Bear Stearns & Co. (Smaller brokerages, including bucket shops, are essentially just rented offices inhabited by branch managers, stockbrokers, and the occasional "analyst," who usually doubles as a stockbroker. To actually buy and sell stock, they phone their orders to major brokerages.)

The business of clearing trades for smaller brokerages and bucket shops is very lucrative for Bear Stearns, the established industry leader, with 12 percent of all trading volume on the NYSE. The firm long contended it was not aiding and abetting fraud, only clearing trades. Eventually, even the feds saw through the cover (though too late to help thousands of investors).

Starting in late 1997, federal prosecutors and SEC regulators finally took a close look at Bear Stearns concerning illegal trades cleared for A. G. Baron in bogus stocks in which investors had been bilked out of $75 million. SEC enforcement chief Richard Walker concluded after the two-year investigation, "Bear Stearns took actions that directly facilitated Baron's widespread fraudulent activity." Bear Stearns agreed to pay $38.5 million to settle charges and signed the usual consent decree, in which it neither denied nor admitted guilt.

Some might have wished for sterner medicine. The SEC also charged (and such charges were seconded by state D.A. Morganthau) that Richard Harriton, the veteran chief of Bear Stearns's powerful trading unit—credited by many with building the unit—knew of fraud at A. G. Baron but abetted it, and even took steps to keep A. G. Baron in business. Moreover, Harriton personally profited from A. G. Baron, by directing the firm to place pre-IPO stock into secret nominee accounts that he held. Among many egregious shortcomings, Harriton knew that many Baron "buy" trades were unauthorized—made without customers' approval—in order to prop up issue prices. After months of resolutely defending Harriton, finally Bear Stearns agreed to fire him as part of the settlement—but only after Bear Stearns president James Cayne gushed fulsome praise on Harriton and said he was sorry to see Harriton go. Cayne also signed off on a company memo that said of Harriton, "we wish him well."

Harriton, through lawyers, denied wrongdoing. He has paid a $1 million fine and is eligible to become active in the industry within a couple of years, having settled charges that are legally defined only as "negligence" and neither admitted or denied guilt even to that.

But Bear Stearns's role in helping bucket shops trade was so obvious that even the mainstream press was offended. *The New York Times* called the details of the SEC charges against Bear Stearns "lurid" and wondered aloud what other public company would have tolerated such illegal activity for so long.

The charges rang around the world. The *South China Morning Post* reran part of a *New York Times* editorial that said, "Wall Street scandals come and go. But the lurid details in the order that Bear Stearns Securities signed ... to settle Securities and Exchange Commission charges have staying power ... a tale of personal and corporate greed relentlessly pursued at the expense of unsuspecting shareholders."

One must wonder what conclusions about ethics and recommendations analysts are to draw when they are employed at Bear Stearns—but then again, the firm did underwrite Planet Hollywood. And flogged the stock almost the whole way to bankruptcy.

## WHERE THE BRASS MEETS THE GOLD
### (Both Metals Are Yellow and Sometimes Hard to Tell Apart)

Some on Wall Street would dismiss Alan Stone as a small player, and the practice of mutual funds and institutions buying up almost all of an IPO and then flipping out on higher prices to retail investors as just necessary business convention. No doubt many on Wall Street regard the pump-and-dumpers as outsiders; the Planet Hollywood IPO as an aberration; Playboy's secondary offering as just aggressive underwriting; Solly telecom analyst Grubman as sui generis; and Wall Street's flogging of Internet stocks such as Priceline.com and eToys.com as nothing unusual given the huge and unpredictable promise of the Internet. Bear Stearns is just clearing trades, nothing more, and Hemant Shah—why, he's an independent analyst. Nothing new here, just some pieces and scraps.

But perhaps a more accurate take is that such events are part of the new Wall Street that has blossomed in the era following rate deregulation in 1975. In something of a parallel to modern journalism, Wall Street is experiencing a blurring of the lines between what's considered right and fair and what is the ne'er-do-well's turf. Just as differences between the tabloids and the "serious" broadsheets—certainly during Presidential sex scandals—are dimming, so too has the line between Wall Street Major and the rest of the industry faded.

Stone and the pump-and-dumpers pay for "research" or just write it themselves. Is that so different from in-house Wall Street analysts and their chronic "buy" signals? Stone and the bucket shops take stock in companies they represent or take public. Is that so distant from the underwriters' allotment of stock, or the pre-IPO equity more and more major underwriters are taking? The pump-and-dumpers run the stock up, then get out. The brokerages and mutual funds run the stock up, then get out.

Some of Stone's clients tank. So, too, did Planet Hollywood, which was underwritten by four major Wall Street firms, and Playboy sank quickly after its secondary offering by two esteemed underwriters, as have Internet stocks too numerous to mention. As academic research has shown, IPOs, as a rule, underperform the market, especially for retail investors who can't buy on IPO day—yet Wall Street sells them again and again and again.

Stone insists he is actually cleaner than the big brokerages: "If I have to, I can walk away from a company and put a sell signal on it. I have other clients. I don't have huge overhead. I have never seen a brokerage put out a sell. They usually have too much inventory [client-company stock], or they want more investment banking business," says Stone. "I can do what I want. An analyst at a Wall Street firm can't do what he wants."

On Wall Street today, it's hard to know whether Stone is just hyping himself, or telling the truth, or some foggy blend of the two.

# 6

# THE SHORTS

*Short traders? I love 'em. Sometimes they are viewed as evil people. But what many of them do is look at the accounting statements. They say, 'Let's check the garbage.' It is good for our society. There are so few analysts willing to say something bad about a company. Shorts are a tonic on the market.*

—HANS R. STOLL

The Anne Marie and Thomas B. Walker

Professor of Finance and Director of the Financial Markets Research Center,

Owen Graduate School of Management, Vanderbilt University

"You gotta have a trigger event," says Stanley Brillo, stopping midstride and holding up a finger to make his point. "You gotta be looking for something that is going to dump the stock. It is not good enough anymore that it is a crappy company with crappy management. Crappy can go on for years. You gotta be looking for a trigger that will send the stock down. Sometimes it is an earnings release, or a material fact that is disclosed in SEC filings, or even some news coverage. But it's got to be something specific."

Stanley Brillo is a short trader, which is to say he makes his money identifying stocks that he believes are headed for the dumper and then selling them short.[1] Selling short sounds somewhat mysterious, or even vaguely sinister, but it is really neither. A short trader usually borrows the shares he wants to sell short from a brokerage or from the trust department of a bank. Both organizations control plenty of their customers' stock and are happy to lend it out, collecting interest on the "loan."

After borrowing the stock, the short seller sells it on the open market. He or she hopes to buy it back later at a lower price and then return the shares to the original owner. If you borrow 100 shares of XYZ stock and sell at $10 a share but buy back two weeks later at $5, then you profited at $5 a share, or $500, before expenses.

There is no contract between short and lender; the lender can "call back" the shares at any time. Obviously, short trading is not for the faint of heart—consider the transaction costs, and the interest to be paid, and the power of brokerages (with lapdog analysts) and mutual funds to move share prices, and the uncertainty about callbacks.

Like many, probably most, market players of his stripe, Brillo won't speak on the record. For one thing, his brokerage firm—a major wire house—won't let him. It's considered bad form for an employee of a major brokerage to indulge in short trading, much less to boast about it openly. Brokerages are supposed to be about selling, not shorting. Beyond that, talking for attribution—and being publicly identified as a short—could cost him his access to corporate insiders, particularly executives of companies whose stock he is shorting. It might also anger one of his firm's corporate clients or alert so-called short busters to what he is doing.

So Brillo (not his real name) keeps a low profile. Not that he is by any means an obscure or retiring figure. A hardened veteran of many a Wall Street tug-of-war, Brillo is one of the premier short traders on the West Coast. Amid the winking and blinking of computer screens, the phones ring almost constantly in his bustling office fifty-five floors above downtown Los Angeles. For the most part, the calls are from clients or other short traders seeking advice, gossip, or commentary.

"Stan Brillo, the boy wonder," he sometimes answers the phone, though he's old enough to be a grandfather, adding: "And, boy, do I wonder."

Brillo plays a demanding game, and he respects its rules, knowing that when he violates them, he can lose big. "I lost a half-million dollars on Yahoo!" he says, referring to the pioneering Internet company whose astonishing stock market performance helped define the dot-com era on Wall Street. "The worst bet of my life. I never lost so much money on a single stock. I stunk to the moon. The good news is that it kept going up after I got out. I could have lost 2 million more. I could have stunk all the way to Jupiter. [Yahoo!] is overvalued, but there was no trigger event out there."

It's the same, he adds, with most Internet stocks. This is in the summer of 1999, just before Internet stocks weakened, in the tech wreck of spring 2000.

"They say Amazon.com won't make money for five years," Brillo observes. "I say it won't ever make money. But you can't short that stock. Not now. But someday. Someday big." (Amazon.com subsequently lost two-thirds of its value.) As Brillo sees it, the biggest short opportunity of all time is out there somewhere just over the horizon. "The Internet stocks have been hyped to the moon," he says. "This will be the biggest bath of all time. It will make the South Sea Bubble look microscopic."

Eventually, he says, the economy will succumb to recession, possibly stagflation. When that happens, equity prices will take a double hit—once due to lower corporate earnings, and again as price/earnings multiples contract. For example, take a company with earnings of $1 a share whose stock is trading at 30 times earnings. That would put its share price at $30. If the company's net income fell to 75¢ a share amid a widespread economic slowdown, it might well see its P/E multiple simultaneously drop to 20 times earnings (still rich by historical standards). This double whammy of declining earnings and shrinking multiples would slash its share price to $15—a 50 percent haircut for investors, but a bonanza for the likes of Stanley Brillo.

"When that day comes, Wall Street will be a short's dream," Brillo says. "It's just a matter of when." He has seen the cycle before.

STANLEY BRILLO WASN'T ALWAYS A SHORT, nor does he only make short plays today. When he sees a good stock he'll buy it. In fact, it was when looking for good stocks that he fell into the short game in the early 1980s, after nearly two decades as a stockbroker. Brillo's clients were, for the most part, wealthy (he rarely took on anyone with less than $250,000 to put in play) and loyal—something increasingly rare in today's financial clime, in which stockbrokers are generally regarded as interchangeable asset allocators. Clients liked him because he had a friendly demeanor and a sharp wit; they listened to him because he made them money.

Brillo's clients were legion and loyal enough that he became known as "a guy who could put away significant amounts of stock." That meant his clients were willing to take major positions in small-cap stocks he recommended. As a result, smaller companies that were unable to get coverage from major or even regional brokerage analysts—a common problem, then and now—began making pilgrimages to Brillo. If they could persuade Brillo, then Brillo's clients would buy in. That would support the stock, even move the stock. It was sort of a microcosm of the type of brokerage/institutional support that large-cap stocks today take for granted.

And so Brillo saw a lot of good companies. And in more than a few cases, he put his clients in their stocks—though only after meeting with management, reading the company's mandatory disclosure statements with the SEC, touring facilities, talking with customers, calling vendors, and doing all manner of other snooping.

Of course, not every supplicant was a hidden beauty. Indeed, as time went on, more and more dubious outfits showed up on his doorstep. "I began to get approached by crappy companies, by the promoters," Brillo recalls. "My initial reaction was a pleasant 'Thanks, but no thanks.' But then, in the 1980s, a lightbulb went off in my head."

Brillo realized that if a company looked truly awful, and still looked that way even after thorough efforts to uncover some redeeming qualities, there was probably money to be made shorting its stock. "Voilà!" he says. "I had a new business."

Put that way, short trading may sound simple. In reality, it's anything but. The best short traders earn their reputations (and their money) by performing extensive research on companies—not only perusing their financial statements for signs of questionable accounting but also checking on the sometimes checkered careers of their top executives. In addition, smart shorts often talk with both current and former employees, call up both vendors and customers, check state and federal court files, and wade through the records of government regulatory agencies. They also visit factories and sales outlets to see for themselves how the business actually operates. In brief, where many brokerage analysts leave off, short traders begin.

"It takes far more work to short a stock than to just buy it on an analyst's recommendation," Brillo says. Indeed, he adds a bit whimsically, "I am not sure short-trading research is a good use of a stockbroker's time. A broker who simply relies on brokerage research has twice as much time to do selling and prospecting for clients. I spend a lot of time researching. I may not be a good business model."

And as Brillo concedes, it's not only that short selling takes more work. In recent years at least, short sellers have had to buck an overall trend. The markets of the 1980s and 1990s were so relentlessly bullish that even weak companies were buoyed by the rising tide.

Internet stocks may be the prime example (at least until the first half of 2000), but many companies are selling at historically high multiples despite so-so or even somewhat soft fundamentals. With run-of-the-mill issues in the late 1990s typically selling for as much as 15 to 30 times earnings—and blue chips trading up to twice that level—even the dogs of the market commanded price/earnings ratios that would have been eye-popping just five or ten years earlier. It is worth remembering that in the 1980s—remember that long-ago time?—the price/earnings ratios of stocks were in the teens. The average stock on the S&P 500 index traded at between 10 and 13 times earnings in 1985, and between 14 and 17 times earnings at the end of the 1980s. In the late 1990s, typical blue chips were trading at more than 30 times earnings, an all-time high, which was sustained into 2001.

That the shorts may have been right about many of these companies being overvalued in the second half of the 1990s didn't do them much good. In the merger frenzy of the era, such companies often wound up being bought by other companies, usually at a premium to market. Although buyers repeatedly came to regret such acquisitions (as in the McKesson-HBO merger, discussed in an upcoming chapter), that didn't help the short trader. Too, an activity known as short busting—large owners of stock manipulating prices upwards, to rout short traders—became somewhat institutionalized.

So it was that over the course of the 1990s most shorts were driven to the wall, or over it. But not all of them. Brillo, for one, certainly managed to do all right for himself swimming against the tide. How? In the case of Koo Koo Roo Inc., he successfully bet against a company whose shareholders and management were counting their chickens before the eggs hatched.

## COCK-A-DOODLE-DOO

In the early 1990s, "everybody" in Los Angeles seemed to like Koo Koo Roo diners—and in media-crazed Los Angeles, the word "everybody" generally meant people living in the wealthier, western side of town. Koo Koo Roo was right for the "in crowd"—a fast-food chain specializing in healthy skinless marinated chicken. Even junk bond impresario Michael Milken was espied dining there frequently, a fact duly noted in Wall Street circles.

At the time, what some called the Warren Buffett school of investing was in vogue. Buffett, the billionaire investment guru, advised investors to buy shares in companies whose products or services they themselves had used and liked. The idea was to put your money into "something you could understand." By those standards, the Los Angeles–based Koo Koo Roo seemed a sure thing. Its restaurants were usually busy, and the food was pretty good. With outlets springing up slowly but steadily in upscale locations throughout southern California, it looked like a perfect candidate for national franchising—why, anybody who ate there could see that.

According to company lore, it was exactly this sort of thinking that inspired Koo Koo Roo's first chairman, Kenneth Berg. A well-heeled former mortgage banker (he had sold his title firm to Primerica in 1985 for $125 million), Berg fell in love with the bird meat in 1990, when he stopped in for a quick meal at one of the two original Koo Koo Roos, near Beverly Hills. He liked what he ate—and when he looked around at his fellow diners, he saw a clientele of generally upscale people enjoying themselves, too.

Following Buffett's dictum, Berg decided to invest. Before long, he had persuaded the restaurant's founders, brothers Michael and Raymond Badalian, to sell him half the company. His idea was to "do a Ray Kroc"—take a small hamburger stand and grow it into a McDonald's empire.

There's a world of difference between mortgages and the poultry-while-you-wait business, however. Some locations floundered. By 1991, there were five Koo Koo Roos grossing just under $4 million—that was growth, but hardly the national empire of which Berg dreamed. Berg blamed the Badalians for the tepid expansion, complaining that they had starved the menu of new items and had sandbagged moves to take the chain up-market.

Like other investors who have sunk a lot of dough into a venture without much to show for it, Berg decided to go public. It is a good way to raise capital when banks won't lend, and recoup original investments while retaining control and a major hand in any upside pots. In October 1991, Koo Koo Roo's IPO came to market at $5 a share. At that point, the Badalians decided to sell out. No one seemed to want their opinion anymore, and they didn't know how to run a big publicly held company. All they knew was how to run a restaurant that made money.

Unshackled from the chain's thrifty founders, Berg replaced Koo Koo Roo's plastic knives and forks with real silverware, put flowers on the tables, and banished the Formica. He also expanded the menu, adding lentils, stewed eggplant, cucumber salad, and other somewhat chichi items not usually consumed at fast-food joints. But Berg still could not make any money. Sales rose, from just over $5 million in 1993 to just under $40 million in 1996, but every year saw more red ink than the year before. By 1996, with some twenty-seven outlets in operation, Koo Koo Roo was posting annual losses of nearly $9.3 million.

All the same, the company was well regarded by analysts. In part, that was because of junk bond king Michael Milken. Throughout the mid-1990s, there were persistent rumors that the storied Milken would take a stake in Koo Koo Roo. In fact, Milken had looked into the idea and decided to pass. Nonetheless, *Forbes* magazine breathlessly reported that in 1996, "Milken's family trust offered to put $55 million into Koo Koo Roo, which Milken believed could become a $1 billion business."[2] It hardly mattered that Milken had never actually made such an offer. Koo Koo Roo was associated with the Milken name.

Milken or not, Koo Koo Roo at least looked like a chain that would need financing for future growth, or might be the kind to do an "industry roll-up"—the acquisition of other restaurant chains, for conversion to Koo Koo Roo. Berg was a wheeler-dealer, no doubt about that. With that bit of investment banking business possibly on the table as an appetizer, Salomon Bros. analyst Paul Westra said he liked the stock. So did Schroder Wertheim's Wayne Daniels. What could be better: good food at a chain that even the great Milken had thought would be a good investment?

According to Brillo, the positive publicity was the result of a coordinated effort by Koo Koo Roo and its backers to boost the stock. It was the public-relations end of the battle between shorts like Brillo—who thought the stock should go down—and the Koo Koo Roo shareholders and management, who wanted the stock to go up. In 1996, Koo Koo Roo's management was clearly winning the battle.

To be sure, the shorts had a lot of ammunition. The fast-food business was a mature industry, and Koo Koo Roo had been showing nothing but widening losses. But in the heady mid-1990s, PR counted a lot more than fundamentals. In the second quarter of 1996, Koo Koo Roo stock hit $10 a share, double its initial offering price.


WHAT EVERYBODY FORGOT, SAYS BRILLO, is that a company is supposed to make money. Koo Koo Roo's food was fine, he concedes. The problem was that it appealed mainly to the well-to-do—which meant its outlets had to be located in the better parts of town. "Better spots means better rents," says Brillo. While Koo Koo Roo talked of the future, Brillo read the quarterly financial reports and other disclosure documents. He thought the former mortgage banker Berg was too glib, a finance guy who didn't really understand (or care about) the prosaic side of fast food, which is that money is made in small amounts on each transaction.

Brillo thought that Berg's background explained a lot about the failings of the Koo Koo Roo model. Light, low-fat fast-food fare would work just fine in trendy spots like Beverly Hills and Brentwood (a very upscale neighborhood in Los Angeles), but in other, more meat-and-potatoes locations—which is to say, the bulk of America—it might not sell as well.

"We tend to forget that here in Los Angeles we eat differently than almost anyplace else, both in terms of variety and health consciousness," Brillo points out. "But can such a concept sell nationally? The guy in Cleveland might wonder why he has to pay $9 for some dry chicken."

Brillo was exaggerating, but only a little. The average cost of a Koo Koo Roo meal was about $8.70. This figure was disclosed in the company's financials, but nobody seemed to talk about it much—perhaps because most people who read financial statements don't think $8.70 is a lot to pay for lunch. You can sell lunch for $8.70 in Beverly Hills, where the Badalians originally set up shop. Selling fast food outside of Beverly Hills is a different proposition.

Brillo noticed that $8.70 was well above the $6 or so it cost to buy lunch at most fast-food outlets. The average tab at Boston Market, a bigger publicly held chicken outfit (which also tanked), was just $5. "Koo Koo Roo was not expensive, but it was at the high end of the fast-food range," says Brillo. "And if they were going to make money, the price would have to go even higher."

To explain Koo Koo Roo's need for higher prices, Brillo points to disclosure documents the company filed with the SEC in 1006. "The average [Koo Koo Roo] restaurant employs thirty to forty staff members," the company reported, "including an experienced full-service general manager, a skilled production chef, [and] a personnel manager, along with shift leaders, cooks, turkey carvers, salad makers, and other service personnel." It was sort of a white-collar fantasy of what a fast-food diner should be like.

Reflecting this extravagance, Koo Koo Roo's overhead sucked up an astonishing 24 percent of revenues in 1996. That was more than four times the industry norm of 5.5 percent. (Given the great disparity between Koo Koo Roo's numbers and the industry norm, one might be forgiven for suspecting that Koo Koo Roo management actually hid operating expenses by counting them as overhead so as to obscure the fact that the chain lost money on operations.) "Yeah, it was the *Queen Mary* of fast-food joints," says Brillo. "Or maybe I should say the *Titanic*."

Management promised overhead would decrease as the number of

Koo Koo Roo outlets increased, and it did somewhat. Still, Koo Koo Roo remained a gold-plated operation until the bitter end, with quirky but bulky "nonoperating" costs eating up the bottom line.

Perhaps most bizarre was Berg's decision to take the company into the art studio business. In 1996, he bought a string of ceramics shops called Color Me Mine, in which customers could paint and then fire pottery. The stores were to be located near the chicken restaurants. The theory was that Koo Koo Roo customers would flock to Color Me Mine, or vice versa, a novel sort of bird-clay synergy. The connection was lost on Wall Street, and on customers as well. "Maybe some of the plates they made in Color Me Mine could be used in the Koo Koo Roos," quips Brillo. "But they weren't close enough to share ovens. I didn't see the synergy."

Undaunted, Berg continued to promise that the numbers would improve. "It was always next year," Brillo recalls. "They always said Koo Koo Roo would make money next year."

TO KEEP ITSELF AFLOAT AMID THE rising tide of red ink, Koo Koo Roo issued more common stock, more preferred stock, more warrants, and more convertible bonds. Although all the issuing of stocks and bonds kept investment bankers well fed, the underwriting had a decidedly unfavorable impact on Koo Koo Roo shareholders. To be sure, without the fresh dough the new stocks and bonds brought in, the company would have been skewered even earlier than it was. But the new cash was a double-edged sword. Not only was the poultry purveyor losing larger amounts of money every year, but by issuing new equity and debt instruments that could be converted into equity, it was effectively diluting its stock.

"I suppose there was an upside," Brillo says with a smile. "If you looked at income on a fully diluted basis, losses per share were smaller. The red ink was getting spread out on more and more shares."

Koo Koo Roo's money-raising abilities have since become minor legend on Wall Street. In 1995, Iacocca Capital Partners L.P.—as in Lee Iacocca, the popular former Chrysler chieftain—served as placement agents for $14.3 million in common stock and warrants. (Typical of the loosey-goosey way in which shares were created by Koo Koo Roo, Iacocca himself invested only about $50,000 but ended up owning 386,500 shares.) In March 1996, $33 million in equity was raised through the sale of new convertible preferred and common stock. In February 1997, another issue of convertible preferred stock raised an additional $29 million. To put it another way, in the mid-1990s, Koo Koo Roo was able to raise more than $75 million in fresh equity capital—an amount comparable to what it booked in sales in the same time frame.

This sort of thing couldn't go on indefinitely, of course, and it didn't. To Brillo, waiting for his opportunity to short the overvalued stock, it was only a matter of time before Koo Koo Roo's skinless marinated chickens finally came home to roost. "When you look at Koo Koo Roo, you think of chicken. But you should think of turkey," says Brillo.

In Brillo's view, there were two likely trigger events: "First, they had to report their financials every quarter, and every quarter they had to report losses. The management was the type that would always promise eventual profits but could never deliver. That was setting up the eventual downfall."

And then there was the huge overhang of convertible stocks and bonds that the company had sold, often with onerous conditions. For example, the convertible preferred stock issued by the company in February 1997 contained a provision allowing for it to be converted at an increasing discount to the market price of Koo Koo Roo stock—a discount that eventually reached as much as 25 percent. In other words, as Koo Koo Roo stock floundered, the convertible was exchangeable into more and more common shares. It was an increasingly dilutive time bomb. "It was dilution, dilution, dilution," says Brillo. "If the bonds converted, it would dilute the original shareholders by more than two-thirds. There was no way the stock could stand up to a conversion like that."

And eventually the bonds did convert. By the end of 1997, Koo Koo Roo's float had increased from 15 million shares to 50 million shares on a fully diluted basis. Perhaps not too surprisingly, the price of its stock plummeted, falling from $10 in mid-1996 to as low as $1.44 in late 1997. In December, Mark Weaver of the Motley Fool

Web site wrote that Koo Koo Roo "stock certificates may be not worth more than a paper place mat."[3]

Koo Koo Roo investors got roasted alive. Stanley Brillo, who had seen the collapse coming, feasted on his winnings. "Yeah, I went out and ordered filet mignon," he said. Although Koo Koo Roo ultimately merged with several other restaurant chains (also struggling), it was delisted from the Nasdaq in February 2000 for failing to meet market capitalization requirements. The stock was trading at well under a dollar per share.

IN MOST REGARDS, HOWEVER, KOO KOO ROO was an exception. Plenty of worse-run companies did just fine on Wall Street in the 1990s, their stockholders rescued by eleventh-hour mergers, while shorts gnashed their teeth and scrambled to cover their positions. Indeed, had Koo Koo Roo enjoyed stronger institutional backing—had its stock and bond offerings been underwritten by a well-connected major investment bank rather than by the relatively obscure Santa Monica firm, Cappello Capital Corp., that handled the transactions— it might still be a winner on Wall Street, albeit under new ownership and management.

In the main, the 1990s turned shorts into an endangered species. By the summer of 1999, publisher Michael Murphy of the *Overpriced Stock Service,* a short-friendly California newsletter, was wondering aloud if anybody was reading his tip sheet anymore for anything more than academic amusement. "There are hardly any shorts left," he complained. "I'd say there is about 10 percent of the money invested in fundamental short positions compared to what there was five or ten years ago. The market ... has killed the business. Now when I talk to people about short ideas, they are politely interested, but they aren't going to do anything about it."[4]

To be sure, the short interest tables published in financial newspapers still show plenty of short action. But as Murphy points out, these tables don't reflect true, fundamental shorting. Most of the short interest they report is merely programmed investing, in which computerized trading models short certain stocks while going long on others. According to industry estimates, fully 98 percent of all short selling these days reflects such programmed trading. Hedging one's bets is actually a very conservative investment strategy.

"Actual people," says Murphy, "people who do fundamental research and then short a stock—and then stick with their convictions—they have almost gone the way of the saber-toothed tiger." In large part, that's the result of the long boom that characterized the economy in general and Wall Street in particular for most of the 1990s. Strong economic growth, fading inflation, and rising multiples are a hard combination to beat.

There is, however, more to the decline of short trading than that. The fact is, the 1990s saw brokerages, mutual funds, and other key Wall Street players declare war on shorts. Their motivation was clear. In a world where not the fundamentals but the perception of a stock has become paramount—witness Amazon.com, or Yahoo!, or the early buzz about Planet Hollywood, the Playboy surge, or an entire blue-chip sector trading at more than 30 times earnings—in such a world, the investment establishment has a very real stake in preserving "value" at the expense of incisive analysis. Short traders, with their skepticism and tendency to raise embarrassing questions, get in the way of that effort.

"You think when a brokerage analyst puts out a sell signal, it's his investment bankers who get angry?" Murphy asks. "You should see how angry the mutual funds get. A sell signal punches a hole in their holdings. And short traders do the same thing, but worse. The mutual funds and the brokerages don't want the short traders breathing."

The big boys' growing irritation with shorts led to the rise of what became known as "short busting." Although the practice has a long if not necessarily distinguished history (remember PaineWebber analyst Peter Butler's efforts to save Memory Metals), it took a big step toward informal institutionalization in 1991, when the maverick analyst Ray Dirks began publishing his *ShortBusters* newsletter. The newsletter's subscribers, who included many brokers and fund managers, comprised a kind of shareholders mafia that Dirks dubbed "the ShortBusters Club." Under his leadership, the group quickly made its presence felt on Wall Street.

The attention the ShortBusters Club attracted did not mark Dirks's first brush with celebrity. Back in 1973, he had made headlines in the notorious Equity Funding scandal. Dirks discovered that Equity Funding Corp., a giant Los Angeles–based insurance company, was actually a sham, based on certain inside, material information. What made Dirks forever controversial was his decision to privately warn his institutional clients to get out of the stock while publicly maintaining a "buy" rating on Equity Funding for the market at large (meaning ordinary investors). In a widely cited decision, the U.S. Supreme Court ruled ten years later that what Dirks did was entirely legal. Ever since, brokerage analysts have been free to get their big clients in or out of a stock before a big move without having to worry about any legal consequences. By extension, the ruling strongly reaffirmed the right of analysts to tell their big clients—the institutions, such as mutual funds, and even their own trading departments—of a pending "buy" or "sell" signal first, before telling the market as a whole.

Now Dirks saw another chance to help the big boys. By acting together, he preached, "longs" could drive short traders out of the market. When the shorts trash a stock, he said, large shareholders should band together and buy in. That will boost prices, forcing the shorts to cover their positions. In turn, that will push up prices even more. In the process, the shorts will get dirtied, and bad.

Dirks's approach was not exactly novel. The idea of trying to organize shareholders in an effort to crush shorts is as old as Wall Street. In particular, the notion of semicoordinated antishort warfare had been growing on Wall Street for perhaps twenty years, as brokerages and mutual funds grew increasingly powerful. Indeed, a few seminal battles had demonstrated the potential effectiveness of such tactics.

In the fall of 1988, for example, Charles Keating's American Continental Inc. conducted a major squeeze aimed at short traders who were loudly predicting the imminent demise of the troubled Lincoln Savings, of which American Continental was a major stockholder. Among other things, American Continental hired a proxy-solicitation firm to persuade its fellow Lincoln stockholders not to lend their shares to shorts. It also provided loans to enable Lincoln shareholders who owned stock on margin to buy their shares outright, thus making the securities unavailable for lending to shorts. The squeeze worked. For the remainder of 1988, the price of Lincoln stock went up. In the process, many shorts were routed.

As it turned out, of course, the shorts' pessimism regarding Lincoln Savings was more than justified. The thrift went belly-up the following year. Nonetheless, Keating's drive on shorts showed what could be done even in a hopeless situation.

What Dirks brought to the party was his considerable promotional skills. He ran ads touting his *ShortBusters* newsletter in financial publications, and he talked up his ideas with financial journalists, who always regarded Dirks as good copy.

Although his newsletter certainly suggested stocks prime for short busting—among them Wells Fargo, Marriott, McDonnell Douglas, and Conseco—Dirks insists he wasn't part of any coordinated effort to boost prices. And it's certainly true that money managers and brokerage bosses are an imperious, independent-minded lot, guided as much by cynicism as by the lust for profit. It is hard to get them to join a cause, any cause.

Nonetheless, at its height, Dirks's ShortBusters Club had a full-time director, claimed 2,200 members, including the largest mutual funds—among them giant Fidelity Magellan, which was widely considered the most aggressive short-busting outfit on the Street. Noted *The Wall Street Journal* in 1994: "Traders say fund managers from big mutual funds such as Fidelity Investments used the club's monthly newsletter as a tip sheet to buy heavily shorted stocks, sending the price up and punishing short sellers betting on a price decline."[5] Fidelity in public kept a straight face and insisted it bought stocks for potential appreciation, nothing more.

There is no way of knowing exactly how much capital Dirks amassed for short-busting ambushes, or how much was deployed on a battle-by-battle basis. The total certainly dwarfed the relatively meager resources of shorts, who taken as a whole probably never managed as much as $10 billion. The mutual funds alone had hundreds of billions of dollars at their disposal. Collectively, the ShortBusters could have called upon literally trillions of dollars. The short-long battle of the 1990s was like David versus Goliath, except David didn't have his sling.

Officially, Dirks's ShortBusters Club lasted only four years, disbanding in 1994 for reasons that seemed to have as much to do with Dirks's mercurial temperament and bumptious public life (he was forever embroiled in disputes with the SEC, or changing firms, or indulging in some public feud) as with anything else. But by the time ShortBusters formally called it quits, the famed Feshbach Bros., whose Palo Alto–based firm once managed $600 million—and who were seen as point men for the short-trading community—had been crushed, put out of business. "They were finished," says Michael Murphy. "And everybody else was in hiding."

The demise of the Feshbachs was a sweet triumph for Dirks. Indeed, he'd once told columnist Dan Dorfman that the only reason he started ShortBusters was to get the Feshbachs. "I like to think to some degree I turned the tide," Dirks said, reminiscing in 1999. "The Feshbachs were huge, they were smart, but they were also abusive. They were good at getting publicity. But I have some experience at that myself."[6]

According to Dirks, although the Feshbachs "lost huge" on a few deals in which "they were short on stocks that went way up," what drove them out of business wasn't their own financial losses. Rather, it was the extent to which the efforts of the ShortBusters Club scared off their clients. "By the time the Feshbachs left the business, they had only $20 million under management," says Dirks. "They didn't lose it all—most of the decrease was people leaving their fund." In other words, even if the Feshbachs themselves weren't spooked, their patrons were—and without the millions upon millions it takes to battle the large mutual funds, the Feshbachs had to bow out.

With the downfall of the Feshbachs, other short funds shriveled up as well. "The other short funds weren't as big or as smart as the Feshbachs," Murphy says. "They were just imitators. So when the Feshbachs folded up their tent, the other tents folded up, too." The shorts were busted, in other words.

In the end, Dirks and his short-busting efforts wound up fundamentally altering the landscape of Wall Street. Although the

ShortBusters Club itself was relatively short-lived, it served as a catalyst, teaching the big institutional owners and brokerage trading
departments the benefits of hardening their positions, of working
together to crush shorts.

As Charles Keating had demonstrated, it's not really all that hard
for the big boys to shut down a short-trading operation once they put
their mind to it. To begin with, since short traders have to borrow
stock before they can sell it, mutual funds and brokerages can cripple
their efforts by deciding not to lend them any. Moreover, brokerages
and funds can demand the return of shares they have previously lent
out to shorts—and, under SEC rules, a short trader must return borrowed stock when asked.

And woe to the short who has to return borrowed shares after large
fund managers have decided to push up the price of the stock he is
shorting. Remember that as the price rises, the short must cover his
position—that is, he must buy shares to replace the borrowed ones
he's required by law to return. With the big boys not selling, the short
will find that his efforts to buy only jack up prices even more.

Did it take a Ray Dirks to point out these facts of Wall Street life
to the securities industry? Not really. "If you are a large mutual fund,
you are in business to make money, and you make money by being
long on a stock," notes money manager Charles Engleberg of San
Francisco–based AmeriCal Securities. "If you see there is a lot of
short interest on a stock, and you know if you call back the stock
[from shorts to whom you've loaned shares] then the price of that
stock will go up, then you do that. That's not a conspiracy, that's just
part of the game."[7]

Of course, whether the calling back of shares is done in concert
with other mutual funds or merely with the implicit knowledge
among large market players that large short positions can be profitably exploited by callbacks, the effect is the same: the shorts will
be crushed.

And so they were. As the 1990s came to a close, only one high-
profile short trader left was on Wall Street. And even he generally
steered clear of stocks that had major brokerage or mutual fund
backing.

IN MANY REGARDS, MANUEL ASENSIO MAY have been the bravest man on Wall Street in the 1990s—a short, and in your face about it. Financial historians might someday call him the Last of the Mohicans. Asensio seems to manufacture controversy—indeed, in December 2000, the National Association of Securities Dealers (NASD) regulators sanctioned Asensio for not properly reporting short trades to monitoring agencies and for misleading advertising. He was censured and fined $75,000.

It hardly seems to matter to Asensio. While most shorts have been reduced to skulking along Wall Street's back alleys, Manuel Asensio promenades right down the middle of the street, taking on all comers. On which stocks is Asensio short? You don't have to guess—he posts his picks on his Web site (www.asensio.com) for all to see. All the stocks he has ever shorted are there, in full view. The posting bespeaks a bravado even sell-side brokerage analysts don't dare to match. A former investment banker with Bear Stearns & Co., the Cuban-born, Harvard-educated Asensio is happy to publicize his record, even in an ultrabullish era. Over the course of the 1990s, Asensio's boutique investment banking shop, Asensio & Co., targeted a total of about twenty-five companies. "Of the stocks we shorted in the 1990s," he claims, "the average decline in values is 80 percent."

Asensio's firm has a staff of six researchers, each of whom is paid what Asensio describes as being at least three to four times as much as a typical college professor. Why compare his people to college professors? "The quality of research they do is extraordinary," says Asensio. "This is not a game for amateurs."[8]

Asensio has prospered by tackling what he calls "fraudulent" companies. After he finds a company he thinks is ersatz, he researches it in detail, doing such legwork as checking management's past work histories. Once his suspicions of fraud are confirmed, he posts his conclusions on his Web site and tells anybody in the media who will listen just what he thinks. It is short trading at its most bare-knuckled.

A classic example of Asensio's technique was his 1998 attack on Turbodyne Inc., a Canadian manufacturer of turbochargers whose stock started out on the Vancouver exchange and then migrated to the

Nasdaq and put its headquarters in Woodland Hills, a suburb of Los Angeles. What piqued Asensio's interest was the startling fact that despite as best as he could tell virtually no sales of its "revolutionary" turbocharger, the company was able to boast a market capitalization approaching $700 million.

His firm's report on the company, released in August 1998, was typically blistering. "Turbodyne does not possess any patents on any ignition, combustion, fuel or intake design or product that offers engine manufacturers any new technology in emission reduction or output," it began. The report went on to charge that faith in Turbodyne products was a "false perception that has been purposely cultivated by management in order to defraud investors."

Among other things, Asensio noted that while Turbodyne claimed to have deals in the works with fourteen companies, no business arrangement had ever borne fruit. Asensio also pointed out that a man Turbodyne had identified as a United Nations official—and who had conferred "special U.N. recognition" and support upon Turbodyne for turbocharger applications in developing nations—had in fact left the U.N. before conferring the bogus recognition. Asensio concluded his report with a prediction that Turbodyne stock—then trading at $17 a share—would soon fall below $1 a share.[9]

From the short trader's perspective, Asensio's stunning summertime assault on Turbodyne amounted to a near knockout. Before August was ripped off the calendar, Turbodyne had fallen to $5 a share. In 1999, the Nasdaq investigated Turbodyne, curious about the company's pattern of news releases promising huge, pending sales and deals, but little real revenue when the dust settled. In March, the regulatory agency delisted the company, as a result of its inquiries.

As uncompromising as it was, Asensio's debunking of Turbodyne was hardly his most tumultuous such campaign. He waged an even more ferocious battle against Diana Corp., a Milwaukee-based purveyor of packed beef and pork products that in 1994 decided to transform itself into a telecommunications company.

What Diana did was buy (for $200,000) some telephone-switching technology from an outfit named Sattel Communications Corp., which had spent a mere $44,000 developing it. Over the following year, Diana launched a publicity blitz, putting out no fewer than six-teen press releases aimed at convincing the world—or at least gullible investors—that its new technology would revolutionize the tele-phone-switching capabilities of Internet service providers.

Investors took the bait. In 1996, Diana stock soared from $5 a share to as high as $120, giving the diminutive company a market cap-italization of $600 million. Suspicious of the run-up, Asensio hired an engineer to evaluate Diana's technology. On October 14, 1996, he issued a detailed analysis that concluded "it couldn't possibly live up to the company's claims."

To hear Asensio tell it, the company was nothing more than a "fraud." Indeed, he claimed that was putting it mildly. The huge in-crease in Diana Corp. shares, he said, was the result of nothing less than a conspiracy among brokerage analysts and institutional stock buy-ers. "The inordinately large stock purchases and subsequent buy rec-ommendations of a number of prominent and respected brokers and analysts could not possibly have been based on due diligence," he charged, "because even the most cursory groundwork would have revealed Diana's 'miracle Internet telephone switch' to be nothing but a cheap, unsophisticated, and obsolete product with no sales potential."

As part of *his* due diligence, Asensio had investigated the back-grounds of the executives who ran both Diana and Sattel. In the process, he found that a number of them had previously been involved with companies whose stock had suddenly shot skyward, only to collapse amid recriminations. In particular, Diana's chief executive had served as president of Summa Four Inc., a telecom-munications firm whose stock jumped by 250 percent in 1994. It later lost all the gain and 40 percent more besides in a stunning turnabout that provoked a raft of shareholder lawsuits, which were consolidated into an unsuccessful, and ultimately dismissed, class-action suit.

But Asensio was adamant that there was more to the Diana saga. "The Diana fraud required more than just a phony product and energetic promoters," he insisted. "It required the complicity of analysts and brokers who were willing to unload a grossly overval-ued security on uninformed investors." An example of this: "In July 1996, Hambrecht & Quist, whose analyst Joe Noel had been recommending Diana at more than double its still-inflated price, agreed to be retained by Diana as advisers, even after the fraud had been exposed."

Once he starts throwing punches, Asensio does not like to back off. Also in July 1996, Asensio noted, the New York–based money management firm of Dawson-Samberg Capital bought 323,000 shares of Diana stock at an average price of $31.73. "However," he reported, "Asensio & Co. discovered that Arthur J. Samberg, a principal of Dawson-Samberg, was able to purchase 20,000 [shares] of Diana's stock for his own account in a privately negotiated transaction at a cost of $20.50 a share." The private sale of stock to money managers, for their personal accounts, at below-market prices—it doesn't get much uglier than that.

Asensio went on to charge Diana and Dawson-Samberg Capital with what amounted to out-and-out stock manipulation. As Asensio told it, on October 15, 1996, the day after he published his scathing critique of Diana's technology, the company put out a press release claiming that he had more or less rigged his engineering report on its switches. Diana then arranged for trading in its stock to be halted. When trading resumed, Dawson-Samberg Capital began buying heavily, which started Diana's stock climbing again. According to Asensio, the idea was to make it seem as if the market had looked at Asensio's report and discounted it.

Usually the combined action of brokerages and money managers can sustain a stock and rout the shorts. As described earlier, the brokerages and money managers have immense financial resources and superior market intelligence. With their online systems and buddy networks, they are able to know—or at least make very good guesses about—where, when, at what price, and by whom shares are being traded.

In this case, however, Diana was so demonstrably a weak company and Asensio such a determined adversary that it was the short trader who prevailed. As Asensio sums it up, "The ruse worked only briefly. On October 16, Diana stock traded down once again. Diana was also forced to withdraw its untrue claim about our soliciting a negative research report."

Ultimately, Diana stock was delisted from the Big Board and wound up having to pay out $8 million to settle nine shareholders suits.[10]

In one sense, the Diana Corp. story should be reassuring. After all, in the end, the investor who checked the fundamentals—Asensio— was rewarded, while the promoters were exposed and punished. As far as Asensio is concerned, however, not all the bad guys got what they deserved. "I won't comment on whether there was a short squeeze on Diana," he says. "But I can tell you, people supported that stock long after it was clear it was a fraud. There were analysts who supported the stock when it was grossly overvalued, and mutual funds that bought it. I won't say more than that." When speaking about such activities in general, he wonders why the SEC does not investigate such goings-on.

Interestingly, Asensio was actually short on Biovail—of Hemant Shah fame—in 1997, and he posted the fact that he was short on his Web site (unlike Shah, who kept his short activities from the public). But Asensio changed his position after Biovail kept posting good earnings, quarter after quarter. "[Biovail] is not a fraud company," Asensio says. "We never accused that company of being a fraud company. That was a short-term short." Asensio won't say what prompted him to believe something was wrong with Biovail even in the short term, but one can make an educated guess.

AS NOTED IN CHAPTER 3, investors who follow the recommendations of brokerage analysts generally wind up underperforming the market, because brokerage analysts tend to be overly bullish about the stocks they cover. So what about short sellers? Are they routinely too bearish? As it happens, they're not. The fact is, short sellers seem to be better at stock-picking than brokerage analysts (perhaps because shorts are free of the baggage brokerage analysts carry).

According to a 1995 Harvard Business School working paper entitled "An Empirical Investigation of Short Interest," the stocks singled out by short sellers as being overvalued generally do tend to decline. After studying data on monthly short positions for all Big Board and

Amex stocks between 1976 and 1993, the paper's coauthors, Professor Paul Asquith of Yale and Professor Lisa Meulbroek of Harvard, noted finding "a strong negative relation between short interest and subsequent returns, both during the time the stocks were heavily shorted and over the following two years." Indeed, they reported that 9 percent of all companies whose stocks were heavily shorted went bankrupt or otherwise wound up being liquidated. They went on to point out that price drops are particularly pronounced among stocks "which are heavily shorted for more than one month" and that the pattern held true over the entire eighteen-year period they studied.

The overall track record of short sellers is good enough, Asquith and Meulbroek said, and prudent investors should pay close attention. "Whether or not short sellers profit ... the finding that heavily shorted stocks underperform the market has important investment implications," they noted. "If an investor already owns a stock that develops high short interest, the clear and strong advice is to sell the stock immediately." By maintaining a diversified portfolio that is resolutely culled of heavily shorted stocks, they added, investors would perform better than otherwise. With the dogs cleansed from a balanced portfolio, returns are likely to beat market averages—something mutual funds, as a rule, have not been able to do.

The Harvard study is doubly interesting because it debunks the old Wall Street myth that heavily shorted stocks must rise in price, since shorts must ultimately go out and purchase the stocks they are betting against in order to cover their positions. The belief was that the resulting buying pressure inevitably pushes up the price of shorted stocks.

Of course, the eighteen-year-period studied by Asquith and Meulbroek ended in 1993—just as short busting was becoming sport among large mutual funds and brokerages. It would be interesting to update the study, with an eye to determining whether the large brokerage/mutual fund combines have actually gained the ability to levitate stocks semi-permanently, thus reducing the predictive power of heavy short interest.

To be sure, even before 1993, the short's life was not an easy one. As Asquith and Meulbroek noted in their paper, "Prices do not adjust for long periods even though short interest is consistently high. This finding suggests that some stocks may be mispriced since available information is not incorporated." In other words, even after shorts have figured out that a stock is no good, a higher-than-justified price may persist for a time—and all the while, the shorts will remain vulnerable to having their borrowed shares called back.

With this in mind, the authors pointed out that from the standpoint of market efficiency, some of the regulations governing shorts may be too onerous. The reason, they suggested, is Wall Street's culture of optimism, which makes "short sales more costly"—which in turn "decreases the adjustment speed of prices to private information, especially to bad news." In particular, they singled out the rule that bars short sales on "down-ticks" and the one that requires shorts to return borrowed shares immediately on demand instead of within some contractually agreed upon period of time.

In the end, though, Asquith and Meulbroek concluded that the excessive optimism of brokerage analysts was hardly Wall Street's only problem. "Even if the analyst bias slows the dissemination of negative firm-specific information," they noted, "the analysis of the paper suggests that market inefficiency may run deeper."

Deeper? As deep as the unwillingness of the brokerages and mutual funds to let their stocks get trashed by a bunch of shorts, however accurate the shorts' analysis may be?

IN THE LATE 1990S AND INTO THE PRESENT, the question for investors is this: given the relatively small number of short traders left in the market who are willing to voice skepticism or otherwise provide fertile soil for contrary points of view, how is one to value stocks properly? To be sure, as we saw in the case of Hemant Shah, not all shorts are saints. Even Asensio has been rapped on the knuckles by regulators. But shorts do make a valuable contribution to the investment community—too valuable a contribution for anyone to be complacent about the extent to which the brokerages and the money managers have bullied shorts off the Street.

Indeed, Wall Street today perhaps bears resemblance to Japan's stock market of the 1980s. Seemingly nothing can bring it down. Like Japan, it is institutionally protected on the one hand, and buoyed up by the generally good economics of sustained growth and low inflation on the other. But as we saw in the 1990s, Japan's house of cards did eventually collapse—long and hard. At the end of the 1990s and into the next decade, Japan's market was still trading at roughly one-third 1980 levels.

In this vein, we would probably do well to remember the tale of legendary financier Bernard Baruch, himself an occasional short seller more than eighty years ago. Back in 1915, Baruch was dubious about the prospects of a high-tech growth company of the day, the Brooklyn Rapid Transit Co., and he was short on the stock. The company's financial reporting was spotty to say the least, but it had just hired the former governor of New York, Russell Flowers, to be its chairman. The stock quintupled on the glad tidings.

Baruch was not impressed, figuring it would take more than reputations to bring in money, and it was the fundamentals that counted. As it turned out, the public was forced to see things the same way: Flowers suddenly died, and the stock started sinking. But the Morgan, Rockefeller, and Vanderbilt trusts were backers of the stock, as powerful in their day as the combines of mutual funds, money managers, bank trust departments, and major brokerages are today. Brooklyn Rapid stock was propped up for months—perhaps allowing the trusts to exit, no one will ever know—and then plummeted. For sure, many individual investors were crushed in one of the period's many busts.

Baruch was summoned before the U.S. Congress as if he had been the miscreant, not those who hyped Brooklyn Rapid or supported the stock. The climate was against Baruch. Then as now, however, there were many in America who did not like short sellers. After the panic of 1916—in which some shorts profited hugely when wildly inflated stocks tumbled like tenpins—legislation was introduced in Congress to ban the practice.

The reaction of government and regulators then, or the regulatory panoply now in place constraining short traders, is par for the course. In principle, it is certainly odd that short sellers cannot have a contract defining when they must return borrowed shares. The SEC rules banning shorts from selling when a stock is going down are another oddity. Odd, but not unusual. At one time or another, short selling has been banned, or heavily and unfavorably regulated, by nearly every stock exchange in the world. Just as with their heroic battle to save fixed commissions, Wall Streeters love free enterprise—except in their own industry.

Fortunately, Baruch and a few others were able to talk Congress out of a complete banning of short traders. "I believe if you had a market without short-selling, that when the break comes ... and when [securities] start to fall down, there might be a crash that would engulf the whole structure," Baruch testified. "And there is also this, if I may add: that the short seller ... continuously calls the attention of the man who is long on securities or the individual who might become long, to the defects, you might say, of those securities. And you might in that way keep people from buying securities at extraordinarily high prices."

What Baruch argued then still holds true today. Regulators would do well to leave short sellers alone. Indeed, they might even consider ways to increase their role and influence, so that the market would be less likely to have huge booms followed by busts. It is the boom-bust cycle that hurts, that causes banks to extend loans that can't be repaid, and lures investors to buy when price/earnings multiples already exceed norms by double.

Unfortunately, Baruch's ideas are not much in vogue these days. Indeed, as we have seen, short sellers have been all but obliterated on Wall Street. This fact alone should give pause to those who have been socking away their retirement money in the hot stocks of the era.

# 7

# THE GOOD GUYS

S o where can investors turn for good advice and analysis? In this
era of powerful brokerages with their captive analysts and
stockbrokers, of huge institutional funds intent on preserving
the "value" of swollen portfolios, and of time-pressed media turning
to brokerage analysts for commentary, this may be the most perplex-
ing question investors face.

Today's small investors find themselves in a pickle much like that
of a would-be litigant who lives in a small town with only two lawyers
to choose between and a single courthouse. The first lawyer is well-
educated, diligent, and expert on the finer points of courtroom procedure. The second is a lazy boozer—but he's drinking buddies with,
and campaign financier for, the local judge.

In a similar way, investors must choose between independent analysts, many of whom do good, earnest work, and brokerage analysts,
whose motives may be suspect but who are powerfully connected to
fleets of stockbrokers, to brokerage trading departments, and to powerful mutual fund managers—and thus have the ability to move a
stock price, at least for a while, and to "sponsor," or support, a stock
for months and even years at a time.

There are squadrons of independent analysts watching Wall Street
who conduct fine research, run Web pages or issue newsletters or
monthly reports, and have no financial axes to grind. The problem is,
most of them specialize in mining small-cap stocks for value—and
though such issues were once regarded as "growth stocks," in recent
years most small caps have been snubbed by the big institutions. As

discussed earlier, the giant investment pools that dominate Wall Street don't buy small caps because of their thin floats and resulting lack of liquidity—not to mention the expense of employing the platoons of researchers that would be required to perform due diligence on them. Moreover, because most small-cap companies lack serious underwriting potential, mainstream brokerage analysts generally ignore them.

As a result, the small caps seriously lagged the blue chips in value for the whole of the 1990s, and into the next decade. An investor who followed the recommendations of the independent analysts and picked good-quality, undervalued small-cap stocks in the 1990s most likely fell far behind the mutual fund managers who bought blue chips. One did even better just buying blue-chip index funds.

That's not to say independent analysts should be ignored. The fact is, there are some good ones out there whose advice is usually worth considering. None of them can guarantee returns, of course, especially if the market does correct and blue-chip price/earnings multiples move down from the current 30 or so toward historical norms of about half that; if the blue chips rumble down, they'll probably squash the small caps underneath them as well. But good analysis is worth seeking out, if only to hone one's own sleuthing skills.

Herewith, a few such good guys. The following list is not intended to be complete but rather to be suggestive of the kinds of "good guys" that are out there and of how individual investors can go about ferreting out the truth about stocks on their own.


HOWARD M. SCHILIT IS A PERFECT example of what is wrong with Wall Street. That's because there is only one Schilit, and he doesn't work for any brokerage. He works for himself, on retainer for the 250 or so institutional clients who pay dearly for his research.

Time and again, Schilit has exposed publicly held companies that have juiced their earnings through telltale accounting gimmicks. These include such stunts as recording dubious receivables as actual income, counting one-time gains as operating profits, and shifting expenses out of the quarter in which they were incurred and into a later period—later, when current management may have already left, stock bonuses under arm, for new executive adventures.

Schilit knows numbers. A professor of accounting at American University and founder of the Center for Financial Research & Analysis in Rockville, Maryland, he wrote the highly regarded 1993 book *Financial Shenanigans: How to Detect Accounting Gimmicks and Fraud in Financial Reports.* In some regards, the book itself is a commentary on the reading habits of individual investors today—it barely sold, says Schilit. The financial best-sellers are books that convince investors they will be able to make a bundle on Wall Street, or select winning mutual funds.

What is most interesting about Schilit—certainly within the context of this book about Wall Street analysts—is that his financial sleuthing is performed using nothing but publicly reported numbers. Schilit doesn't have clandestine meetings with disgruntled employees, or call a target company's vendors, or try to develop a personal relationship with a company's treasurer. Nor does he hire gumshoes to learn the real deal on shipments or product quality.

Schilit will be the first to admit he has few friends in corporate boardrooms and so does not have access to inside information. Rather, he and the seven analysts who work for him simply comb through publicly available financial reports filed with the SEC and other regulatory agencies. It's there they find the dirt: hiding right out in the open, where anyone (especially brokerage analysts) could see it, if they knew how to look—or didn't deliberately look the other way.

Wall Street analysts detest Schilit. It's easy to see why. He points out what they should have red-flagged but didn't. And he makes it look easy. A classic case in point was Schilit's 1997 debunking of HBO & Co. (now McKesson-HBOC), an Atlanta-based designer of computer software for the health care industry. What Schilit did with HBO was what he usually does with companies that catch his notice: he just followed his nose.

What piqued his interest was that HBO was thriving in an industry that had been going through wrenching economic changes. Throughout the 1990s, insurance companies, HMOs, and government programs such as Medicare cut way back on how much they were willing to reimburse doctors and hospitals for their services. As a result, health care became a famously slow-paying industry. But while everyone else in the sector seemed to be struggling, HBO was growing like Topsy—or so it claimed. Largely as a result of acquisitions, the company reported an astonishing 55 percent year-to-year increase in revenues.

When one firm buys a lot of other similar firms in the same field, it is said to be "doing an industry roll-up." Wall Street loves roll-ups. They mean big fees for investment bankers, who perform advisory work in mergers and acquisitions and arrange for new issues of stock and bonds to finance acquisitions. But for investors, there is a problem. "Roll-ups get sloppy when they keep buying, especially if it is the only way to boost numbers," says Schilit. "The due diligence [on acquired companies] begins to fade."[1] As he once told *BusinessWeek* magazine, "It is not a question of will a roll-up blow apart. It's almost always a question of when."

Armed with these insights, Schilit went looking for more hints of what was really going on at HBO. He didn't have to go far. He had only to read the quarterly financial reports the company filed with the SEC (financial disclosure statements for all companies are now available to all at www.sec.gov). On April 14, 1997, Schilit's Center for Financial Research issued an eight-page report that was sharply critical of HBO. In it, Schilit noted that though HBO's receivables were getting older and older (which is to say its customers were taking longer and longer to pay their bills), the company was booking more and more receivables as current income.

To be sure, in the often arcane world of accounting, it can be kosher to count unpaid receivables as income. But some judgment is required. If a company's receivables are aging over time, something may be amiss. At the very least, a portion should be set aside as a reserve and not counted as income. As almost anybody who ever ran a business knows, the older your receivables get, the less chance you have of ever getting paid in full, if at all.

HBO's receivables were certainly getting older. At the end of 1995, their average age was 80 days. By the first quarter of 1997, that figure had grown to 115 days. Yet the company blithely continued counting them as revenue. Even worse, as its receivables got older, the proportion the company set aside as a reserve against bad debts got smaller, dropping from 5.01 percent in 1995 to just 3.16 percent in 1996.

Word of Schilit's report leaked out on April 15, and HBO stock took a 25 percent haircut. The mainstream Wall Street analysts who followed HBO didn't just ignore what Schilit had to say. To the contrary, they attacked him—viciously. No fewer than six analysts lambasted his report publicly, three of them actually issuing written rebuttals that impugned Schilit and his ethics. HBO officials derided him as a short. In fact, Schilit and troops abstain from speculating in stocks they cover.[2]

On April 16, 1997, analyst Dirk Godsey of Hambrecht & Quist told the *Atlanta Journal and Constitution,* HBO's hometown newspaper, that the company's fundamentals were strong. "They just reported solid earnings," Godsey said. "They had a great quarter."

Two days later, Michael Samols of Robertson, Stephens (now Banc of America Securities) charged that Schilit's report "contains significant errors, regurgitates old news, and demonstrates poor judgment." Samols also issued a written report of his own rebutting Schilit's conclusions. For some reason, his brokerage declines to make copies of it available anymore.

Analyst Scott A. Remley of Robinson-Humphrey, a regional brokerage headquartered in Atlanta, echoed Samols almost word for word. Schilit's findings, he claimed, were filled with "numerous factual errors and/or information that is irrelevant to the [company's] fundamentals."

In fact, Schilit's report was not erroneous, nor did it contain any factual errors. It was only a careful review of financial numbers that HBO had filed with the SEC, pointing out the aging receivables and the decrease in reserves for bad debts. HBO was selling to an industry that was struggling with declining reimbursement for services rendered. Those were facts, not judgment calls.

Just over a year later, in August 1998, Schilit issued a second report on HBO. This time the reaction of mainstream brokerage analysts was strangely muted. Maybe their big institutional clients had gotten out of HBO already. Once again, Schilit reported that HBO's receivables were getting older and older—they averaged 118 days in the second quarter of 1998, compared to 110 days in the same period a year earlier. Moreover, HBO was now counting as income something it called "unbilled receivables."

If this wasn't novel accounting, it surely was on the creative side of the fence. "Unbilled receivables" were monies that HBO believed it was owed under existing contracts but for which it hadn't yet even billed customers. The company did not reveal exactly how it had calculated this income, leaving shareholders in the dark.[3]

Not surprisingly, HBO's cash flow—that is, the amount of real money coming in—was declining. In the second quarter of 1998, cash flow from operations fell to 54 percent of reported income; in previous quarters, it had sometimes actually exceeded revenues. For better or worse, the company was accumulating piles of receivables, under complicated contracts that might or might not be contested, with customers who might or might not pay.

Schilit's second report also mentioned some unusual charges, or reversals of previous charges, taken by HBO. They all pointed to a company trying to "make numbers" quarter by quarter.

Despite all the problems, shareholders in HBO lucked out in January 1999, when San Francisco–based health care services giant McKesson Corp. bought the company in a $14 billion stock swap. The deal was vetted by two top-line investment banking firms: Bear Stearns for McKesson and Morgan Stanley Dean Witter for HBO. Evidently, no one at McKesson and none of the investment bankers read Schilit's work, or if they did, they resolutely ignored it.

For HBO shareholders, the buyout was proof of the sports adage "It's better to be lucky than to be good." (As mentioned, it is also a reason why short trading is so difficult. A crappy company can be bought out at a premium.) But for McKesson shareholders, now shareholders of McKesson-HBO, it was as if a Trojan horse had been let into the compound.

It took barely three months before the real story came to light. In April 1999, McKesson was forced to report that more than $44 million in previously recorded revenues didn't exist. The problem was—

you guessed it—bogus revenues reported by HBO. With annual revenues totaling $21 billion, McKesson was big enough to take the hit, a loss of $44 million representing merely a nick, not a gouge, in its profits.

But after that, a lot started to look ill at McKesson-HBO. With more and more revenues of the former HBO beginning to look suspect, the McKesson-HBO board dismissed the chairman, Charles McCall (who was from the HBO side of the aisle), and the chief executive officer, Mark Pulido, resigned. Other executive heads rolled, and four major accounting firms were brought in to try to clean up the mess. Talk was of restating profits going back two years, and earnings forecasts going forward were reduced. McKesson-HBO stock, which had peaked at $90 a share in 1998, then traded around $65 before irregularities were publicly announced, fell to $33. About $10 billion of market capitalization evaporated in the last tumble, and $10 billion before that, when the stock evidently drifted in anticipation of the bad news.

Now even the mainstream analysts wondered aloud. Anthony Vendetti, a Gruntal & Co. analyst, said McKesson-HBO wasn't returning his phone calls, and so he couldn't find out what was going on. But Kenneth Abramowitz, an analyst with Sanford C. Bernstein & Co., held out hope that Year 2000 problems were delaying some payments to McKesson-HBO and the situation could improve in the new millennium. Interestingly, McKesson-HBO stock never really recovered from the financial accounting fiasco, and into fall 2000 the company's stock traded in the $25-a-share range.

A question about the McKesson-HBO situation begs to be asked: How come only Schilit called it? Schilit may be a smart forensic accountant, but he is only human. There are plenty of brokerage analysts loaded with business and accounting degrees just as impressive as his, plenty of other analysts with brains to burn. So why does it so often seem as if Schilit's firm is the only one that can ferret out financial shenanigans? What about all those highly paid analysts at the major Wall Street brokerage houses?

Like so many other knowledgeable observers of the securities industry, Schilit answers the question by noting the Wall Street imperative to make money on investment banking. "In general, we are better trained in understanding the quality of earnings than most analysts," he says. "But there are a lot of analysts out there, so why aren't at least some of them finding out what we find out? The answer is what you would expect. Their compensation is driven by being friendly to the investment bankers, helping them generate deals. Their jobs, their careers would be placed in jeopardy if they wrote reports that killed important investment banking relationships. HBO, with its rollups, was a good investment banking client."

Schilit adds, "Not only will analysts be silent about the problems we pointed out, the analysts will dutifully write rebuttal after rebuttal in order to endear themselves to clients such as HBO."

Schilit is a particular fan of watching cash flow, accountant talk for real money coming in the front door. Companies that have worsening cash flows bear close inspection.

Unfortunately for average investors, Schilit does not sell his services cheaply. That's why almost all his subscribers are institutions. However, Schilit does have an instinct for fairness that seems to be common among those who rummage through corporate reporting, and he says he will eventually begin posting his reports on the Internet, perhaps with a six-week delay.

The delay may seem unfair, for the stocks Schilit criticizes typically drop by about half following his initial report. But Schilit says the market is slow on the uptake, and many stocks don't fall for several months. In the meantime, investors should watch cash flow, and keep checking the Internet to see if Schilit's Center for Financial Research & Analysis has launched its Web site.

ANOTHER VALUABLE RESOURCE FOR small investors is the Red Chip Review, a seven-year-old Portland-based research house devoted to covering small-cap stocks—or as the firm likes to put it, "Discovering tomorrow's blue chips today." Red Chip makes its money solely by selling research, not by investment banking. Individual investors or institutions can subscribe to its reports, either online or through regular delivery of monthly bulletins. Investors familiar with *Value*

*Line*'s monthly updates, which fit into a three-ring binder, will instantly recognize the Red Chip Review format.

Red Chip is run by Marcus Robins, a former analyst and money manager who, along with his wife and six students from a popular investment class he taught at Portland State University, started the business in his basement in 1993. By 1999, the firm boasted a staff of thirty.

Although there are more than 8,000 small-cap stocks traded in U.S. public markets, Red Chip focuses on what it considers the 300 or so best of them—and it often has the field to itself. "Most small-cap stocks have nobody, or just one analyst, covering them," says Robins.[4]

In promoting its services to subscribers, Red Chip reminds investors what has always been true about small caps: that because they are undercovered, there must be some gems in the rough waiting to be found. Robins puts it this way: "Investors haven't been able to track individual small-cap stocks the way they have followed the blue chips. [As a result,] small-cap stocks are inefficiently priced. In other words, the price you pay for any given small cap may be artificially low because few investors know about it. Analysts for big Wall Street investment firms don't follow the small caps. The financial press doesn't write about them. And thus the market doesn't accord them the value they deserve."

It's a persuasive argument. But it also raises a troubling question. Isn't the undervaluing of small-cap stocks likely to grow even worse as the power of large brokerages and mutual funds continues to increase?

Robins concedes that mutual funds and brokerages are increasingly able to influence market prices, evidently for years at a time. But he believes the fundamentals will eventually rule. Good-quality small-cap companies with steadily growing earnings, he insists, should appreciate more in the years ahead than blue chips, with their outsized price/earnings ratios.

"I don't know if it will take a market meltdown," he says, "but you will see a shift in the trend of the market. You will see a return to old-fashioned analysis and emphasis on the fundamentals."

Another perhaps less satisfying but equally likely scenario is that small-cap companies, seeking recognition on Wall Street Major, will merge or be acquired in industry roll-ups. Clumped together, small-cap companies could become large enough to warrant investment banking attention from the big brokerages and liquid enough for the big mutual funds.

"If only a small fraction of the huge pool in mutual funds becomes devoted to small caps, you will see huge appreciation," predicts Robins.

Robins is a great believer in investor discipline. By following certain principles, he says, individual investors (or even smaller institutions) can identify the sort of small caps that might one day become big caps. Robins calls these potential blue-chip stocks "red chips" (hence his firm's name), and he says they can be distinguished by the following characteristics:

➤ 20 percent compounded annual growth rate
➤ 20 percent return on investment
➤ Less than 20 percent ownership by institutions
➤ More than 20 percent ownership by insiders

In addition to looking for these basic criteria, Robins likes to visit corporate headquarters and kick the tires—almost literally. A favorite pastime of his is to check out the top executives' automobiles in the company parking lot. "If you see the top guy is driving a Ferrari and acting like a little king, then you know there are risks there," he says. "With a small-cap company, the company often is the chief executive." (Robins notes with pride that his company's original office furniture, handmade from plywood, is still in service.)

For small-cap investors and devotees of Red Chip, the good news is that the firm's research can hit home runs. In just the first seven months of 1999, stocks identified as "top picks" by Red Chip analysts appreciated by 44.5 percent, easily besting market averages.

Be forewarned that 1999 was an unusually good year for Red Chip Review. Robins admits 1998 was a bust, as Wall Street shunned small caps, along with anything else with the whiff of risk about it. Indeed, when the performance of the firm's picks is compared to that of the

S&P 500 as a whole, the whole second half of the 1990s was tough for Red Chip.

As noted, it remains very difficult to make money on Wall Street as a research-only shop. As 1999 came to a close, Red Chip announced it had been acquired by Roth Capital Partners, an Orange County, California–based securities brokerage and investment banking shop. But Robins and Byron Roth, chairman of the brokerage, both insisted that Red Chip independence was sacred and would not be affected by the merger. The Web site is www.redchip.com.

MARK HULBERT, FOUNDER OF *Hulbert's Financial Digest,* doesn't research small-cap *or* big-cap stocks. What he does is gauge the performance of investment newsletters and report which of them have the best track records (and, by inference, which have the worst). His *Financial Digest* is a valuable resource for stock market players who base their investment decisions on what the newsletters have to say.

As anyone who has ever contemplated buying investment advice knows, it seems every investment newsletter claims it contains crucial news of immediate import—and that its picks outperform the market. The good news is that some actually do, at least during a bull market.

The bad news, as Hulbert's ratings demonstrate, is that most don't. And even more deliberately muddy the waters by making their advice blurry or conditional, which allows them to claim to have made the right call if things break right or to have stayed on the sidelines if they don't.

Like many other professional skeptics who specialize in pointing out the emperor's lack of clothing, Hulbert is regularly vilified by the people he writes about. In 1998, for example, a group of newsletter writers started a rumor that Hulbert was "under investigation by the SEC." As it turned out, SEC investigators had been in contact with Hulbert—but only to check the claims of a newsletter author who had run ads touting his tip sheet as being "Number One With Hulbert." Hulbert confirmed the claim, and the investigators went away satisfied.

It seems no calumny is too base to dump on Hulbert's head. James

Dines of *The Dines Letter* has been particularly vicious, suggesting that Hulbert has "dined out on English beef" (i.e., contracted Mad Cow disease), that he has "discovered a new use for old clothes—he wears them," and even that Hulbert's baby was said to resemble its father ... until it was turned faceup. Maybe it should be mentioned that Dines's standing in the newsletter world fell a bit in the 1990s, and Hulbert's narrow-eyed assessments didn't help. Such personal attacks, needless to say, do not alter the numbers on which Hulbert's ratings are based or the conclusions he draws from them.

Hulbert found his vocation when he attended an investment seminar in New Orleans in 1979. Fresh out of Oxford University, armed with a master's degree in philosophy, politics, and economics, he found himself bewildered by a slew of newsletter authors, all of whom claimed titanic profit records. In those pre-Internet days, newsletters were red-hot. It sometimes seemed as if every other former financial journalist or disaffected analyst was talking about starting a new one. (The goal, according to the mantra of the day, was "getting 1,000 subscribers—that's all you need—at $200 each.")

Hulbert's idea of offering a "newsletter on newsletters" was a hit from the start. Over the years, he has become a regular on financial-news television shows, a columnist for *The New York Times*, and a favorite source of quotes for financial journalists. He even has a popular Web site (www.hulbertdigest.com).

What studying the Annandale, Virginia–based *Hulbert's Financial Digest* will teach you is that very few newsletters outperform the market over extended periods, the same result obtained by mutual funds and brokerage analysts (the latter actually manage to *under*perform the market, of course). Even the newsletter ranked No. 1 for performance in 1999, *The Prudent Speculator*, just barely beat the Wilshire 5000 index over the fifteen-year period ended June 30, 1999—and in any case, it experienced considerably more volatility than the market as a whole. By volatility, market professionals generally mean a "more volatile" portfolio will tend to go up more than market averages in a bull market and down more in a bear market. Moreover, *The Prudent Speculator* at times recommended taking margin positions—a risky strategy that's not for everyone and that exaggerates volatility.

Still, there are newsletters with eye-popping returns for those willing to get killed in downturns in exchange for beating the upsurges. As of mid-2000, for example, the newsletter *OTC Insight* had posted a 36.6 percent annually compounded returns on its recommendations—for the previous ten-year period. Not a fluke, and not bad, although it should be noted that in the summer of 1998, when stocks weakened, *OTC Insight* stocks nosedived. It's a good-times newsletter.

After two decades of rating and ranking Wall Street tip sheets, *Hulbert's Financial Digest* seems to confirm for newsletters what innumerable academic and industry studies have found to be the vexing reality: measured long enough, the performance of virtually any selection scheme will regress to slightly below market averages, or somewhat worse. The fact is, the very best performing newsletters of the past ten and fifteen years have all relied on strategies much riskier than investing in an index fund, yet have barely beat the indexes, and even then they have occasionally underperformed the indexes. Hulbert's conclusion: "I tell people to put a large portion of their stock investments into index funds. And to not have all of their investments in the stock market."[5]

MARKETS WORK EFFICIENTLY ONLY IF investors are well informed and behave rationally. But as well-known Wall Street contrarian David Dreman points out, investors are neither omniscient nor always rational. As a result, inefficiencies inevitably emerge—and where there are inefficiencies, he notes, there is an opportunity to make money.

Dreman has spent a professional lifetime following a common-sense rule: If everybody is hot to buy something, then that something is probably overpriced. Similarly, if no one is interested, it's probably underpriced.

If there were a Dreman's Law, it would probably read something like this: "Buy solid companies that appear to be out of market favor, as measured by their low price-to-earnings, price-to-cash-flow, or price-to-book-value ratios or high yields."

Among Dreman's more valuable nuggets of wisdom: Don't make

investment decisions based on a past trend of correlations. In other words, beware of the new mutual fund that claims to be a sure thing because it has "back tested" its strategy, plugging in historical data to see how the fund might have performed over the past five or ten years. The problem with such claims, Dreman points out, is that history never quite repeats itself. If it did, gold would be selling at several times its current price, and investments in Japan would be booming. Neither, of course, is the case.

Dreman also recommends that investors diversify, perhaps considering junk bonds for yield, and avoid investing in IPOs, which as a group have a long track record of underperforming the market—Dreman cites academic studies that the median return on IPOs from 1970 to 1990 was minus 37 percent.

What about hot IPO issues? Forget about it. "[N]obody but the largest money managers, mutual funds, or other major investors" can buy into those, Dreman says, and they usually do so solely for the purpose of flipping out—à la Planet Hollywood.

For those with fortitude, Dreman suggests jumping into the market during and right after a major world crisis, such as the Persian Gulf War or the summer 1998 meltdown of Asian financial markets. To learn more, you can read Dreman's book, *Contrarian Investment Strategies: The Next Generation.* Or you can put your money where his mouth is, via his Dreman Value Management LLC, in Red Bank, New Jersey.


FOR NEARLY SEVENTY YEARS NOW, the *Value Line Investment Survey* has been the stock market bible for many an inveterate investor, particularly those inclined to do their own stock picking. Indeed, *Value Line's* six-inch-thick, black three-ring binder with gold print—in which data-laden monthly installments are stored—has been a staple of stock market warrens for generations. It can be found in most public libraries and at virtually every business school. There is a good reason for all this. In terms of objective, impartial research, *Value Line's* seventy analysts are unparalleled, and its investment formulas seem to bear fruit in a steady if unspectacular fashion.

Founded in 1931, Value Line Publishing Co. ranks some 1,700 stocks in ninety industries according to what the company calls its Timeliness Ranking System. Although this system has been in use since 1965, it is still considered a recent innovation in Value Line circles and in company literature. Stocks are ranked by computerized formula, based on earnings performance of the past twelve months, and safety. Stocks with greater volatility—stocks that gyrate more than market norms—get lower rankings, in general. The Timeliness System was an effort to induce some element of "when to buy" into *Value Line* surveys, which historically just ranked companies by quality. Even yet, the prevailing *Value Line* temperament is to buy and hold, not trade. If you buy a true quality company and hold, when you buy doesn't matter that much, in the world of *Value Line* investors.

And in 1983, *Value Line* also introduced a "Technical Ranking," based on a stock's price performance in the last fifty weeks. This was probably a concession to the reality that there is a lot of "momentum" buying today on Wall Street, and so when a stock gets hot, more investors are drawn off the sidelines and into the stock, sustaining the upward push for a while longer.

Not surprisingly, *Value Line* is highly rated by *Hulbert's Financial Digest*. Indeed, as heralded by *Barron's* in July 2000, *Value Line* has outperformed every other newsletter rated by Hulbert for the twenty-year period ended June 2000.[6] For investors who believe in solid companies and think in terms of years and decades, Value Line may be just the ticket.


TECHNICALLY SPEAKING, BURKENROAD REPORTS IS a student project. However, its research is as professional as you'll find. Founded in 1993, Burkenroad Reports is produced by a group of undergraduate and graduate students at Tulane University's A. B. Freeman School of Business. It focuses mainly on small- and mid-cap stocks issued by companies in the southeastern United States. Most of these stocks are ignored by Wall Street Major and are only sporadically covered by the declining number of regional brokerages in the Southeast.

Pressing the flesh and looking at facilities is an important part of the

Burkenroad routine. "We meet with top management, visit company sites, and publish investment research reports, which are sent to more than 3,000 individual and institutional investors," says Professor Peter Ricchiuti, who supervises the Burkenroad project.[7] Among other things, Ricchiuti teaches his crew of budding analysts that corporate managers, bogged down in their own work, are often unaware of competitive developments at rival firms or that a vendor may be getting ready to hike prices. As a result, he trains his students to contact a company's competitors and vendors in search of information that management would not necessarily disclose—or even know about.

The reaction to Burkenroad's work from money managers is more than encouraging. According to Ricchiuti, a typical response is, "You may not be that experienced, but at least you are objective. With brokerage analysts, you wonder if the whole thing is just predicated on future corporate finance deals. I would rather have what you offer, knowing it was put together without an ax to grind."

Indeed, some of Burkenroad's "buy" recommendations are almost endearing. Take SCP Pool Co., a Covington, Louisiana, swimming-pool-supply outfit that the collegiate analysts recommended at the beginning of 1999. As the Burkenroaders noted, SCP Pool had some real muscle. It was the largest company in an easily understood industry, and it was making careful acquisitions. It was also buying back its stock. Based on its analysis, Burkenroad predicted the company's annual earnings would hit $1.31 a share in 1999, up from $1.10 the previous year. At the time, the stock was trading at $15.125—just 11.5 times earnings. It was, in other words, a good, old-fashioned small-cap growth stock—and trading for a commonsense multiple, to boot! By the summer of 1999, SCP Pool stock was trading at $26.25. Not a bad recommendation, by anyone's standard.

Because of their good financials, many Burkenroad picks turn out to be good takeover candidates. Indeed, of the thirty-six companies Burkenroad covered in 1999, six were acquired by larger firms in the first eight months of the year, all at premiums to market. Obviously, without investment bankers to feed (and influence their judgment), the Tulane stock pickers can concentrate on spotting good investments.

The principles they follow make eminent sense. Before they put a "buy" signal on a stock, it must meet a number of stiff criteria, among them the following:

➤ Low price-to-book-value and price/earnings ratios, compared with the average for small-cap stocks

➤ Relatively low proportion of institutional ownership

➤ Heavy management ownership of stock

➤ Little analyst coverage

➤ A price/earnings ratio that is less than projected three-year earnings-per-share percentage growth rate—i.e., a stock trading at 15 times earnings should have an annually compounded growth rate exceeding 15 percent

➤ Some catalyst for change, such as new management, or some new ability to deliver a product for less, or some new but tested and increasingly successful business venture

Not surprisingly, Burkenroad graduates find themselves in demand on Wall Street. Over the past several years, many have gone to work for major brokerages. One wonders how well their sterling training and freewheeling analysis are appreciated in the big leagues.

STANDARD & POOR'S IS ANOTHER ONE of those stalwart Wall Street names whose reputation actually turns out to be well earned. Its main claim to fame is its daily stock index known as the S&P 500, and its main business is rating corporate bonds. But S&P is also one of Wall Street's premier research shops. An excellent repository of information and advice for the individual investor, the firm has offered first-rate securities analysis since before the Civil War, its work untainted by any involvement in either the brokerage or underwriting businesses.

Of particular interest to individual investors, S&P maintains a user-friendly Web site (www.personalwealth.com) that contains a remarkable plethora of financial and investment information, all of it accessibly written and concise—and much of it available at no charge to anyone who logs on. There are free tutorial pages for neophytes, and market commentary and economic overviews for more sophisticated sorts. One can even construct an online portfolio and then check in at any time during trading hours to see how it's doing.

For the modest price of a subscription, one can access a broader array of recommended stocks, plus thick industry reports. But that may be overkill. The S&P site offers enough free information and advice to overwhelm all but the most addicted Wall Street junkies. Indeed, the site is so well packaged, authoritative, and free of conflicts of interest that it is difficult to recommend that anyone pay for investment advisory or tip services at S&P or elsewhere.

The site's core strengths are its respect for fundamental analysis and healthy skepticism of Wall Street fads and company proclamations. Perhaps most important (and delightful), it is not reluctant to pan stocks or summarily remove lagging mutual funds from its "recommended" lists.

To take a day more or less at random, consider the downbeat report S&P analyst Howard Choe wrote about shoe retailer Just For Feet Inc. on August 25, 1999. Justifying the two-star (or "avoid") rating he gave the company, Choe noted, "Sales rose 29 percent, but cost of goods sold surged to 70 percent of sales as heavy markdowns were necessary to lower inventories ... Northeast superstores performing below plan ... Stock trading at historic lows but has little attraction with co.'s poor sales trends and losses."

On the same day Choe stepped on Just For Feet, another S&P analyst, Mark Cavalone, reiterated his "avoid" rating on the shares of Canadian-based Newbridge Networks Corp., a maker of computer networking equipment. The problem: "balance sheet weaknesses" were too glaring to justify even a "hold" on the stock.

Contrast these crisp no-confidence votes with the woozy cheerleading efforts that Bear Stearns, Wertheim Schroder, and other brokerage analysts conducted on behalf of Planet Hollywood, or Credit Suisse First Boston and ING Barings's relentless drumbeating on behalf of Playboy Enterprises. Interestingly enough, on the same day that Cavalone urged caution regarding Newbridge Networks, BancBoston Robertson Stephens analyst Paul Silverstein reiterated a "buy" recommendation for the stock—of course, as a research-only firm, S&P doesn't have to worry about keeping the investment bankers happy.

Standard & Poor's is not even averse to financially slugging an initial public offering in the nose. On its August 7, 2000, Web site, S&P analyst Mark Basham called ChipPAC, a semiconductor chip packaging company slated to go public later in August, underwritten by Credit Suisse First Boston, a stock to avoid. Basham noted the company had reported improving profits but that black ink increased only because of a change in the estimated depreciable lives of equipment and machinery from five to eight years. This resulted in depreciation expenses for the quarter being $6.7 million lower than they would have been otherwise. "Importantly, we have serious doubts that the actual useful life of the company's equipment is eight years. Competitor Amkor Technology depreciates its equipment over three to five years." Now that is a report worth reading.

Not all is doom and gloom at S&P. The firm also makes its share of "buy" recommendations and upgrades. Its Web site even contains a list of "10 Hot Stocks." S&P, in other words, is no den of bears. It is simply an impartial investment service willing to call the game as it sees it.

THESTREET.COM IS MAYBE A LITTLE TOO SMART or glib for its own good. Certainly, you don't have to spend much time at this Web site to get the impression that it is run by a bunch of New Yorkers who think they are smarter than the market, or at least smarter than a lot of the morons in it. They may be right on the latter count—though, of course, it takes more than talking tough and being smart to beat the market.

The point is, TheStreet.com isn't afraid to put the needle into the balloon of Wall Street fads, an attitude the market—and investors—can always use more of.

For example, writing in the summer of 1999, a time when Internet stocks dominated the IPO game—and when big first-day price run-ups were still common—Street columnist Herb Greenberg had no compunctions about tearing into one new Internet issue that had soared for no reason other than the general enthusiasm for companies with a dot-com in their name. "Pump and dumpers are having a field day … at the expense, no doubt, of the little guy, who will almost certainly get walloped," he warned. "Anything, and I mean anything, that goes up that quickly—on a relatively small float—almost always falls just as quickly, if not faster, after this kind of buying frenzy." Of course, Greenberg was pretty much validated by the dot-com meltdown of 2000.

Such adversarial writing is not often seen in most print financial journals, and certainly not in the mainstream dailies, in which the determination to be neutral or "objective" often seems to mean not tipping off readers to what amounts to legal fraud (*Barron's* and *Forbes* deserve recognition for looking underneath rocks on occasion). Perhaps this is because Web culture prefers putting the reader and the writer next to each other and then butting out. Or maybe TheStreet.com simply has smarter writers who are more confident about taking on Wall Street. Whatever the reason, the sort of blunt commentary favored by TheStreet.com is more valuable for investors.

Like S&P's Web site, TheStreet.com contains tons of information about virtually every aspect of the market. But while the S&P site basically provides what amount to well-written reports from a research house, TheStreet.com's offerings read more like journalism, with knives unsheathed, on occasion. TheStreet.com has a sharper edge than S&P, more often—and more enthusiastically—bringing hidden corporate problems to light and more willingly labeling aggressively touted IPOs as overheated.

To be sure, however enterprising they may be, the site's reporters are not likely to ferret out more than a fraction of the duds posing as winners on Wall Street. Still, it's an excellent source of information for investors who like to feel they are a part of the market and want to immerse themselves in Wall Street culture, or at least the Web version of such.

CHICAGO-BASED ZACKS INVESTMENT RESEARCH, well known for the data it compiles on consensus earnings estimates, maintains an excellent Web site (www.zacks.com) that offers an essential piece of information that investors can't get anywhere else: an objective ranking of the best-performing security analysts.

Unlike Major League Baseball players, whose batting averages are routinely and widely printed in the newspapers almost every day in season, brokerage analysts have never been publicly ranked on the basis of their earnings estimates and trading recommendations. Until recently, the closest analysts came to this sort of scrutiny was *Institutional Investor* magazine's annual "all-star" survey. Unfortunately, "Eye-Eye" compiles its rankings on a somewhat clubby basis, using such subjective criteria as "industry knowledge" and "accessibility" (to institutional clients). As a result, it is all but worthless to individual investors.

Now Zacks has come to the rescue, with a Web site that ranks the top ten analysts in forty-eight different industry groups, based not on their relationships with money managers but on the accuracy of their forecasts and/or the quality of their "buy" recommendations. (Alas, Zacks does not rank the worst analysts.)

It shouldn't be surprising that there is much on the Zacks Web site to daunt investors who want to follow analyst recommendations. Since 1998, Zacks has constructed a stock portfolio made of "analysts' top picks." These are stocks that are followed by more than three brokerage firms and are currently recommended as a "Strong Buy" by each of the analysts following the company.

The results are ugly. In 1998, the analysts' portfolio fell 11.5 percent, compared with an 8.2 percent contraction of the Russell 2000 index and a 28 percent increase in the S&P 500. In the first eleven months of 1999, the analysts' top-picks portfolio fell another 12 percent, versus a 7.6 percent increase in the Russell 2000 index and a 19 percent increase in the S&P 500. Indeed, investors who went along with analysts' top picks in 1998 and 1999 lost 22.1 percent of their portfolio, cumulatively and still counting. They also missed a historic bull market.

Wonderfully informative, the Zacks Web site represents a huge step in the direction of bringing accountability to a profession that has long avoided scrutiny. However, the Web site is not always user-friendly, and its analysts' rankings are updated only twice a year. Unfortunately, it remains easier to judge the performance of any Major League Baseball player than to know the stock market batting average of even major analysts. Given the increasing millions of Americans who are betting on the stock market, in retirement accounts and to finance their children's education, one might well wonder at such a situation. Surely the media could educate and then regularly inform readers as to which analysts have good stock "buy" signals. But then, the huge national brokerages have become major media advertisers.

Nevertheless, for now, by carefully reading the Zacks site, an investor can figure out which stocks have the blessing of the few analysts who sport winning records. Whether those records will mean anything over the long haul, of course, remains to be seen.

For investors who want specific stock trading advice based on continuously updated track records, there is finally an answer: the Pasadena, California–based iExchange.com (www.iexchange.com). It is a self-described "democratic" site in which anyone with an online computer can either become a guru or seek out a guru's advice. "You can have your CFA [chartered financial analyst badge] or you can be Joe Sixpack. We will hold you accountable and rank your performance," said David Eisner, president and CEO of the new online business. "We add the attributes of online—it's fun, and everyone is equal—to accountability."[8]

The heart of iExchange is its ranking system. Analysts select stocks and pick target prices and dates by which those prices should be breached—and post their selections on the site. Then iExchange ranks the quality of the selections, based on performance, from the investor point of view. It is hoped that over time, analysts with proven track records will develop followings and get a lot of "hits."

It is perhaps surprising to learn that Frank Baxter, chairman of Jefferies & Co., a brokerage based in Los Angeles, is an investor in iExchange. Doesn't iExchange pose a threat to brokerages, which have long used analyst recommendations to help sponsor initial public offerings and other investment banking business? Is Baxter hedging his bets?

"Well, you are subscribing to the fallacy of displacement," said

Baxter. "For example, that television would displace movies or radio. Not every good idea wipes out other good ideas."

A big part of a brokerage analyst's job is to maintain good relations and a flow of information to large institutional trading clients and to work with the investment banking department in helping to sell deals. That turf is not iExchange.com's, points out Baxter. So there will be room for iExchange, brokerage analysts, and even more market watchers in the future, predicted Baxter. "The cost of information is going down. There will be more barometers than ever in the future measuring analyst performance."[9]

From Baxter's lips to God's ears.

# 8

# TO REGULATE OR
# NOT TO REGULATE

A by-product of the unprecedented public interest in our markets and the accompanying explosion in media focus has been the proliferation of financial analysts providing commentary to the public.... What troubles me is what purports to be utterly unbiased analysis could, in fact, be shaped by unspoken pressures between the analysts and the companies they follow....

The vast majority of analysts speaking to the public today work for [brokerage] firms that have business relationships with the companies the analysts follow....

Today, analysts are under increased pressures to look for and attract business and to help the firm keep the business it has. Analysts are expected to be key players in the road show promoting securities to be issued in conjunction with a firm's investment bankers. An analyst's compensation is often based partially upon trading desk and investment banking profits....

I read that according to one study, sell recommendations account for 1.4 percent of all analyst recommendations, while buys comprised 68 percent. Certainly, the growth in the market has had something to do with this lopsidedness. But I can't help but wonder what else is driving the number of buys to exceed sells by 8 to 1, when in the early 1980s that ratio was roughly 1 to 1. Part of the explanation [is] ... a direct correlation between the content of an analyst's recommendation and the amount of business his firm does with the issuer....

*I worry that investors are being influenced too much by analysts whose evaluations read like they graduated from the Lake Woebegon School of Securities Analysis—the one that boasts that all its securities are above average. And I worry that investors hear from too many analysts who—whether they realize it or not—may be just a bit too eager to report that what looks like a frog is really a prince. Well, that's just not the way it is: every investor and every analyst must beware that—to paraphrase a very different type of analyst—sometimes a frog is just a frog.*

*I don't know how much of this is apparent to investors....*

—ARTHUR LEVITT

SEC Chairman, April 13, 1999, in speech to the Securities Industry Association

IN THE COMING FEW YEARS, the Securities and Exchange Commission faces a fundamental decision of how much—or whether—to regulate securities analysts. The current regulations pertaining to analysts—a body of law extending back more than sixty years, and almost completely formulated before the 1980s—are far more protective than restrictive. There are but few no-nos for analysts. Analysts can't personally dump stock while keeping a buy signal on, and they can't aggressively "front-run" their own recommendations—e.g., buy a wad of stock in a small-cap company, and put out aggressive "buy" signals, and then sell out. Obviously, they can't knowingly tell lies about a company, in hopes of moving the stock.

But otherwise, SEC law pertaining to analysts provides them with virtual carte blanche. It is legal for analysts to tell major clients—institutional investors—that they will issue a "buy" or "sell" signal prior to doing so. Even more notably, analysts can tell their own trading departments that a "buy" signal is forthcoming. In the case of a hot analyst, such as a Henry Blodget or a Mary Meeker, this is close to being a license to print money—and essentially, to put it mildly, a constant temptation. Consider the profits to be earned at CIBC Oppenheimer if the trading department moved into Amazon.com stock before Blodget's now-famous "buy" signal went out, shooting the Internet bookseller from under $150 past $400 a share. (Securities brokerages argue that tipping off trading departments is just good business practice; it allows the trading department to assemble stock to service ensuing retail demand.)

The law regarding analysts and information about publicly held companies is remarkably loose as well. Analysts who receive material disclosures before the market can trade in their own accounts on those disclosures, or tell their major clients.

To some extent, SEC regulations reflect the facts of life for many, perhaps all, governmental regulatory agencies. The only people or interest groups who really care about any government agency, who will lobby, conduct public relations, closely follow the legislative action— and spend the bucks—are those regulated by that particular agency. The securities industry lobbies the SEC and the U.S. Congress every business day, and a lot of nights. The National Association of Securities Dealers (NASD), which operates under the aegis of the SEC and which monitors such industry practices as stockbroker hiring and trading, not only is financed by the industry, but its various governing boards are made up of industry denizens. Small investors, spread out and unorganized, have little clout in this picture. It is the age-old problem of government: the conflict between the diffuse public good and intense narrow greed.

Additionally, the body of SEC law pertaining to analysts was developed in the 1930s through the 1960s, when by steeped tradition analysts were the resident academics of the Street, virtually kept behind the so-called Chinese wall that shielded them from the banking and trading departments. This is how securities brokerage Shearson Hamill & Co. Inc. was operated in 1972, as described by a Twentieth Century Fund report: "Moreover, Shearson had a policy, again quite common, that forbade formal 'buy' recommendations being issued for the securities of investment banking clients."[1]

But the tradition, the Chinese wall between brokerage analysts and investment bankers, was never codified, and as we have seen, analysts have thrown down the green eyeshades and picked up pom-poms and spears for investment banking and corporate finance. The tradition that may have obviated the need for law has weakened to the point of becoming a farce.

At times, one wonders what it would take to prompt SEC action against an analyst at a major brokerage. Aside from the 1991 action against Peter Butler of PaineWebber for his efforts on behalf of Memory Metals, SEC actions against analysts at major brokerages have been rare, if not nonexistent. The SEC public relations department is at a loss to provide any examples of disciplinary actions taken against brokerage analysts for too-obviously ignoring red flags while flogging stocks in the past twenty years. The disciplinary record of brokerage analysts is sparklingly clean.

That's no accident. Rather, as former SEC chief economist Gregg Jarrell notes, it's deliberate policy. "Throughout the course of history, the SEC has seen fit to give brokerage analysts a favored, coddled status," says Jarrell, now a professor of finance at the University of Rochester's Simon Business School. "If you take a long look at the regulatory model the SEC has in place, it puts analysts into very privileged positions. They have been anointed to give information to the public. Their reports get widespread dissemination. They have immunity. If they are 'taken in' by glib management or are too optimistic about a company, they can't be sued. They have safe harbor, and the government gives them that safe harbor."[2]

But looked at from the side of investors at large, the SEC laws for analysts are as if the NFL adopted rules that allowed a particular player to run out onto the field, foul every other player in sight, and perhaps even wear the uniform of the opposing team, but never draw a flag. As mentioned earlier, current law as determined by the Supreme Court in 1983, in the famed Ray Dirks–Equity Funding case, makes it legal for analysts even to spill inside information to big customers first, then to the market.

THIS REMARKABLE LAXITY AND LATITUDE accorded analysts in their professional conduct is strikingly different from the securities law that pertains to almost every other professional associated with public companies or with the underwriting process. For the most part, insiders who reveal material information about a publicly held company to friends and associates before sharing it with the public can be prosecuted for their actions. If convicted, or if they sign a consent decree, they face disgorgement of profits, fines at treble profit, even the prospect of jail time, not to mention years of expensive legal wrangling with the SEC. This applies to company officers, corporate counsels, and auditors, and U.S. attorneys have even applied insider trading laws to workers in the shops that print stock prospectuses (though with mixed success). Woe to the ink-stained little guy, but brokerage analysts are exempt from this law, as determined by regulation and by the high court in the land.

Nor does current SEC regulation or securities law address the emergent market realities of the 1990s and current era—the awesome size of mutual funds and the scope and scale of brokerages and their trading departments. Once more of a patchwork industry comprised largely of regional brokerages, today the securities business is national in perspective, with the larger brokerages having branches in every state, tens of thousands of stockbrokers under one roof, and even captive money management firms or aligned insurance companies (which are major stock market investors). Many brokerages today, of course, are owned by bank holding companies. A single brokerage, Merrill Lynch, had $1.81 *trillion* directly under management as of mid-2000. An analyst's buy signal today is as much a bugle call to rally the formidable troops as anything else.

Any basic economic or market analysis must yield to this reality: Markets with lots of small buyers and sellers are competitive and can be properly called free markets. Markets with a few huge titans become less competitive, subject to manipulation. And in symbiosis with the huge brokerage industry, the mutual fund trade, minuscule before 1975, now manages multitrillions of dollars. Market concentration and heft do translate into market power.

Further, former SEC chief Levitt has justifiably wondered in public about growing *commercial* banking conflicts that now attend to analysts, as more and more brokerages become owned by or aligned with banks, such as U.S. Bancorp Piper Jaffrey, and Citigroup (Citibank)–Salomon Smith Barney.

As THIN AND AGING AS THE VEIL OF SEC regulation of analysts may be, however, it is still gauzy enough to mislead investors into thinking there is real oversight in this area—and to encourage financial reporters to quote brokerage analysts as legitimate market soothsayers. After all, brokerages—the main employers of analysts—are licensed by the NASD, and that industry trade and regulatory entity operates under SEC authority. Given these official connections, it's no wonder the investing public—particularly the millions of less-sophisticated investors who have been socking away nest eggs in 401(k) and other retirement programs—may assume that the NASD and the SEC do monitor and regulate the behavior of analysts, particularly the ones who work for brokerages.

The reality, of course, is that the SEC has all but lost control of the game. Analysts today are media stars, some of them, like Blodget or Shah, quoted hundreds of times a year in financial media. And as we have seen, most feel no compunction about working with investment bankers to solicit business for the brokerages that employ them (indeed, Hemant Shah and Jack Grubman, telecom analyst at Salomon Smith Barney, are both investment bankers *and* analysts).

Even if the public is fuzzy on the topic, academics, market professionals, and evidently former SEC Chairman Levitt are well aware of how relations between analysts and investment bankers have changed. But even they have no easy answers to the question of how to regulate.

Stephen Buser, chairman of the finance department at Ohio State University and one of the nation's leading experts on security analyst regulation, concedes as much. "The cat is out of the bag, and the myth of the Chinese wall between investment banking and the analysts is over," he says. "But how you would enforce regulations in this area is a very difficult proposition."[3]

As Buser notes, the prospect of more strictly regulating analysts raises questions that are nearly metaphysical in their complexity. For instance, would you prosecute an analyst for making an honest mistake? How about a young analyst under heavy pressure from his brokerage? How do you draw the line between an honest mistake and a dishonest one? All business people, almost by definition, are optimists—so analysts are, too. Do you prosecute optimism? Can you prosecute unconscious self-deception? And what about freedom of speech? Do you throw people in jail for being fierce proponents of a stock, online or otherwise? If jail time isn't part of the equation, does the law have teeth?

Despite a growing awareness within academia and the professional investment community—and even of late, the financial media—that the integrity of brokerage analysts has been compromised, the SEC as it stands now is flat-footed. Levitt, perhaps sensing an intractable problem—or at least one in which the industry will not brook action—promised in 1999 that he would ask a lot of people, especially ordinary investors, a lot of questions about analysts. But he didn't promise any concrete steps, and he left office before doing anything. It's hard to blame Levitt for the old "let's study the problem" sidestep favored since time immemorial by public officeholders of all stripes (with the modern-day spin of talking to regular folk, and not only experts, about solutions).

The former general counsel to Chairman Levitt, Greg Corso, was quoted in June 2000 in the Web-oriented *Industry Standard* magazine to the effect that analysts warranted additional scrutiny. Retail investors "are the ones most likely to be influenced by free research," said Corso. "It is particularly acute in financial news, CNBC and the like. So many people are watching, but you never hear [the analysts] disclose they are related [have conflicts]," said Corso.

To be sure, the SEC under Levitt has taken some steps to modifying analyst behavior. In October 2000, the SEC promulgated Regulation FD (Fair Disclosure), which is admirably simple in concept. Under the new rule, material information pertaining to and held by public companies must be disclosed to one and all at the same time. In other words, a public company may not make selective disclosure to favored analysts.

Some say this will improve analyst objectivity, including John Coffee, the widely quoted securities law professor at Columbia University. No longer will analysts fear being ostracized by public company managements, if they put out a "sell" signal on a stock. Under Regulation FD, a public company cannot legally bar such an analyst from analysts' meetings or phone calls (nor anymore any member of the public), nor leak the real dope to other analysts, while excluding the offender.

"FD makes it less possible to bribe analysts," said Coffee. Whisper numbers, those carefully leaked indicators of pending quarterly earnings, should disappear over time. Still, even SEC insiders concede that analysts increasingly face the welter of conflicts from all directions—the investment banking departments, the institutional owners of stock, their own trading departments. One might even snidely ask if any valuable information was ever gleaned from management, as the company line is usually pretty well known. And where is the avalanche of sell signals, following Regulation FD? (There has been none.) Anyway, should not analysts be developing sources apart from management, such as vendors, former employees, delivery people, and competitors? Regulation FD is probably good rule-making, but its very existence paints a rather dismal picture of analysts fretfully pacing in corporate lobbies, awaiting latest word of the company's fortunes. Now, no one will be pushed out on the sidewalk.

The SEC has also evidently informally asked the NYSE and the NASD to meet to discuss possible new rules or regulation of analysts, but as of early 2001 there was nothing to show except some private meetings, to which no reporters were invited. The three regulatory groups are toying with the idea that there should be "an oral disclosure" made on financial television shows, to the effect that the analyst might have conflicts of interest, said SEC spokesman Chris Ullman.

But little else is in the works. As of late 2000, according to another SEC spokesman, John Heine, the commission was not conducting any "formal study of the regulations on analysts," nor did it plan to. "There is no staff study in progress or anything like that," Heine said. The NASD, the self-regulatory body for the industry, is similarly indifferent. Indeed, it has completely absolved itself of any responsibility for analyst regulation, deferring to the SEC.

OF COURSE, IT IS EASY TO CARP ABOUT the SEC, but it is harder to suggest workable alternatives. What could—or should—the SEC do?

Experts such as Buser suggest that one possible course of action is simply to retreat, making official what is true in practice. The idea here is that ineffective regulation may be worse than no regulation, since it gives market participants—especially small, novice investors—a false sense of security. The University of Rochester's Professor Jarrell seconds that sentiment. "The SEC either has to figure out a way to get financial information to the public that is communicated clearly without conflict, or they have to think about a strategic retreat," he says.

According to this way of thinking, the SEC might require that analyst commentary be accompanied by a boilerplate disclosure statement. It might state: "The analyst's recommendations are not licensed by, registered with, or regulated by the SEC, nor must the analyst disclose any conflicts of interest that exist with regard to his recommendations. The analyst or the analyst's employer may own a part of, or have or seek business with, the company the analyst is covering, and the analyst's compensation may be related to his employer's ability to achieve and maintain such business relationships. There is no aspect of the analyst's recommendations that requires full or even partial disclosure."

Investors would thus be put on notice that an analyst might be operating with a conflict of interest—even if the notice comes in the dull form of boilerplate, which is usually ignored. It is difficult to imagine such a long-winded advisory being routinely read over the airwaves, for obvious practical reasons.

Such warnings, however, do not represent the only hope for honest analysis. There is also the much-ballyhooed Internet, whose unrivaled power to disseminate information has already had a profound effect on the securities industry. As we have seen, because of the Internet, never before have small investors enjoyed such ready access to so much information about stock markets and publicly held companies.

Ohio State's Professor Buser, for one, suggests that online chat rooms devoted to the stock market and individual companies could wind up providing individual investors with the guidance and protection that the SEC itself is unable—or unwilling—to offer. A loyal Buckeye, Buser cites as a model the evolution of chat rooms devoted to Ohio State football recruiting prospects. In the pre-Internet days of yore, reporters and fans relied mainly on professional recruiters and a few experts as the authoritative voices on recruiting. In recent years, however, a number of chat rooms devoted to the subject have sprung up online and now serve as rival sources of information. At first, Buser notes, the quality of information offered by the chat rooms was amateurish. But over time, it improved—in some cases, radically. Participants whose contributions proved to be consistently reliable developed a following, and their "handles" (or aliases) came to be respected. Before long, professional recruiters began reading what was posted in the chat rooms, and even chatting themselves. In what Buser labels a kind of "reverse Gresham's law," good information drove out bad.

There is hardly a widely traded publicly held company around today that doesn't have an Internet chat room devoted to it, and in the case of Planet Hollywood, chatters were busily warning of the restaurant chain's demise years before it flopped. Although the quality of commentary in such rooms varies wildly—it should be noted that even Planet Hollywood had supporters to the bitter end—it is often superb.

Indeed, an increasing number of financial reporters have started to turn to stock market chat rooms for insights, although the difficulty (especially on deadline) of seeking comment from online chatters or ascertaining their credibility remains a daunting hurdle. It's still both easier and safer for journalists, especially those with big-name news organizations such as *The Wall Street Journal* or CNBC, to interview an acknowledged expert—very often, a brokerage analyst—than some unknown chat-room participant who might be a short trader in disguise. If some sort of "equal time" approach could become the norm in financial journalism, however, as it is in other arenas, such as civic-issues reporting, this might help level the playing field for investors at large. In this vein, if one analyst got on the air to tout a stock, an effort would be made to find another analyst or short trader to offer a competing view.

Beyond the chat rooms are a growing number of Web sites aimed at providing the sort of watchdog function the SEC should offer but doesn't or can't. One such, located at www.techstocks.com, actually maintains a list of "Stocks That Should Be Investigated by the SEC." There is even a self-styled "queen" of cyber vigilantes, a fifty-two-year-old art historian from Milan, Italy, who goes by the online moniker "Janice Shell." She likes to spend twelve hours cruising the Web, finding bogus offerings and then posting her findings on the tech-stocks site. The fact remains, however, that despite the growing number of savvy investors posting commentary on the Web, scams, rip-offs, and such mainstream foolishness as the underwriting of overhyped Internet stocks by well-known brokerages continue to proliferate.

There are powerful, smart organizations with staying power—brokerages and institutional investors—with specific and dread financial interests in maintaining, increasing, and manipulating the market value of shares. Against these large institutions, individual investors are unorganized, and less knowledgeable, and often have but fleeting interest in particular stocks, or even the whole market. In truth, for Buser's "reverse Gresham's law" even partially to take effect, there will probably have to be a prolonged market correction. Short of that, nothing much is likely to change.

A SECOND OPTION FOR THE SECURITIES industry—which was fleetingly mentioned in the 1930s and received even briefer mention in the 1970s, before May Day 1975—is the forced separation of investment banking from brokerage operations. The market has evolved some brokerage-only securities firms, such as Charles Schwab and most of the other discount firms. Brokerages such as A.G. Edwards & Sons Inc. used to thrive with minuscule investment banking departments, which were largely insignificant to the bottom line.

Additionally, the market has brokerages that are only investment banking shops, with almost totally institutional client bases. Before it formed DLJdirect, the online brokerage (which it later spun off), New York brokerage Donaldson, Lufkin & Jenrette Securities Corp.

(now Credit Suisse First Boston) had virtually no retail clients, other than some very high net worth individuals. In the early 1970s, such brokerages as Morgan Stanley & Co. and First Boston Corp. were underwriters only, with no retail distribution. They survived on long relationships with leading corporations and with institutional clients.

The problem is that almost all the old-line underwriting firms have merged into retail shops, à la Morgan Stanley Dean Witter, following a successful model pioneered by Merrill Lynch more than a generation ago. What Merrill showed, with other brokerages following suit, was that having a captive retail distribution arm is immensely profitable, both for the underwriting departments and for large institutional clients. It is nice to have a place to dump those shares.

Columbia University law professor and securities industry expert John Coffee gives no chance that the U.S. Congress will ever legislate a split between the underwriting and retail arms of brokerages. "If anything, it is going the other way," said Coffee. "The financial industry is evolving into full-service conglomerates, with the wiping out of Glass-Steagall."[4] Coffee was referring to the Financial Services Modernization Act of 1999, which effectively eliminated legal barriers established between the commercial banking, securities, and insurance industries in 1933.

A second problem is that exclusively retail shops to date have found no way to support research. One would think the retail brokerages could form alliances with the Red Chip Reviews, the Standard & Poor's, the Value Lines of the world, and provide research free of investment banking influences, but to date there has been no major move in this direction (although some online brokerages have links to the S&P Web site, an excellent arrangement).

At any rate, the SEC is hardly renewing any long-dormant interest in forcing a split between investment banking and retail brokerage operations, according to SEC spokesman Heine. The gentlemanly Heine's tone of voice just barely hinted that the idea of forcing a split between brokerage retail and investment banking operations ranked up there with establishing an SEC outpost on Mars.

IT IS NOT DIFFICULT TO UNDERSTAND the complacency of the public regarding brokerage analysts, or the corresponding lack of resolve or interest at the SEC, Levitt's April 1999 speech notwithstanding. Through the 1990s few investors had much reason to complain—a ten-year bull market hides a multitude of sins. The year 2000 kicked some investors in the stomach, but it was hardly a 1929, or even a 1987, when the market corrected by 25 percent in October. If anything, the public seems to have accepted the new Wall Street, much as the nation increasingly accepts legalized gambling and state lotteries. Wall Street offers a chance to get rich, or at least it advertises as much, and it sells the illusion nicely. And with a twenty-year bull run, there is a dose of reality in the marketing.

True, as a group, analysts continue to overestimate earnings and underperform the market. True, initial public offerings are usually dogs—especially for retail investors who buy after trading begins— but there are some spectacular home runs, too, and the public has never complained about jackpot systems. Think Las Vegas. Anyway, the sustained bull has made almost everyone a winner, even if most investors lag the indexes.

But what if the S&P 500 should trade back down to a point where price/earnings ratios approach the long-term historical norm—a correction that could easily exceed 50 percent, and one considered not unlikely by more than a few market sages?

Unfortunately, as was seen following the sell-off in the late 1960s, many investors will not return to Wall Street perhaps for a generation, permanently reducing stock values and starving companies for equity capital in the meantime. Companies starved for equity will grow more slowly, becoming worth even less and harming the economy. This is a concern voiced by Fed chief Alan Greenspan.

AS 1999 TURNED INTO 2000, GREENSPAN continued his contorted public remonstrations that the stock market was overvalued, and probably by quite a bit. Of course, back in December 1996, when the Dow traded in the 6,400 range, Greenspan criticized the "irrational exuberance" of investors, which given the power of brokerages, mutual funds, and other institutional players must be viewed as a crack at the Wall Street establishment itself. But Greenspan's 1996 comments were listened to for all of a day before becoming ancient history. The Dow marched forward and upward, crossing through 11,000 in 1999 and wandering around that mark for the next two years.

In the waning days of August 1999, speaking at a Jackson Hole, Wyoming, financial confab, Greenspan again called the rise in U.S. stocks inexplicable. He went so far as to say that investors were finding it difficult to gauge the true value of stocks they own, partly due to fishy corporate accounting practices but also due to the market's predilection to follow "herd instincts." Greenspan, ever circumspect in his public commentary, came as close as one could come to calling the U.S. stock market a bubble without saying so forthrightly. He first called the strength and length of the bull market "extraordinary" and then noted that in such markets "small exogenous events" can cause market turmoil. The specter of Greenwich, Connecticut–based Long-Term Capital Management, the highly leveraged hedge fund that tanked in the summer of 1998, spooking financial markets worldwide, probably came to Greenspan's mind.

Greenspan expanded upon the point, stating that "collapsing confidence is generally described as a bursting bubble, an event incontrovertibly evident only in retrospect.... To anticipate a bubble about to burst requires the forecast of a plunge in prices previously set by the judgments of millions of investors, many of whom are highly knowledgeable about the prospects for specific companies that make up our broad stock-price indexes."

The salient point is that investors who brave risk one day can lose their nerve the next, opined Greenspan. So the historically sky-high price/earning ratios of 1998 through 2000—the result of investors and brokerage/money manager combines who feel the bull down to their bones—could shrink rapidly should some investors get cold feet. The shrinkage could be "rapid"—a bubble bursting, Greenspan all but said.

As if to presage Greenspan's comments, in late August 1999, just a few days before Greenspan's speech, it was announced that Merrill Lynch's top stock market guru—Charles Clough, fifty-seven, a twelve-year-veteran of Merrill—was leaving the brokerage "to spend more time with his family and his church." Clough, an ordained Roman Catholic deacon, said he wanted to be more active in the Our Lady Help of Christians church, in Concord, Massachusetts. Nevertheless, *The Wall Street Journal* said Clough had committed Wall Street's "cardinal sin: being bearish and wrong." Like Greenspan, Clough had been wary of stock prices for years, a trait shared with other older titans of the market, such as Warren Buffett and George Soros.[5]

Both Clough and Merrill fell over themselves to portray the parting as thoroughly amicable, and there is scant evidence to the contrary. Yet Merrill's vast fleet of stockbrokers and institutional salespeople were known to be unhappy with Clough's carefulness and his recommendation that investors might want to bulk up on bonds. When he departed, Clough called on long-term investors to have 55 percent of their portfolios in bonds and 40 percent in equities, with 5 percent on the sidelines. Not exactly bullish, which is, after all, Merrill Lynch's symbol.

Merrill's director of private-client research affirmed that a new asset allocation model would be speedily ginned up after Clough's departure, as Clough's model caused "problems and consternation" at the brokerage. Read, "Very soon, a new model will say buy stocks." Of course, Clough was wrong through August 1999, as had been Buffett, Soros, and even the legendarily well-informed Greenspan, a man who never saw a data stream he didn't like to read and keep around the office. The market marched forth into 2000, a relentless juggernaut able to crush under its wheels even luminaries like the aforementioned. The indexes did, of course, flatten out in 2000, while Internet stocks took a bath. Beginning of a long-term correction? Nobody really knows.

But for individual investors, the questions remain: Are Greenspan and his fellow market conservatives wrong on the fundamentals? Or have we entered a "new era" when stocks are worth not 15 times earnings but 30 times? Or (more cynically) is Greenspan only naive about the power of institutional investors and brokerages to promote stocks and maintain sky-high price/earnings ratios, given the comfy environment of low inflation and steady economic growth?

IT COULD BE THAT GREENSPAN & CO. are wrong, relics of the dinosaur age of investing. Maybe stocks will rise, and rise interrupted, and maybe Internet stocks are worth 400 times revenues, and maybe never again will a recession darken prospects across the face of America. Maybe an ongoing productivity boom will unleash untold wealth on investors and workers alike.

More likely, however, is that someday the fundamentals will reassert themselves on Wall Street. In the late 1960s, when the economy was growing at 5 percent a year (about double the 1990s rate of growth) and productivity was increasing even more sharply than in the late 1990s, there were also dramatic predictions of a bountiful future—a future so rich that the four-day workweek would likely be the next norm (for one-worker families, no less) and the Dow would scale heights figuratively suggested by the country's ambitious space and moon-landing programs. Instead, it is well to remember, from 1967 through 1982 the Dow Jones Industrial Average treaded water, posting a level of 1,000 in both years. For fifteen years stocks, in the vernacular of the day, were not "where it's at."

The American financial future has a way of rarely being so bright as hoped or so grim as feared. Boomers and doomsayers should recognize that real increases in general living standards and profits, all through history, have been won by hard work and innovation sustained over years and decades. While different eras have ushered in different spectacular inventions—commercial electricity, computers, lasers, the "magic metal" aluminum, the "green revolution," robot manufacturing, plastics, and jet aircraft—the rise in overall living standards and profits was in fact a pedestrian march that spanned generations, never an overnight boom. The Internet, the miracle invention that some boomsters still say will change the way business (maybe life) is conducted, will likely take its place among other advancements, in mankind's three-steps-forward, two-steps-back struggle for a better life.

For specific companies in a free economy, the rule has always been that fat profits will spur remorseless competition, and thus lesser profits, if any. Throughout history, almost every investment boom has been followed by a bust. In the 1990s, the pied pipers—read brokerages and their analysts, the hypesters and the Web touts, and Wall Street poseurs of all stripes—trumped the adherents of fundamental investing. As tech stocks soared, and as blue chips routinely traded for more than 30 times earnings, the Greenspans, the Buffetts, the Cloughs, and the Soroses were pushed back on their haunches, sputtering futile incantations against "irrational" markets. However, gravity cannot be defied forever. Sooner or later, a company has to make enough money to warrant its market value, whether on Wall Street or Main Street. In the 2000s, it already appears the tech-stock mania of the 1990s is in retreat.

But that's of mere passing concern to the pied pipers. They already made their money on the initial public offerings, on the pre-IPO stock they held, on the big underwriting fees. They are only waiting for the next investment "concept" that catches on—or which they can plant—so they can score a new sheet of flute music. Investor beware.

# Notes

## CHAPTER 1
## THE MAN ON THE TELEPHONE

**1.** According to an online literature search of the Dow Jones Publications Library. Hemant Shah may have been quoted in other publications, and especially broadcasts, not tracked by the service.

**2.** See papers in the lawsuit *Biovail Corp. International v. Parker Quillen et al.* Hemant Shah did not respond to telephoned, faxed, and mailed requests for an interview.

**3.** Transcript of the tape recording of a telephone call dated May 20, 1996, presented in the lawsuit *Biovail v. Parker Quillen.* All tape-recorded conversations represented in this book, and their transcripts, emerged in papers pertaining to that suit. The transcripts evidently were deposed from various money managers and brokerages.

**4.** *The Ethnic Newswatch,* March 31, 1996.

**5.** Interviewed by author.

**6.** Interviewed by author.

**7.** Some portion of Shah's trading records became part of the papers generated by the *Biovail v. Parker Quillen* suit.

**8.** See "Biovail, Is the Bloom Off the Rose, or Was There Ever a Rose?" prepared by Jim Wilhelm, director of Richardson, Greenshields, Woodstock, Canada.

**9.** HKS & Co. newsletter, May 1996.

**10.** "Squawkbox," CNBC, RTV transcript, May 23, 1996, 8:30 A.M.

**11.** HKS & Co. newsletter, September 1996.

**12.** See "The Biovail Bet," by Stephen Northfield, *The Toronto Globe and Mail,* November 23, 1996.

**13.** From the deposition of Hemant Shah, February 23, 1998, in the *Biovail v. Parker Quillen* suit.

**14.** Note that Shah's actions on Biovail may have been entirely legal, under current federal law and SEC regulations.

## CHAPTER 2
## AN INDUSTRY TRANSFORMED:
## FROM SLEUTHS TO SALESMEN

**1.** Interviewed by author.

**2.** Interviewed by author.

**3.** Securities Association Industry Fact Book, 2000.

**4.** See *The Transformation of Wall Street,* by Joel Seligman, Houghton Mifflin Co., 1982. Other books include *Abuse on Wall Street—Conflicts of Interest in Securities Markets;* a Twentieth Century Fund Report, Quorum Books, 1976; *The Last Days of the Club,* by Chris Welles, E. F. Dutton & Co. Inc., 1975; and *The Securities Brokerage Industry, Nonprice Competition and Noncompetitive Pricing,* University of California at Davis, by Lawrence Shepard, Lexington Books, 1974.

**5.** See *Serpent on the Rock,* by Kurt Eichwald, HarperBusiness, 1995, and *In Good Faith,* by Kathleen Sharp, St. Martin's Press, 1995.

**6.** See "Will Nasdaq Accord Transform the Market?" by Anita Raghavan and Jeffrey Taylor, *The Wall Street Journal,* August 8, 1996.

**7.** Interviewed by author.

**8.** For growth of securities industry underwriting, see the Securities Industry Association publication *Trends,* January 31, 1997, and March 30, 1999, as well as the SIA *Securities Industry Factbook,* 1998.

**9.** See *Abuse on Wall Street,* cited in footnote number 4, page 365.

## CHAPTER 3
## COMPROMISED RELATIONSHIPS

**1.** Interviewed by author.

**2.** See "The Woman in the Bubble," by John Cassidy, *The New Yorker,* April 26 and May 3 double issue, 1999.

**3.** See "theStreet.com," a column by Gregg Wirth, *The New York Observer,* May 10, 1999.

**4.** Interviewed by author.

**5.** Interviewed by author.

**6.** See "Bad Advice," by Faith Keenan, *Bloomberg Markets,* July 2000.

## CHAPTER 4
## THE PIED PIPERS WITH GOLDEN FLUTES

**1.** "Planet Hollywood Expected to Be Among Stars of 1996," *The Toronto Globe and Mail,* February 23, 1996.

**2.** Ibid.

**3.** Ibid.

**4.** See "Will Planet Hollywood's IPO Be Down to Earth," *The New York Times,* March 24, 1996.

**5.** See "Bear Stearns New Purchase Recommendation: Planet Hollywood International Inc.," Joseph Buckley, June 4, 1996.

**6.** See Schroder Wertheim & Co., Inc., research report on Planet Hollywood, May 22, 1996.

**7.** See "Planet Hollywood Plans Revolve Around Logo—Merchandizing Is Where the Money Is for Restaurant Chain," by Susan Stroher, *Orlando Sentinel,* October 14, 1996.

**8.** Ibid.

**9.** Interview by author.

**10.** See "Lost Appetite: Fame Proves Fleeting at Planet Hollywood," by Richard Gibson, *The Wall Street Journal,* October 7, 1998.

**11.** See "Playboy—Leveraging the Only Global Multimedia Men's Brand Name to Accelerate Cash Flow and Asset Value," Credit Suisse First Boston, May 24, 1999.

**12.** See "Playboy Enterprise Inc.," research report, ING Barings, May 12, 1999.

**13.** See "Private Sector," by Stan Schiesel, *The New York Times,* May 23, 1999.

**14.** See "The Superstar Who Wears Two Hats," by Geoffrey Smith, *BusinessWeek,* October 5, 1998.

## CHAPTER 5
## THE PIED PIPERS (BRASS FLUTE VERSIONS)

**1.** See *SEC v. Peter E. Butler,* 90, Civ. 4508 (wcc) U.S. District Court for the Southern District of New York, litigation release No. 13264, June 8, 1992. See also "Analysts Frequently Own the Stocks They Tout," by John R. Dorfman, *The Wall Street Journal,* January 7, 1992.

**2.** Butler himself got a little bent over Memory Metals. The U.S. District Court in New York entered a final judgment against Butler in 1992, six years after his misdeeds. The court found that Butler had violated an anti-fraud provision of the Securities and Exchange Act of 1934, by engaging in a scheme to defraud the market and to affect the market price of Memory Metals. The court found that Butler had made materially misleading statements about Memory Metals to boost the stock, or was reckless in not knowing that they were misleading. Butler, who consented to the final judgment without admitting or denying guilt, was barred from the industry for six months and fined $37,249.

**3.** See "Small Stock Fraud Is a Big-Time Problem," *The Portland Oregonian,* March 23, 1998, and also "Investment Fraud Is Soaring Along with Stock Market," by Leslie Eaton, *The New York Times,* March 30, 1997.

**4.** See "Wanna Great Stock? Just Phone Barry Davis and the Sleaze Hotline," by Eric J. Savitz, *Barron's,* March 25, 1991, and also "The Anatomy of Penny Stock Fraud," by Joseph Perone, *The Newark Star-Ledger,* August 20, 1995, and "Penny Stocks, Big-Bucks Fraud," by Eric J. Savitz, *Barron's,* December 6, 1993.

**5.** See "More on Memory Metals: The Troubled Little Company Stirs Fresh Controversy," by Kathryn Welling, *Barron's,* September 9, 1987.

6. See "Eighty-Five Brokers Are Charged with Allegedly Bilking Customers," by Michael Schroder, *The Wall Street Journal,* June 17, 1999.

7. See "Florida Brokerage A. S. Goldmen Is Indicted in Stock-Fraud Case," Associated Press, July 8, 1999, and also "NASD's National Adjudication Council Fines A. S. Goldmen $150,000," June 14, 1999, a NASD news release. See also "NASD Scrutinized over Security Leaks," Dow Jones Business News, July 19, 1999.

8. See "Former A. S. Goldmen Executive Charged in Plot to Kill Judge," by Colleen Deboise, Dow Jones Business News, August 9, 2000, and *Newsday,* December 23, 2000.

9. See "U.S. Attacks Stock Fraud on Internet," by Michael Schroder and Rebecca Buckman, *The Wall Street Journal,* October 29, 1998.

10. See "Chief of SEC's Enforcement Unit Vows to Battle Internet Stock Fraud," by Judith Benis, *The Wall Street Journal,* April 5, 1999. Also, author interview with Ken Israel, SEC Administrator in district office, Salt Lake City.

11. "Now We'll Never Know the Truth about Bear Stearns," by Gary Weiss, *BusinessWeek,* May 8, 1999.

## CHAPTER 6
## THE SHORTS

1. Interviewed by author.

2. "Koo Koo Who?" by Robert C. La Franco, *Forbes,* November 18, 1996.

3. See "How Did It Find Trouble," by Mark Weaver, the Motley Fool, December 11, 1997.

4. Interviewed by author.

5. "Now You Can't Call Short Busters," by William Power, *The Wall Street Journal,* August 17, 1994.

6. Interviewed by author.

7. Interviewed by author.

8. Interviewed by author.

9. See "False Publicity Bars Turbodyne from Trading," by Benjamin Mark Cole, *The Los Angeles Times,* April 20, 1999.

10. See "$8 Million Settlement Proposed," by Kathleen Gallagher, *The Milwaukee Journal Sentinel,* April 7, 1999.

## CHAPTER 7
## THE GOOD GUYS

1. Interviewed by author.

2. See "Anatomy of a Shareholder Slaughter," by Janet Rae-Dupree, *Business-Week,* May 17, 1999. See also "HBO & Co.," April 14, 1997, by the Center for Financial Research and Analysis.

3. See "HBO & Co.," August 19, 1998, by the Center for Financial Research and

Analysis.

**4.** Interviewed by author.

**5.** Interviewed by author.

**6.** See "Special Delivery," by Robin Goldwyn Blumenthal, *Barron's,* July 17, 2000.

**7.** Interviewed by author.

**8.** Interviewed by author.

**9.** Interviewed by author.

## CHAPTER 8
## TO REGULATE OR NOT TO REGULATE

**1.** See footnote number 4, Chapter 2.

**2.** Interviewed by author.

**3.** Interviewed by author.

**4.** Interviewed by author.

**5.** See "Leading Merrill Lynch Stock Strategist Will Leave Firm by End of Year," by Charles Gasparino, *The Wall Street Journal,* August 27, 1999.

# Index

## ABOUT BLOOMBERG

Bloomberg L.P., founded in 1981, is a global information services, news, and media company. Headquartered in New York, the company has nine sales offices, two data centers, and 79 news bureaus worldwide.

Bloomberg, serving customers in 100 countries around the world, holds a unique position within the financial services industry by providing an unparalleled range of features in a single package known as the BLOOMBERG PROFESSIONAL™ service. By addressing the demand for investment performance and efficiency through an exceptional combination of information, analytic, electronic trading, and Straight Through Processing tools, Bloomberg has built a worldwide customer base of corporations, issuers, financial intermediaries, and institutional investors.

BLOOMBERG NEWS℠, founded in 1990, provides stories and columns on business, general news, politics, and sports to leading newspapers and magazines throughout the world. BLOOMBERG TELEVISION®, a 24-hour business and financial news network, is produced and distributed globally in seven different languages. BLOOMBERG RADIO™ is an international radio network anchored by flagship station BLOOMBERG® WBBR 1130 in New York.

In addition to the BLOOMBERG PRESS® line of books, Bloomberg publishes *BLOOMBERG® MARKETS, BLOOMBERG PERSONAL FINANCE™*, and *BLOOMBERG® WEALTH MANAGER*. To learn more about Bloomberg, call a sales representative at:

| | | | |
|---|---|---|---|
| Frankfurt: | 49-69-92041-200 | São Paulo: | 5511-3048-4530 |
| Hong Kong: | 85-2-2977-6600 | Singapore: | 65-212-1200 |
| London: | 44-20-7330-7500 | Sydney: | 61-2-9777-8601 |
| New York: | 1-212-318-2200 | Tokyo: | 81-3-3201-8950 |
| San Francisco: | 1-415-912-2980 | | |

For in-depth market information and news, visit BLOOMBERG.COM®, which draws from the news and power of the BLOOMBERG PROFESSIONAL™ service and Bloomberg's host of media products to provide high-quality news and information in multiple languages on stocks, bonds, currencies, and commodities, at **www.bloomberg.com**.

## ABOUT THE AUTHOR

BENJAMIN MARK COLE has been a financial writer for the past twenty years. He began his career in journalism as a researcher and reporter for *U.S. News & World Report* in Washington, D.C. After four years with *U.S. News,* covering the federal budget, finance, and economics, Cole returned to his native Los Angeles to help launch the daily financial paper *Investor's Daily* (now *Investor's Business Daily*). Cole later joined the staff of *The Los Angeles Herald Examiner.* As a reporter for the newspaper's money page, he wrote about the Southern California economic picture, manufacturing, corporate finance, and securities. In 1986, his investigation of insurance-policy scams was cited by the Hearst newspaper group as "the best business story of the year" for the entire chain. Later that year Cole moved to the *Los Angeles Business Journal,* where he covered the securities industry, government, and general economic news. In 1997 he won the Best Feature Story of the Year award from the Association of Area Business Journals in a national competition. Subsequently, he has written weekly national columns on the securities industry for Knight-Ridder Financial and Bridge Information Systems. Cole currently writes the *Los Angeles Business Journal*'s "Wall Street West" column. In addition, he writes a weekly column on private equity markets for Direct Stock market (dsm.com), an online marketplace for private venture deals, and also freelances regularly for *The Los Angeles Times,* among other publications. Cole is a graduate of the University of California at Berkeley, with a master's degree from the Lyndon B. Johnson School of Public Affairs at the University of Texas at Austin.